ALCOHOL AND DRUG ABUSE

Methadone-Related Overdose Deaths: Factors and Prevention Measures
Maxime G. Lejeune (Editor)
2010. ISBN: 978-1-60876-066-4

Underage Drinking: Examining and Preventing Youth Use of Alcohol
David Edvin and Samuel Harald (Editors)
2010. ISBN: 978-1-60876-141-8

ALCOHOL AND DRUG ABUSE

UNDERAGE DRINKING: EXAMINING AND PREVENTING YOUTH USE OF ALCOHOL

DAVID EDVIN
AND
SAMUEL HARALD
EDITORS

Nova Science Publishers, Inc.
New York

For permission to use material from this book please contact us:
Telephone 631-231-7269; Fax 631-231-8175
Web Site: http://www.novapublishers.com

LIBRARY OF CONGRESS CATALOGING-IN-PUBLICATION DATA

Underage drinking : examining and preventing youth use of alcohol / editor, David Edvin and Samuel Harald.

p. cm.

Includes bibliographical references and index.

ISBN 978-1-60876-141-8 (hardcover : alk. paper)

1. Youth--Alcohol use--United States. 2. Youth--Alcohol use--United States--Prevention. 3. Minors--Alcohol use--United States. 4. Minors--Alcohol use--United States--Prevention. 5. Drinking of alcoholic beverages--Government policy--United States. I. Edvin, David. II. Harald, Samuel.

HV5135.U424 2009

362.292083'0973--dc22

2009038423

Published by Nova Science Publishers, Inc. ✦ New York

CONTENTS

PREFACE

Alcohol use by persons under the age of 21 has been identified as a major public health problem. Studies report that it increases the risks for disability and may be detrimental to the developing brain. Minors who drink are more likely to commit suicide, break the law, or be victims of violence. Alcohol is implicated in nearly one-third of youth traffic fatalities. Underage drinking remains a far more prevalent problem than the use of illicit drugs or tobacco products. While most underage drinking prevention laws are passed by states, there has been legislative activity and interest at the federal level to support states' efforts to curb the problem. Issues of concern to policy makers include the ineffective enforcement of "zero-tolerance" laws prohibiting underage drinking, and the online sale of alcohol to minors. This chapter highlights the ongoing problems that stem from underage drinking and the steps being taken by the government to curb this problem. This chapter consists of public documents which have been located, gathered, combined, reformatted, and enhanced with a subject index, selectively edited and bound to provide easy access.

Chapter 1 - Alcohol abuse affects the physical, mental, and fiscal health of millions of people every year. A number of programs can effectively treat alcohol dependence or abuse; however, many people who need treatment may not use these services or even recognize the need for them. Increasing the public's awareness of the signs of alcohol problems, expanding screening for alcohol problems in primary care and in emergency departments, and ensuring that individuals are matched to appropriate intervention and/or treatment services may help to save or improve the lives of alcohol abusers, their families, and other citizens in our communities.

The National Survey on Drug Use and Health (NSDUH) gathers information that can help to provide a better understanding of alcohol treatment needs, service utilization, and barriers. NSDUH classifies persons as needing treatment for an alcohol problem if they met the criteria for alcohol dependence or abuse or if they received specialty alcohol use treatment in the past year.[1,2] Respondents were asked if there was any time in the past year when they felt they needed treatment for their alcohol use but did not receive it. Persons who felt the need for treatment but did not receive it were asked about their reasons for not receiving treatment. *The NSDUH Report* presents 2007 estimates of alcohol treatment need, receipt of treatment, and perceived need for treatment, as well as 2004 to 2007 combined estimates on the reasons for not receiving alcohol treatment among persons aged 12 or older.

Chapter 2 - Alcohol use by persons under age 21 has been identified as a major public health problem. Studies report that it increases the risks for disability and may be detrimental to the developing brain. Minors who drink are more likely to commit suicide, break the law, or be victims of violence. Alcohol is implicated in nearly one-third of youth traffic fatalities. The total annual cost of underage drinking is estimated at $62 billion. On March 6, 2007, the Office of the U.S. Surgeon General issued an official call to increase efforts to curb underage drinking.

The prevalence of alcohol consumption by minors is measured by three federally funded national surveys: the National Survey on Drug Use and Health (NSDUH), the Youth Risk Behavior Survey (YRBS), and Monitoring the Future (MTF). There are an estimated 10.8 million underage drinkers in the United States. More than 2 million are classified as heavy drinkers, and nearly 7.2 million are classified as binge drinkers, meaning that they have had more than five drinks on one occasion.

Although the consumption of alcohol by youth has dropped steadily over the past decade, recent data suggest that 74.3% of individuals in grades 9-12 have used alcohol on multiple occasions, 43.3% regularly consume alcohol, and 25.5% engage in binge drinking. Underage drinking remains a far more prevalent problem than the use of illicit drugs or tobacco products.

While most underage drinking prevention laws are passed by states, there has been legislative activity and interest at the federal level to support states' efforts to curb the problem. Issues of concern to policy makers include the ineffective enforcement of "zero-tolerance" laws prohibiting underage drinking, and the online sale of alcohol to minors. According to recent research, millions of minors either buy alcohol online or know an underage friend who has done so. In recent years, state and national policy makers have proposed restrictions on home delivery of alcohol ordered from Internet sites.

This chapter describes the extent of alcohol use by youth, federal surveillance systems for monitoring underage drinking, judicial and legislative activity on this issue, and various policy implications.

Chapter 3 - In 2006, a majority (53.9 percent) of American adolescents and young adults aged 12 to 20 had used an alcoholic beverage at least once in their lifetime.[1] Young people aged 12 to 20 consumed approximately 11.2 percent of the alcoholic drinks consumed in the United States in the past month by persons aged 12 or older.[2] Research shows that underage drinkers tend to consume more alcohol per occasion than those over the legal minimum drinking age of 21.[3] Studies also have linked early drinking to heavy alcohol consumption and alcohol-related problems in adulthood.[4,5] For example, in 2006, 16.3 percent of adults aged 21 or older who had first used alcohol before the age of 15 met the criteria for alcohol dependence or abuse in the past year compared with 2.4 percent of adults who first used alcohol at age 21 or older.[6] Research also shows that early initiation of alcohol use is associated with higher likelihood of involvement in violent behaviors, suicide attempts, unprotected sexual intercourse, and multiple sex partners.[7,8]

The National Survey on Drug Use and Health (NSDUH) asks persons aged 12 or older to report the frequency and quantity of their alcohol use during the 30 days prior to the interview. Respondents who drank alcohol in the past 30 days also are asked for the number of days they consumed alcohol in the past month and the average number of drinks consumed per day on the days they drank.[9]

This chapter focuses on the frequency and quantity of past month alcohol use among underage drinkers (i.e., persons aged 12 to 20 who consume alcohol). Comparisons of the quantity and frequency of alcohol use in the past month also are made between underage drinkers and drinkers aged 21 or older. All findings presented in this chapter are based on combined 2005 and 2006 NSDUH data.

Chapter 4 - Underage alcohol use is a widespread problem with significant health and safety consequences. This is the third Federal Trade Commission report on efforts by the alcohol industry to reduce the likelihood that alcohol advertising will target youth, by its placement or content. This chapter provides data about how industry members allocate promotional dollars; data on compliance with the industry's advertising placement standard (requiring that at least 70 percent of the audience for advertising consist of adults 21 and older); analysis of external review of advertising complaints; and an update on the FTC's "We Don't Serve Teens" campaign.

Chapter 5 - Alcohol is the drug of choice among young people in the United States, and alcohol use constitutes one of the principal public health issues for this population. Approximately 5,000 persons under 21 years of age lose their lives each year as a result of underage drinking, and early initiation of alcohol use is associated with increased risk of subsequent alcohol use disorders and increased risk of involvement in violent behaviors, suicide attempts, and a variety of other problematic activities. In response to this issue, this study presents findings from the 2002 to 2006 National Surveys on Drug Use and Health (NSDUHs) on the use of alcohol by persons aged 12 to 20.

Chapter 6 - In 2006, more than one in four persons aged 12 to 20 in the United States, or about 10.8 million persons, drank alcohol in the past month (i.e., were current drinkers).[1] Nearly one in five persons aged 18 to 20 drove under the influence of alcohol in the past 12 months in 2006,[1] and each year approximately 1,900 people under the age of 21 die as a result of alcohol-involved motor vehicle crashes.[2] In addition, early initiation of alcohol use is associated with increased likelihood of unprotected sexual intercourse and multiple sex partners.[3,4]

The 2006 National Survey on Drug Use and Health (NSDUH) asked past month alcohol users aged 12 to 20 how they obtained the last alcohol they drank and where they were when they consumed it. *The NSDUH Report* examines age-related changes in the locations where male and female underage drinkers use alcohol. It also examines differences by college enrollment and living situation for those aged 18 to 20. Findings presented in this chapter are based on 2006 NSDUH data.

Chapter 7 - Although the use of alcohol is illegal for persons under the age of 21, its use constitutes one of the principal public health issues for this age group,[1] and reduction of underage alcohol use is a top public health priority of the Federal Government.[2] Many of the efforts to prevent or reduce underage alcohol use attempt to reduce the availability of alcohol to underage drinkers. Data from 2006 and 2007 National Surveys on Drug Use and Health (NSDUHs) indicate even with efforts to reduce availability, underage drinkers are able to obtain alcohol.

The NSDUH Report examines how current (i.e., "past month") drinkers aged 12 to 20 obtain alcohol, by age group and gender. The 2006 and 2007 NSDUHs included items that asked past month alcohol users aged 12 to 20 how they obtained the last alcohol they drank. This chapter also presents data on the prevalence of current underage alcohol use and findings on the average number of drinks that underage drinkers had on their last occasion of alcohol use, depending on where they obtained alcohol. All findings presented are annual averages based on combined 2006 and 2007 NSDUH data.

In: Underage Drinking
Ed: David Edvin and Samuel Harald
ISBN: 978-1-60876-141-8

Chapter 1

ALCOHOL TREATMENT REPORT*

National Survey on Drug Use and Health

IN BRIEF

- In 2007, 7.8 percent of persons aged 12 or older (an estimated 19.3 million persons) needed treatment for an alcohol problem in the past year
- Of those who needed alcohol treatment in the past year 8.1 percent received treatment at a specialty substance use treatment facility, 4.5 percent did not receive treatment but felt they needed it, and 87.4 percent did not receive treatment and did not perceive a need for it
- Only one quarter (27.9 percent) of those who did not receive alcohol treatment but felt they needed it made an effort to get treatment in the past year
- Averages for 2004 to 2007 show that the most common reasons given for not receiving alcohol treatment among those who felt the need for it were not being ready to stop using alcohol (42.0 percent) and cost or insurance barriers (34.5 percent)

Alcohol abuse affects the physical, mental, and fiscal health of millions of people every year. Increasing the public's awareness of the signs of alcohol

---

* This is an edited, reformatted and augmented version of a National Survey on Drug Use and Health publication dated April 2009.

problems, expanding screening for alcohol problems in primary care and in emergency departments, and ensuring that individuals are matched to intervention and/or treatment services may help to save or improve the lives of alcohol abusers, their families, and other citizens in our communities.

The National Survey on Drug Use and Health (NSDUH) gathers information that can help to provide a better understanding of alcohol treatment needs, service utilization, and barriers. NSDUH classifies persons as needing treatment for an alcohol problem if they met the criteria for alcohol dependence or abuse or if they received specialty alcohol use treatment in the past year.[1,2] Respondents were asked if there was any time in the past year when they felt they needed treatment for their alcohol use but did not receive it *The NSDUH Report* presents 2007 estimates of alcohol treatment need, receipt of treatment, and perceived need for treatment, as well as 2004 to 2007 combined estimates on the reasons for not receiving alcohol treatment among persons aged 12 or older.

Need for Alcohol Treatment

In 2007, 7.8 percent of persons aged 12 or older (an estimated 19.3 million persons) needed treatment for an alcohol problem in the past year. The rate of treatment need for an alcohol problem was twice as high for males as for females (10.9 vs. 4.8 percent), and the rate of treatment need for young adults aged 18 to 25 was 2 to 3 times higher than that of other age groups (17.2 percent for persons aged 18 to 25 vs. 5.5 percent for those aged 12 to 17 and 6.5 percent for those aged 26 or older) (Figure 1).

Service Utilization

Of the 19.3 million persons who needed alcohol treatment in the past year, 8.1 percent (1.6 million) received treatment at a specialty facility in the past year (Figure 2). Among persons who needed treatment for alcohol use, adults aged 26 or older were more likely than adolescents and young adults to have received treatment at a specialty facility (9.7 vs. 5.9 and 5.1 percent, respectively) (Figure 3). There was little difference by gender.

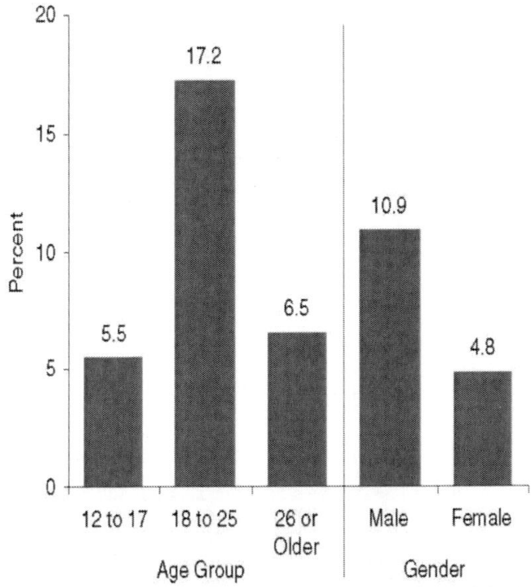

Source: 2007 SAMHSA National Survey on Drug Use and Health (NSDUH).

Figure 1. Needed Treatment for an Alcohol Problem in the Past Year among Persons Aged 12 or Older, by Demographic Ccharacteristics: 2007.

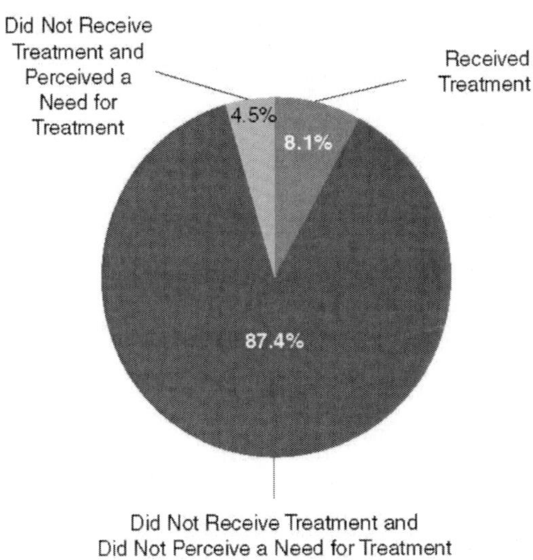

Source: 2007 SAMHSA National Survey on Drug Use and Health (NSDUH).

Figure 2. Receipt* of and Perceived Need for Alcohol Treatment in the Past Year among Persons Aged 12 or Older Who Needed Treatment: 2007.

Nearly nine tenths (87.4 percent) of individuals who needed treatment neither received it nor perceived the need for it (Figure 2). Only 4.5 percent perceived a need for treatment but did not receive it (i.e., had a perceived unmet need). About one quarter (27.9 percent) of the 859,000 persons who had a perceived unmet need for alcohol treatment made an effort to get it in the past year.

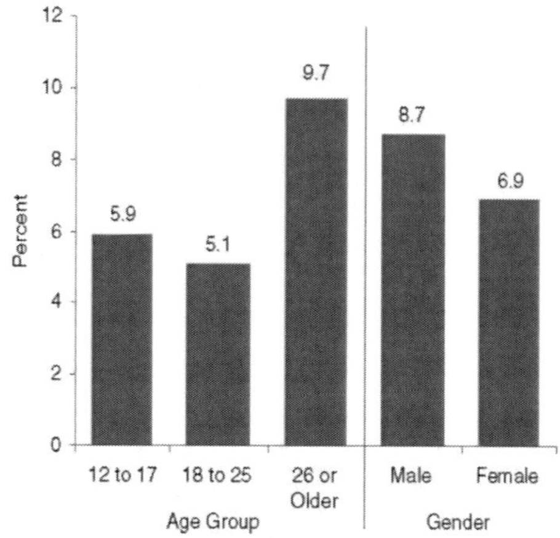

Source: 2007 SAMHSA National Survey on Drug Use and Health (NSDUH).

Figure 3. Received Treatment for an Alcohol Problem in a Specialty Facility in the Past Year among Persons Aged 12 or Older in Need of Treatment, by Demographic Ccharacteristics: 2007.

Barriers to Receiving Alcohol Treatment

Individuals who needed but did not receive alcohol treatment at a specialty facility and who felt a need for alcohol treatment were asked to indicate the reasons for not receiving it. Averages for 2004 to 2007 show that the most common reasons given for not receiving treatment were not being ready to stop using alcohol (42.0 percent) and cost or insurance barriers (34.5 percent) (Figure 4).[3] Other reasons included social stigma associated with receiving treatment (18.8 percent), access issues (11.7 percent), not feeling the need for treatment or thinking they could handle the problem without treatment (11.6 percent), and not knowing where to go for treatment (11.1 percent).

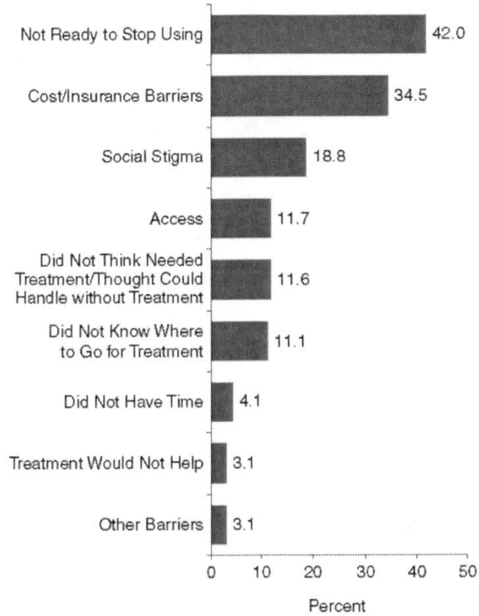

Source: 2004 to 2007 SAMHSA National Surveys on Drug Use and Health (NSDUHs).

* Refers to receipt of treatment in a specialty facility (see End Note 2).

** Respondents could indicate multiple reasons; thus, these response categories are not mutually exclusive. *"Cost/insurance barriers"* include "no health coverage and could not afford cost," "had health coverage but it did not cover treatment or did not cover cost," and other-specify responses of "could not afford cost; health coverage not indicated." *"Social stigma"* include "might cause neighbors/community to have negative opinion," "might have negative effect on job," "did not want others to find out," and other-specify responses of "ashamed/embarrassed/afraid" and "afraid would have trouble with police/social services." *"Did not think needed treatment/thought could handle the problem without treatment"* include "did not feel need for treatment," "could handle the problem without treatment," and other-specify responses of "could do it with support of family/friends/others" and "could do it through religion/spirituality." *"Other barriers"* include "no transportation/inconvenient," "no program having type of treatment," "no openings in a program," and other-specify responses of "no program had counselors/doctors with whom you were comfortable," "services desired were unavailable or you were currently ineligible," and "attempted to get treatment but encountered delays."

Figure 4. Reasons** for Not Receiving Alcohol Treatment in the Past Year among Persons Aged 12 or Older Who Needed Treatment and Who Perceived a Need for It: 2004 to 2007.

Discussion

A large number of Americans are in need of alcohol treatment but do not receive it; most of those who do not receive treatment also do not perceive a need for it. Even among those with a perceived unmet need for alcohol treatment, only about one quarter made an effort to get treatment. Among those with a perceived unmet alcohol treatment need, the most common reason given for not getting alcohol treatment was not being ready to stop drinking. These findings highlight the need to increase the public's awareness of the signs of alcohol dependence or abuse, the need for increased alcohol screening in multiple health care settings, and wider dissemination of information on treatment availability and cost.

ALCOHOL TREATMENT: NEED, UTILIZATION, AND BARRIERS

- In 2007, 7.8 percent of persons aged 12 or older (an estimated 19.3 million persons) needed treatment for an alcohol problem in the past year
- Of those who needed alcohol treatment in the past year 8.1 percent received treatment at a specialty substance use treatment facility, 4.5 percent did not receive treatment but felt they needed it, and 87.4 percent did not receive treatment and did not perceive a need for it
- Only one quarter (27.9 percent) of those who did not receive alcohol treatment but felt they needed it made an effort to get treatment in the past year
- Averages for 2004 to 2007 show that the most common reasons given for not receiving alcohol treatment among those who felt the need for it were not being ready to stop using alcohol (42.0 percent) and cost or insurance barriers (34.5 percent)

The National Survey on Drug Use and Health (NSDUH) is an annual survey sponsored by the Substance Abuse and Mental Health Services Administration (SAMHSA). The 2007 data used in this chapter are based on information obtained from 67,870 persons aged 12 or older, and the 2004 to 2007 combined data are based on information obtained from 271,740 persons aged 12 or older. The survey collects data by administering questionnaires to a representative sample of the population through face-to-face interviews at their place of residence.

End Notes

[1] NSDUH defines dependence on or abuse of alcohol using criteria specified in the Diagnostic and Statistical Manual of Mental Disorders (DSM-IV), which includes such symptoms as withdrawal, tolerance, use in dangerous situations, trouble with the law, and interference in major obligations at work, school, or home during the past year. For details, see the following resource: American Psychiatric Association. (1994). Diagnostic and statistical manual of mental disorders (4th ed.). Washington, DC: Author.

[2] Specialty substance use treatment is defined as treatment received at drug or alcohol rehabilitation facilities (inpatient or outpatient), hospitals (inpatient services only), and mental health centers. Specialty substance use treatment excludes treatment in an emergency room, private doctor's office, self-help group, prison or jail, or hospital as an outpatient.

[3] For this section, data from the 2004 to 2007 NSDUHs were combined to gain a sufficient sample size in order to produce estimates that met the standard NSDUH precision criteria.

In: Underage Drinking
Ed: David Edvin and Samuel Harald
ISBN: 978-1-60876-141-8

Chapter 2

ALCOHOL USE AMONG YOUTH*

Andrew R. Sommers and Ramya Sundararaman

SUMMARY

Alcohol use by persons under age 21 has been identified as a major public health problem. Studies report that it increases the risks for disability and may be detrimental to the developing brain. Minors who drink are more likely to commit suicide, break the law, or be victims of violence. Alcohol is implicated in nearly one-third of youth traffic fatalities. The total annual cost of underage drinking is estimated at $62 billion. On March 6, 2007, the Office of the U.S. Surgeon General issued an official call to increase efforts to curb underage drinking.

The prevalence of alcohol consumption by minors is measured by three federally funded national surveys: the National Survey on Drug Use and Health (NSDUH), the Youth Risk Behavior Survey (YRBS), and Monitoring the Future (MTF). There are an estimated 10.8 million underage drinkers in the United States. More than 2 million are classified as heavy drinkers, and nearly 7.2 million are classified as binge drinkers, meaning that they have had more than five drinks on one occasion.

---

* This is an edited, reformatted and augmented version of a CRS Report for Congress publication dated January 2008.

Although the consumption of alcohol by youth has dropped steadily over the past decade, recent data suggest that 74.3% of individuals in grades 9-12 have used alcohol on multiple occasions, 43.3% regularly consume alcohol, and 25.5% engage in binge drinking. Underage drinking remains a far more prevalent problem than the use of illicit drugs or tobacco products.

While most underage drinking prevention laws are passed by states, there has been legislative activity and interest at the federal level to support states' efforts to curb the problem. Issues of concern to policy makers include the ineffective enforcement of "zero-tolerance" laws prohibiting underage drinking, and the online sale of alcohol to minors. According to recent research, millions of minors either buy alcohol online or know an underage friend who has done so. In recent years, state and national policy makers have proposed restrictions on home delivery of alcohol ordered from Internet sites.

This chapter describes the extent of alcohol use by youth, federal surveillance systems for monitoring underage drinking, judicial and legislative activity on this issue, and various policy implications.

INTRODUCTION

On March 6, 2007, the Office of the U.S. Surgeon General issued an official call to increase efforts to curb underage drinking.[1] "We can no longer ignore what alcohol is doing to our children," said Acting Surgeon General Kenneth Moritsugu. "Alcohol," he continued, "is the most heavily abused substance by America's youth."[2] The nation, he implored, must "attempt to change attitudes toward drinking."

In light of recent research demonstrating that alcohol may harm the adolescent brain and that individuals who start drinking before the age of 15 are five times more likely to have alcoholrelated problems later in life, the Acting Surgeon General announced six basic goals:

- Fostering changes in American society that facilitate healthy adolescent development and help prevent and reduce underage drinking.
- Engaging youth and all social systems that interface with youth in a coordinated effort to prevent and reduce drinking and its consequences.

- Promoting understanding of underage drinking in the context of development and maturation that considers individual adolescent characteristics and environmental, ethnic, cultural, and gender differences.
- Conducting additional research on adolescent alcohol use and its relationship to development.
- Improving surveillance on underage drinking and its risk factors.
- Ensuring that all policies are consistent with the goal of preventing and reducing underage alcohol consumption.

Although drinking by persons under the age of 21 is illegal in all states, people aged 12-20 drink almost 20% of alcohol consumed in the United States.[3] In 2004, there were more than 142,000 emergency room visits by youth aged 12-20 as a result of injuries and other conditions linked to alcohol consumption.[4] Each year, data suggest, approximately 5,000 young people under the age of 21 die as a result of underage drinking.

The economic toll of underage drinking in the United States in 2001 was an estimated $61.9 billion.[5] It has been reported that medical care, work loss, and pain and suffering directly associated with underage drinking cost $2,207 annually for each young person in the United States.[6]

Low educational achievement and high absenteeism rates are common among underage students who drink alcohol. These youth often have problems with social integration, are more prone to fighting, and are often disinclined to participate in healthier activities such as intramural sports. They have a higher risk of being engaged in illegal activities and participating in unprotected sex.[7]

SURVEILLANCE

Although many national surveys collect information about alcohol consumption, three federally funded studies most comprehensively cover aspects of underage drinking.

National Survey on Drug Use and Health (NSDUH)

NSDUH is the primary source of statistical information on illegal drug use by the U.S. population. Sponsored by the Substance Abuse and Mental Health

Services Administration (SAMHSA), NSDUH collects data in interviews at each respondent's place of residence. Survey items aim to provide the drug prevention, treatment, and research communities with current, relevant information on the status of the nation's drug usage, including national and state-level estimates of the past month, past year, and lifetime use of alcohol. NSDUH tracks trends in the use of alcohol and helps identify the consequences of underage alcohol use and the groups who are at greatest risk.

Youth Risk Behavior Survey (YRBS)

The YRBS monitors health risk behaviors, including underage drinking, that contribute to mortality, disability, and social problems among youth in the United States. The YRBS is a national school-based survey fielded by the Centers for Disease Control and Prevention (CDC) and supplemented with data collected by state and local education and health agencies. It is conducted every two years during the spring semester and provides data representative of 9th- through 12th-grade students in public and private schools throughout the United States.

Monitoring the Future (MTF)

Funded by the National Institute on Drug Abuse, MTF annually surveys 8th, 10th, and 12th graders about substance use, including alcohol consumption. Respondents are asked about daily and monthly alcohol use, the quantity of alcohol consumed, and the number of episodes of heavy drinking in the past month. Unlike NSDUH or YRBS, MTF also explores issues of risk and ethics by asking, "How much do you think people risk harming themselves (physically or in other ways)" if they drink daily or if they drink heavily on the weekends. Similarly, survey participants are asked whether they "disapprove" of these behaviors. Each year, a random sample of 12th- grade MTF participants is selected for follow-up studies. These individuals are surveyed by mail every other year until age 30, then every fifth year until age 45. Data from these follow-up surveys allow researchers to investigate questions about the effects of alcohol use over time, such as the following:

- How do different social contexts (e.g., military service, civilian employment, college, unemployment) and social roles (e.g., marital status, parenthood) affect alcohol use by individuals?
- How does the life course of individuals who used alcohol as teens differ from those who did not?

PREVALENCE

The consumption of alcohol by youth has dropped steadily over the past decade. Data from 2005 suggest that 74.3% of individuals in grades 9-12 have used alcohol on multiple occasions, 43.3% regularly consume alcohol, and 25.5% engage in binge drinking (see **Figure 1**).[8] These figures represent absolute declines of 4.8, 7.5, and 7.9 percentage points, respectively, since 1997. Still, underage drinking remains a far more prevalent problem than the use of illicit drugs or tobacco products. According to Monitoring the Future, U.S. high school seniors are 50% more likely to have consumed alcohol more than once than to have ever tried illicit drugs or to have smoked tobacco.[9]

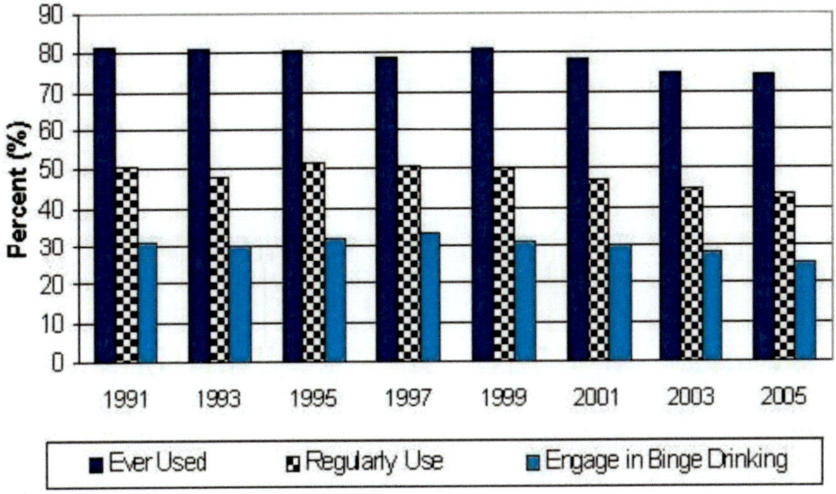

Source: Centers for Disease Control and Prevention, 2005 i; data available at http://www.cdc.gov/yrbss.

Figure 1. Underage Use of Alcohol, 1991-2005.

There are an estimated 10.8 million underage drinkers in the United States. More than 2.0 million are classified as heavy drinkers, and nearly 7.2 million are classified as binge drinkers, meaning that they have had more than five drinks on one occasion.[10] Rates of alcohol consumption differ by gender among individuals aged 12-20. In 2006, drinking was more common among boys than girls in this age category, with males reporting more current alcohol use (29.2% vs. 27.4% for girls), more frequent binge drinking (21.3% vs. 16.5%), and more frequent heavy drinking (7.9% vs. 4.3%). Racial and ethnic differences were also evident. Rates of binge drinking were highest among American Indian/Alaskan Native (23.6%) and white youth (22.7%), followed by Hispanic youth (16.5%), Asian American youth (11.8%), and African American youth (8.6%).[11]

Underage drinking varies by geographic region. Since 2002, it has been higher in the Northeast (32.0%) and Midwest (29.7%) than in the West (28.1%) and South (25.8%).[12] According to the most recent NSDUH data, underage drinking rates in 2006 were similar in small metropolitan (28.9%), large metropolitan (27.8%), and non-metropolitan areas (29. 1%).[13] Unlike in previous years, the rate in rural areas has increased to 28.2% and now exceeds the underage drinking rate seen in large metropolitan areas.[14]

While NSDUH and YRBS ask many similar questions regarding underage drinking, the Youth Risk Behavior Survey includes several unique, noteworthy findings. Among high school students surveyed in 2005, 26% had their first alcoholic drink before age 13; one in three had ridden with a driver who had been drinking alcohol; and over the course of the past month, 10% had consumed alcohol while operating a motor vehicle, and 4.3% had done so while on school property.[15]

Legal Perspectives

The 21st Amendment to the U.S. Constitution gives states the primary authority to regulate the sale and distribution of alcohol within their borders. Hence, most underage drinking prevention laws are passed by states. Today, all states have set the minimum legal drinking at age 21 and have passed zero-tolerance laws that make it illegal for people under age 21 to drive after drinking any alcohol. Despite their demonstrated benefits, legal drinking age laws and zero-tolerance laws generally have not been vigorously enforced.[16] Alcohol purchase laws aimed at sellers and buyers also can be effective, but experts believe that more resources need to be made available for enforcing these laws.[17]

Online Sales of Alcohol

Millions of minors either buy alcohol online or know an underage friend who does, according to an April 2006 study conducted by Teen Research Unlimited (TRU).[18] This survey analyzed a nationally representative sample of youth. Its finding suggest that at least 551,000 individuals (2%) aged 14-20 have purchased alcohol over the Internet; 3.1 million minors (12%) in this age bracket report having at least one friend who has purchased alcohol online. Moreover, nearly 8.9 million Americans (33%) aged 14-20 believe it is possible that they will make an online alcohol purchase before age 21.

The Wine and Spirits Wholesalers of America (WSWA), a trade association representing U.S. alcohol wholesalers, argues that the TRU study underscores the dangers of permitting wine and other alcoholic beverages to be sold online. It is important to note that WSWA has a vested interest in limiting Internet sales of alcohol and ensuring that wine and liquor continue to be sent from distillers or brewers to the distributors it represents, not to the doorsteps of consumers—be they adults or teenagers. The TRU numbers suggest that in 2004 only 9% of teens had visited a website that sells alcohol. However, this 9% figure may be more substantial than is initially evident. Because only 34% of survey respondents reported knowing that it was "possible to purchase alcohol online," another way to frame this finding is that more than 25% of 14-to-20- year-olds who knew alcohol could be purchased via the Internet visited websites that sell beer, wine, or liquor.

Viewed in this light, the TRU study's estimate that 68% of 14-to-20-year-olds report that their parents make no attempt to control online activity, and the report that 75% say their parents are unable to control what they do online, leads some analysts to believe that more minors can be expected to purchase alcohol online in the future.[19] This suggestion is consistent with a 2003 report by the Institute of Medicine, which found that underage individuals are increasingly buying alcohol online and concluded that greater use of the Internet in the future will likely exacerbate this problem.[20] It is also supported by the significant number of teenagers who are being given credit/debit cards by their parents (or guardians).[21]

In recent years, state and national policy makers have proposed restrictions on home delivery of alcohol ordered from Internet sites. It is unclear, however, whether debates over alcohol sales from the Internet are driven primarily by the desire to reduce youth access to alcohol, because prohibitions of home delivery from local retail outlets have not been included in the policy debates on Internet sales. This omission has led some political observers to conclude that policy attention to Internet sales of alcohol may reflect the varying economic interests of local versus national alcohol distributors and retailers—rather than concerns about teen access to alcohol.[22]

Judicial Activity Regarding Internet Wine Sales

In May 2005, the Supreme Court issued a 5-4 opinion in *Granholm v. Heald* (03-1116) 544 U.S. 460 (2005), and consolidated cases.[23] This opinion held that Michigan's and New York's regulatory schemes, which permit in-state wineries to ship alcohol directly to consumers, but restrict the ability of out-of-state wineries to do so, violate the Constitution's Commerce Clause. While the facts of these cases involved wine sales, the Court's opinion has made it more difficult for states to regulate businesses that engage in Internet-based commerce.

At issue was the 21st Amendment, which ended Prohibition in 1933 and granted states the authority to regulate alcohol sales. Nearly half the states subsequently passed laws requiring out-of-state wineries to sell their products through licensed in-state wholesalers, resulting in millions of dollars in state alcohol taxes. However, the Commerce Clause generally prohibits state laws that unreasonably discriminate against out-of-state businesses. That led to the challenges to the Michigan and New York laws.

Justice Anthony Kennedy, who wrote the majority opinion, stated, "States have broad power to regulate liquor. This power, however, does not allow States to ban, or severely limit, the direct shipment of out-of-state wine while simultaneously authorizing direct shipment by in-state producers." The Majority continued, "The differential treatment between in-state and out-of-state wineries constitutes explicit discrimination against interstate commerce," that is "neither authorized nor permitted by the Twenty-first Amendment." Justice Kennedy's opinion was joined by Justices Antonin Scalia, David H. Souter, Ruth Bader Ginsburg, and Stephen G. Breyer.

New York and Michigan defended their laws as necessary to prevent underage drinkers from buying wine without having to show proper proof of age, as well as to prevent tax evasion. The majority rejected these arguments, finding that the states "provide little concrete evidence for the sweeping assertion that they cannot police direct shipments by out-of-state wineries." Justice Kennedy also said that the states' concerns did not justify discrimination. "Minors are just as likely to order wine from in-state producers as from out-of-state ones." Moreover, he noted, minors are no more likely to purchase and consume wine than beer or wine coolers or hard liquor. Finally, the Majority asserted that minors who choose to disobey laws governing alcohol purchase/consumption have more direct means of gaining access to alcohol than methods that involve direct shipping.

Given the decision in *Granholm*, it is anticipated that any effort to regulate online sales of alcohol will face considerable political and legal hurdles, because the Court has ostensibly ruled that the only way to limit Internet sales of alcohol is to treat out-of-state direct sellers (such as Internet- based sales) and in-state direct sellers equally.[24]

POLICY PERSPECTIVES

Legislative Activity

At the federal level, legislative activity has been aimed primarily at coordinating and supporting the states' efforts. The following underage drinking prevention laws have been passed since the 106th Congress:

- Sober Truth on Preventing Underage Drinking Act (STOP Act), 2006: Mandates the Secretary of Health and Human Services to formally enhance the efforts of the Interagency Coordinating Committee on the Prevention of Underage Drinking.[25]
- Science, State, Justice, Commerce, and Related Agencies Appropriations Act, 2006:[26] Provides $25 million for grants to states to enforce minimum drinking age laws, and for technical assistance.
- Consolidated Appropriations Act, 2005:[27] Provides $25 million for grants to states to enforce minimum drinking age laws, and for technical assistance.
- No Child Left Behind Act, 2001:[28] Authorizes the Substance Abuse and Mental Health Services Administration to award grants to local educational agencies to develop and implement programs to reduce alcohol abuse in secondary schools.
- National Police Athletic League Youth Enrichment Act, 2000:[29] Provides for expansion of Police Athletic League Chapters to conduct underage drinking prevention activities in non-school hours.

- District of Columbia Appropriations Act, 2001 :[30] Provides $25 million for grants to states to enforce minimum drinking age laws, and for technical assistance.
- Missing, Exploited, and Runaway Children Protection Act, 1999:[31] Provides funding for community-based alcohol and drug abuse prevention and education services to street youth.

Although no legislation directly addressing the sale of alcohol over the Internet has been signed into law, the 106th Congress did consider a bill that indirectly dealt with this topic: S. 577, the Twenty-First Amendment Enforcement Act. Introduced by Senator Orrin Hatch (R-UT), this bill would have amended the Webb-Kenyon Act to authorize a state attorney general to deal with the consequences of new distribution channels for the sale of alcohol. S. 577 was concerned with "the interstate sale of alcohol," which included purchases made on the Internet and delivered by direct mail. By permitting states to bring actions in federal court for violation of state alcohol laws, it sought to give state attorneys more power to enforce underage drinking laws and to ensure payment of state and local taxes on the sale of alcohol.

In addition, Senator Dianne Feinstein (D-CA) inserted into The Violent and Repeat Juvenile Offender Accountability and Rehabilitation Act of 1999 (S. 254/H.R. 1501, 106th Congress) a provision that would have amended liquor trafficking prohibitions to (1) require persons who ship alcoholic beverages in interstate commerce to label the packages as containing alcohol, (2) require shipping companies to obtain the signature of the person receiving delivery of packages containing alcohol, and (3) verify that that person is of legal age for the purchase of alcohol beverages within the receiving state. None of the aforementioned bills from the 106th Congress were signed into law.

Institute of Medicine Recommendations

The 2003 Institute of Medicine (IOM) report on reducing underage drinking concluded that underage drinking cannot be successfully addressed by focusing on youth alone.[33] Because minors "usually obtain alcohol—directly or indirectly—from adults," the IOM contended, efforts to reduce drinking among teens should also be aimed at adults and industry. The IOM's recommendations, discussed below, included community-based interventions and policy options to limit or prevent underage alcohol consumption.

Prohibit Alcohol Advertisements from Targeting Youth

Long-term exposure to alcohol advertising and promotion increases the likelihood that children will drink. The IOM has called on the alcohol and entertainment industries to shield youth from unsuitable messages about drinking by ensuring that programs do not portray underage drinking in a favorable light. The IOM also suggested that Congress consider restrictions on the alcohol industry, analogous to those placed on the tobacco companies, to prevent marketing practices that disproportionately appeal to minors.

Increase Alcohol Prices Through Excise Taxes

The current tax on alcohol has not kept pace with inflation, observed the IOM, thus reducing the real price of alcohol over time. Thus, alcoholic beverages are cheaper today in real dollars than they were in the 1960s and 1970s. Research indicates that increases in alcohol price are associated with decreased underage drinking.[34] Increasing excise taxes on alcohol, according to the IOM, could provide revenue for strategies to reduce underage drinking.[35]

Public Awareness

Educating the public about the consequences of underage drinking, as well as the existing laws regarding alcohol consumption by minors, could curtail underage drinking. The IOM recommended that the federal government fund and support development of a national media effort as a major component of an adult-oriented campaign to reduce underage drinking. For these public education efforts to be effective, said the IOM, they would need to be combined with better enforcement of existing laws.

Enforcement

The IOM suggested that states or the federal government could consider criminalizing the use of falsified or fraudulent identification in an attempt to purchase alcoholic beverages, as well as criminalizing the provision of any alcohol to minors by adults, except to their own children in their own residences.

End Notes

[1] U.S. Department of Health and Human Services, *The Surgeon General's Call to Action to Prevent and Reduce Underage Drinking*, United States Department of Health and Human Services, Office of the Surgeon General, 2007, at http://www.surgeongeneral.gov/topics/underagedrinking/calltoaction.pdf.

[2] U.S. Department of Health and Human Services Press Office, *Acting Surgeon General Issues National Call to Action on Underage Drinking*, Office of the Surgeon General, March 6, 2007, at http://www.hhs.gov/news/press/2007pres/ 20070306.html.

[3] Susan E. Foster et al., "Alcohol Consumption and Expenditure for Underage Drinking and Adult Excessive Drinking," *Journal of the American Medical Association*, vol. 289, no. 8 (2003), pp. 989-95.

[4] Office of Applied Studies, "Emergency Department Visits Involving Underage Drinking," *The New DAWN Report*, Issue 1, Rockville, MD: SAMSHA, 2006, at https://dawninfo.samhsa.gov/files/tndr02underagedrinking.htm.

[5] Excluding pain and suffering from these costs, the direct costs of underage drinking incurred exceed $20.3 billion each year; Ted R. Miller, David T. Levy, Rebecca S. Spicer, and Dexter M. Taylor, "Societal Costs of Underage Drinking," *Journal of Studies on Alcohol*, vol. 67 (2006), pp. 5 19-528.

[6] For alcohol-related fatalities, the costs of pain and suffering were computed based on the monetary values that people ascribed in experimental settings to not being killed. Similarly, the pain and suffering costs of nonfatal injuries were based on the values associated with different dimensions of functioning, cognition, mobility, sensation, and pain. Methodology details are outlined at http://www.udetc.org/documents/UnderageMethods.pdf.

[7] See http://www.cdc.gov/alcohol

[8] Centers for Disease Control and Prevention, 2005, *Youth Risk Behavior Survey*, available at http://www.cdc.gov/ yrbss.

[9] Lloyd D. Johnston, Patrick M. O'Malley, Jerald G. Bachman, et al., *Monitoring the Future national survey results on drug use, 1975-2005. Volume I: Secondary school students*, NIH Publication No. 06-5883, Bethesda, MD: National Institute on Drug Abuse, 2006.

[10] SAMHSA, *Results from the 2006 National Survey on Drug Use and Health: National Findings*, NSDUH Series H30, HHS Pub. No. SMA 06-4194. Rockville, MD: SAMHSA, Office of Applied Studies, 2006.

[11] NSDUH, 2006, at http://www.oas.samhsa.gov/nsduh/2k6nsduh/2k6Results.pdf.

[12] U.S. Census regions are defined as follows: *Northeast*—Maine, New Hampshire, Vermont, Massachusetts, Rhode Island, Connecticut, New York, New Jersey, Pennsylvania; *Midwest*—Ohio, Indiana, Illinois, Michigan, Wisconsin, Minnesota, Iowa, Missouri, North Dakota, South Dakota, Nebraska, Kansas; *South*—Delaware, Maryland, District of Columbia, Virginia, West Virginia, North Carolina, South Carolina, Georgia, Florida, Kentucky, Tennessee, Alabama, Mississippi, Arkansas, Louisiana, Oklahoma, Texas; *West*—Montana, Idaho, Wyoming, Colorado, New Mexico, Arizona, Utah, Nevada, Washington, Oregon, California, Alaska, Hawaii.

[13] Large metropolitan (large metro) areas have a population of 1 million or more. Small metropolitan (small metro) areas have a population fewer than 1 million, but more than 2,500. Nonmetropolitan (nonmetro) areas are outside of "metropolitan statistical areas," which are geographic clusters defined by the United States Census Bureau that have 2,500 or more individuals and include either a city of at least 50,000 people or an urbanized area of at least 100,000 people.

[14] NSDUH , 2006, at http://www.oas.samhsa.gov/nsduh/2k6nsduh/2k6Results.pdf.

[15] Centers for Disease Control and Prevention, *2005 Youth Risk Behavior Survey*, 2005.

[16] Ralph K. Jones and John H. Lacey, *Alcohol and Highway Safety 2001: A Review of the State of Knowledge*, DOT HS 809 383, Washington, DC: National Highway Traffic Safety

Administration, 2001, at http://www.nhtsa.dot.gov/people/ injury/research/ Alcohol Highway.

[17] David F. Preusser, A.F. Williams, and H.B. Weinstein, "Policing Underage Alcohol Sales," *Journal of Safety Research*, vol. 25, pp. 127-133, 1994.

[18] This study was funded by the Wine and Spirits Wholesalers of America, Inc.

[19] David Carney, "Supreme Court Rules in Internet Wine Sales Case," *Tech Law Journal*, May 17, 2005, available at http://www.techlawjournal.com/alert/2005/05/17.asp.

[20] Richard J. Bonnie and Mary Ellen O'Connell (eds.), *Reducing Underage Drinking: A Collective Responsibility*, Institute of Medicine, Committee on Developing a Strategy to Reduce and Prevent Underage Drinking, Washington, DC: National Research Council and the Institute of Medicine, 2003, at http://www.nap.edu/catalog/10729.html.

[21] In 2005, 11.1% of teens had their own credit cards. Credit card ownership increases steadily with age. Only 6.2% of teens aged 13-14 own credit cards, compared with 13.1% of teens aged 17. Among teens 18 years of age and older, 20.5% have their own credit cards. See the Junior Achievement Interprise Poll on *Teens and Personal Finance 2005*, April 4, 2005, at http://www.ja.org/files/polls/personal_finance

[22] Kelli A. Komro and Traci L. Toomey, "Strategies to Prevent Underage Drinking," *Alcohol Research & Health*, vol. 26, no. 1 (2002), pp. 5-14.

[23] When two or more cases have common questions of law or arise of a common dispute, the Court may "consolidate" such cases and hear them simultaneously. In this instance, the Court consolidated *Granholm v. Heald* (03-1116), *Michigan Beer & Wine Wholesalers v. Heald* (03-1120), and *Swedenburg v. Kelly* (03-1274).

[24] Carney, "Supreme Court Rules in Internet Wine Sales Case," May 17, 2005.

[25] P.L. 109-422, Sec. 2(c)(1), 120 Stat. 2891.

[26] P.L. 109-108, Sec. 5(c), 119 Stat. 2300.

[27] P.L. 108-447, Sec. 2, Division B, Title I, 118 Stat. 2866.

[28] P.L. 107-110, Title IV, Sec. 4129, 115 Stat. 1757.

[29] P.L. 106-367, Sec. 6(a)(2)(B)(I), 114 Stat. 1414.

[30] P.L. 106-553, Appendix B, Title I, 114, Stat. 2762A-65. P.L. 106-553.

[31] P.L. 106-71, Sec. 3(b)(1), 113 Stat. 1042.

[32] U.S. Department of Health and Human Services, 2007, at http://www.surgeongeneral.gov/ topics/ underagedrinking/ calltoaction.pdf.

[33] Richard J. Bonnie and Mary Ellen O'Connell (eds.), *Reducing Underage Drinking: A Collective Responsibility*, Institute of Medicine, Committee on Developing a Strategy to Reduce and Prevent Underage Drinking, Washington, DC: National Research Council and the Institute of Medicine, 2003, available at http://www.nap.edu/catalog/ 10729.html.

[34] Frank J. Chaloupka, Michael Grossman, and Henry Saffer, "The effects of price on alcohol consumption and alcohol-related problems," *Alcohol Research and Health*, vol. 26, no. 1, pp. 22-34, 2002.

[35] If this policy option were pursued, the IOM emphasized that alcohol taxes would have to be indexed to the consumer price index to ensure that they keep pace with inflation.

In: Underage Drinking
Ed: David Edvin and Samuel Harald
ISBN: 978-1-60876-141-8

Chapter 3

QUANTITY AND FREQUENCY OF ALCOHOL USE*

National Survey on Drug Use and Health

IN BRIEF

- Combined 2005 and 2006 data indicate that an annual average of 28.3 percent of persons aged 12 to 20 in the United States (an estimated 10.8 million persons annually) drank alcohol in the past month
- Past month alcohol users aged 12 to 20 drank on an average of 5.9 days in the past month and consumed an average of 4.9 drinks per day on the days they drank in the past month
- Underage drinkers aged 12 to 20 consumed, on average, more drinks per day on the days they drank in the past month than persons aged 21 or older (4.9 vs. 2.8 drinks)

In 2006, a majority (53.9 percent) of American adolescents and young adults aged 12 to 20 had used an alcoholic beverage at least once in their lifetime.[1] Young people aged 12 to 20 consumed approximately 11.2 percent of the alcoholic drinks consumed in the United States in the past month by persons aged 12 or older.[2] Research shows that underage drinkers tend to

* This is an edited, reformatted and augmented version of a National Survey on Drug Use and Health publication dated March 2008.

consume more alcohol per occasion than those over the legal minimum drinking age of 21.[3] Studies also have linked early drinking to heavy alcohol consumption and alcohol-related problems in adulthood.[4,5] For example, in 2006, 16.3 percent of adults aged 21 or older who had first used alcohol before the age of 15 met the criteria for alcohol dependence or abuse in the past year compared with 2.4 percent of adults who first used alcohol at age 21 or older.[6] Research also shows that early initiation of alcohol use is associated with higher likelihood of involvement in violent behaviors, suicide attempts, unprotected sexual intercourse, and multiple sex partners.[7,8]

The National Survey on Drug Use and Health (NSDUH) asks persons aged 12 or older to report the frequency and quantity of their alcohol use during the 30 days prior to the interview. Respondents who drank alcohol in the past 30 days also are asked for the number of days they consumed alcohol in the past month and the average number of drinks consumed per day on the days they drank.[9]

This chapter focuses on the frequency and quantity of past month alcohol use among underage drinkers (i.e., persons aged 12 to 20 who consume alcohol). Comparisons of the quantity and frequency of alcohol use in the past month also are made between underage drinkers and drinkers aged 21 or older. All findings presented in this chapter are based on combined 2005 and 2006 NSDUH data.

Past Month Alcohol Use

Combined 2005 and 2006 data indicate that an annual average of 28.3 percent of persons aged 12 to 20 in the United States (an estimated 10.8 million persons annually) drank alcohol in the past month. Rates of past month alcohol use among persons aged 12 to 20 varied by demographic characteristics. Young adults aged 18 to 20 were 3 times as likely as youths aged 12 to 17 to have used alcohol in the past month (51.4 vs. 16.6 percent) (Table 1). Underage males were more likely than their female counterparts to have drunk alcohol in the past month (29.1 vs. 27.5 percent). Across racial/ethnic groups, the rate of past month alcohol use among persons aged 12 to 20 ranged from 17.6 percent among Asians to 32.3 percent among whites.[10]

Table 1. Percentages of Past Month Alcohol Use among Persons Aged 12 to 20, by Demographic Characteristics: 2005-2006.

Demographic Characteristic	Past Month Alcohol Use	
	%	SE*
Total Aged 12 to 20	28.3	0.31
Age Group		
12 to 17	16.6	0.23
18 to 20	51.4	0.58
Gender		
Male	29.1	0.39
Female	27.5	0.40
Race/Ethnicity**		
White	32.3	0.39
Black or African American	18.8	0.58
American Indian or Alaska Native	26.4	2.43
Native Hawaiian or Other Pacific Islander	18.0	3.76
Asian	17.6	1.59
Two or More Races	25.7	1.82
Hispanic or Latino	25.6	0.69

* Standard error (SE) is a measure of the sampling variability or precision of an estimate, where smaller values represent greater precision and larger values represent less precision.

** See End Note 10.

Number of Days of Alcohol Use in the Past Month

Past month alcohol users aged 12 to 20 drank on an average of 5.9 days in the past month (Figure 1). Underage drinkers aged 18 to 20 consumed alcohol on more days in the past month than those aged 12 to 17 (6.7 vs. 4.6 days). Male underage drinkers used alcohol on more days in the past month than their female counterparts (6.6 vs. 5.1 days). The number of days of alcohol use in the past month varied by race/ethnicity, ranging from an average of 4.2 days among Asians to an average of 8.3 days in the past month among Native Hawaiians or Other Pacific Islanders.

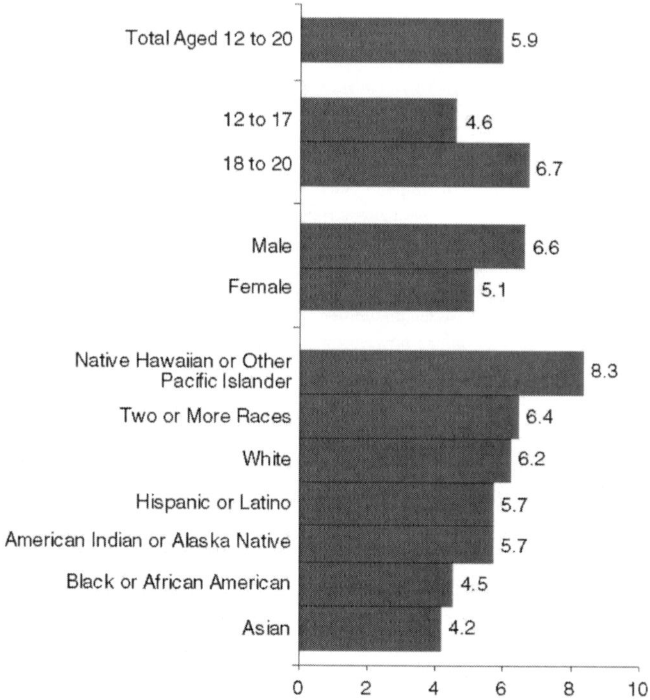

Source: SAMHSA, 2005 and 2006 NSDUHs.

Figure 1. Average Number of Days of Alcohol Use in the Past Month among Past Month Alcohol Users Aged 12 to 20, by Demographic Characteristics: 2005-2006.

Number of Drinks per Day in the Past Month

Past month alcohol users aged 12 to 20 consumed an average of 4.9 drinks per day on the days they drank in the past month (Figure 2). The average number of drinks consumed per day varied by demographic characteristics. Past month alcohol users aged 18 to 20 averaged more drinks per day than their counterparts aged 12 to 17 (5.2 vs. 4.5 drinks). Among underage past month alcohol users, males consumed an average of 5.8 drinks per day on the days they drank in the past month, and females consumed an average of 4.0 drinks per day on the days they drank. Among underage past month drinkers, the average number of drinks consumed per day ranged from 2.8 drinks per day among blacks to 6.4 drinks per day among Native Hawaiians or Other Pacific Islanders.

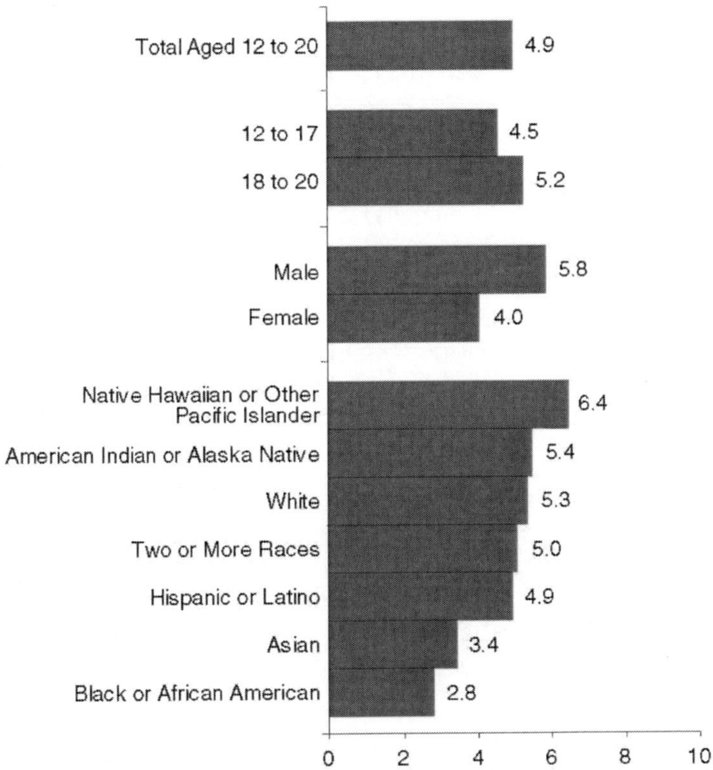

Source: SAMHSA, 2005 and 2006 NSDUHs.

Figure 2. Average Number of Drinks Consumed per Day on the Days Used Alcohol in the Past Month among Past Month Alcohol Users Aged 12 to 20, by Demographic Characteristics: 2005-2006.

Underage Drinkers versus Drinkers of Legal Age

Among past month alcohol users, drinkers aged 21 or older averaged more days of alcohol consumption in the past month than underage drinkers (8.7 vs. 5.9 days). However, underage drinkers consumed, on average, more drinks per day on the days they drank in the past month than drinkers aged 21 or older (4.9 vs. 2.8 drinks).

QUANTITY AND FREQUENCY OF ALCOHOL USE AMONG UNDERAGE DRINKERS

- Combined 2005 and 2006 data indicate that an annual average of 28.3 percent of persons aged 12 to 20 in the United States (an estimated 10.8 million persons annually) drank alcohol in the past month
- Past month alcohol users aged 12 to 20 drank on an average of 5.9 days in the past month and consumed an average of 4.9 drinks per day on the days they drank in the past month
- Underage drinkers aged 12 to 20 consumed, on average, more drinks per day on the days they drank in the past month than persons aged 21 or older (4.9 vs. 2.8 drinks)

The National Survey on Drug Use and Health (NSDUH) is an annual survey sponsored by the Substance Abuse and Mental Health Services Administration (SAMHSA). The 2005 and 2006 data used in this chapter are based on information obtained from 62,602 persons aged 12 to 20. The survey collects data by administering questionnaires to a representative sample of the population through face-to-face interviews at their place of residence.

End Notes

[1] Office of Applied Studies. (2007). *Results from the 2006 National Survey on Drug Use and Health: National findings* (DHHS Publication No. SMA 07-4293, NSDUH Series H-32). Rockville, MD: Substance Abuse and Mental Health Services Administration.

[2] Office of Applied Studies, Substance Abuse and Mental Health Services Administration. (2006, September 28). *Table 7.7B: Alcohol use in the past month and measures of past month alcohol consumption, by detailed age category: 2005.* Retrieved March 13, 2008, from http://oas.samhsa.gov/ NSDUH/ 2k5NSDUH/tabs/Sect7pe Tabs1to66.htm#Tab7.7B

[3] Institute of Medicine (Bonnie, R. J., & O'Connell, M. E., Eds.). (2004). *Reducing underage drinking: A collective responsibility*. Washington, DC: The National Academies Press. [Available at http://www.nap.edu/catalog.php?record_id=10729]

[4] Hingson, R. W., Heeren, T., Zakocs, R. C., Kopstein, A., & Wechsler, H. (2002). Magnitude of alcohol-related mortality and morbidity among U.S. college students ages 18-24. *Journal of Studies on Alcohol*, 63(2), 136-144.

[5] Grant, B. F., Stinson, F. S, & Harford, T. C. (2001). Age at onset of alcohol use and DSM–IV alcohol abuse and dependence: A 12-year follow-up. *Journal of Substance Abuse*, 13, 493-504.

[6] Office of Applied Studies, Substance Abuse and Mental Health Services Administration. (2007, October 18). *Table 7.36B: Alcohol dependence or abuse in the past year among persons aged 21 or older, by age first used alcohol and age group: Percentages, 2005 and 2006.* Retrieved March 13, 2008, from http://oas.samhsa.gov/NSDUH/2K6NSDUH/ tabs/ Sect7peTabs1to47.htm#Tab7.36B

[7] Swahn, M. H., Bossarte, R. M., & Sullivent, E. E., 3rd (2008). Age of alcohol use initiation, suicidal behavior, and peer and dating violence victimization and perpetration among high-risk, seventh-grade adolescents. *Pediatrics*, 121, 297-305.

[8] Stueve, A., & O'Donnell, L. N. (2005). Early alcohol initiation and subsequent sexual and alcohol risk behaviors among urban youths. *American Journal of Public Health*, 95, 887-893.

[9] Respondents with unknown or missing information regarding the number of alcoholic drinks consumed per day on the days that they drank were excluded from this analysis.

[10] Race/ethnicity categories are determined by combining the responses from two separate questions. For this report, respondents identifying themselves as Hispanic were assigned to the Hispanic group regardless of their racial identification. Respondents identifying themselves as non-Hispanic were grouped according to their racial identification. Thus, "white" refers to those identifying themselves as non-Hispanic and white.

In: Underage Drinking
Ed: David Edvin and Samuel Harald
ISBN: 978-1-60876-141-8

Chapter 4

SELF-REGULATION IN THE ALCOHOL INDUSTRY*

Federal Trade Commission

EXECUTIVE SUMMARY

Underage alcohol use is a widespread problem with significant health and safety consequences. This is the third Federal Trade Commission report on efforts by the alcohol industry to reduce the likelihood that alcohol advertising will target youth, by its placement or content. This chapter provides data about how industry members allocate promotional dollars; data on compliance with the industry's advertising placement standard (requiring that at least 70 percent of the audience for advertising consist of adults 21 and older); analysis of external review of advertising complaints; and an update on the FTC's "We Don't Serve Teens" campaign. The report is based on the responses to Special Orders issued to twelve major alcohol suppliers, comments submitted in response to two Federal Register notices, and discussions with a wide range of stakeholders. It provides alcohol supplier data in an aggregate or anonymous fashion.

---

* This is an edited, reformatted and augmented version of a Federal Trade Commission publication dated June 2008.

Allocation of promotional expenditures and related self-regulatory efforts. The Special Orders directed the suppliers to report 2005 expenditures in 22 categories; the suppliers also described efforts to reduce the likelihood that expenditures would be targeted to those below the legal drinking age ("LDA"). The data provided by the suppliers show that about 42 percent of promotional funds are used for television, radio, print, and outdoor advertising; about 40 percent are used to help wholesalers and retailers promote alcohol to consumers; about 16 percent are used for sponsorships; and the final 2 percent are directed to other efforts, such as Internet advertising, other digital promotions, and product placement. It appears that the suppliers keep self-regulatory responsibilities in mind as they engage in promotional efforts, even in cases where the self-regulatory codes do not expressly apply. Nevertheless, as described below, the Commission recommends improvements in standards and practice.

Compliance with the 70 percent placement standard. Prior to 2003, the industry codes permitted placing advertisements in media where as little as 50 percent of the audience was composed of adults and did not specify any placement protocol to support this standard. Between 2000 and 2003, at the Commission's recommendation, the alcohol industry modified its self-regulatory codes to require suppliers to check reliable audience composition data before placing an ad and to make a placement only if that data showed that, historically, at least 70 percent of the audience consisted of adults 21 and older. The Special Orders required the companies to describe their placement practices, and to provide data showing the composition of the audience (that is, number and percent of persons below and above the LDA) for each individual television, radio, magazine, and newspaper advertising placement disseminated in the first six months of 2006.

The responses showed that the suppliers directed their media buyers to follow the steps set forth in the self-regulatory codes, and to conduct periodic after-the-fact audits to determine whether the placements had, in fact, met the 70 percent standard. Advertising placement can be an uncertain process, as it relies on data about past audiences to predict the future. Nevertheless, more than 92 percent of all television, radio, and print advertising placements for which data were available had an LDA audience composition of 70 percent or better when they ran. Further, about 97 percent of total alcohol advertising "impressions" (that is, individual exposures to an advertisement) were due to placements that met the 70 percent target, as placements that missed the target were concentrated in media with smaller audiences. In the first half of 2006, more than 85 percent of the aggregate audience for the twelve suppliers' advertising consisted of adults above the LDA, although some individual companies' aggregates were a few points lower.

External review of advertising. Self-regulation is most effective when an advertiser's internal mechanisms for fostering code compliance are supplemented by a system in which another entity provides consistent, impartial, objective, and public resolution of disputes about whether a particular practice violates code standards. Per earlier FTC recommendations, the three major industry trade associations now have systems for external review of complaints about code compliance. In 2006, the review boards considered twenty-six complaints. Trade association members complied with review board conclusions in all cases where the review board determined that a member had violated the code.

Underage access to alcohol. Restrictions on teen access to alcohol are a proven way to reduce teen drinking. The FTC developed the "We Don't Serve Teens" ("WDST") program to provide parents and other responsible adults with information about the importance of restricting teen alcohol access. A wide range of public and private entities, including federal and state government representatives, consumer groups, the advertising industry, and the alcohol industry, joined the Commission in 2007 to spread the word, "Don't serve alcohol to teens. It's unsafe. It's illegal. It's irresponsible."

Analysis and recommendations. It is evident that the twelve major suppliers have engaged in good faith efforts to respond to the FTC's earlier recommendations, implementing the 70 percent placement standard for print and broadcast media and adopting systems of external review. The Commission believes that additional steps can be taken to reduce the likelihood of targeting those under the legal drinking age, as follows:

- *Advertising in traditional media.* The 70 percent placement standard is consistent with the 2000 census data, showing that approximately 70 percent of the American public is 21 or older. The industry has been largely successful at meeting the 70 percent standard, and, as a result, more than 85 percent of the audience for alcohol advertising placed by the twelve suppliers in the first half of 2006 consisted of persons 21 and older. Thus, the Commission does not recommend a change in the 70 percent standard at this time. Individual suppliers should consider aggregate audience composition when making placements, however, and the trade associations should consider the results of the 2010 Census, when they become available. Further, the Commission has identified practices that will facilitate better advertising placement management, potentially increasing the proportion of placements that meet the 70 percent target. These include:

- trade association adoption of consistent and transparent systems for interpreting demographic data;
- regular training of company personnel about audience composition data, including training by the trade associations on practices calculated to increase compliance with the placement standards;
- "hands on" management of media buyers; and
- maintenance of records that reflect actual buys and show the source of post- placement demographic data.

- *Internet advertising.* (1) Supplier sites. Suppliers who operate websites to promote their brands should use neutral age-entry screens, complemented by tracking tools to prevent minors from back-clicking to change their birth date once they realize that they have been blocked from an alcohol company website based on their age. (2) Online alcohol sales. Sites that sell alcohol should use age-verification technologies to ensure that alcohol is not shipped to underage purchasers. (3) Advertising on independent sites. The suppliers generally applied an informal 70 percent standard when placing advertising on independent sites, and the wine industry's 70 percent standard applies to all media, including the Internet. In the course of this study, the Commission staff recommended that the codes of the beer and distilled spirits industries be modified to extend the 70 percent placement standard to Internet advertising, and to include buying guidelines for Internet advertisements.

- *Other digital advertising.* Other digital advertising currently accounts for only a small fraction of expenditures, but is likely to grow in importance over the coming years. As alcohol marketing efforts expand into new digital areas, such as email and mobile marketing, it is important that suppliers continue to expand their age-screening and verification processes.

- *Sponsorships.* All self-regulatory codes should specify a 70 percent placement standard for sponsorship of events.

- *Product placement in films.* The Commission recommends that suppliers work with film producers to incorporate available demographic data into the analysis of prospective product placements, and place only in films that the producer has a good-faith belief will meet the 70 percent standard.

- *Expenditures to help others promote alcohol.* These expenditures are subject to the existing placement and content provisions of the codes, and are regulated at the state and federal levels. The Commission will continue to monitor this aspect of alcohol marketing, but it does not appear that additional self-regulatory provisions are needed now.

- *External review of complaints.* The Commission recommends that all of the trade associations accept online complaints, competitor complaints, anonymous complaints, and complaints about non-member advertising.

- *Youth access to alcohol.* The Commission continues to encourage all stakeholders concerned about underage alcohol use to support social responsibility efforts, such as WDST, that are designed to reduce youth access to alcohol and the subsequent alcohol-related injury.

Commission commitment to ongoing monitoring. Historically, the Commission has relied on informal inquiries and periodic major studies to monitor self-regulation. The Commission is now implementing a new monitoring system. Each year, the Commission will send compulsory process orders to between two and four suppliers, including smaller suppliers, seeking information about advertising and marketing practices, systems used to prevent deceptive and unfair marketing, and compliance with self-regulatory guidelines. This procedure will allow the Commission to appraise the industry's response to this report's recommendations; evaluate alcohol marketing efforts in new media; and consider efforts to reduce the likelihood that alcohol advertising in such new media will target youth.

I. INTRODUCTION

A. Background

Underage alcohol use is a persistent problem, giving rise to concerns about youth exposure to alcohol marketing. This is the third FTC report on activities related to alcohol and youth, including the status of alcohol industry initiatives to reduce the likelihood that alcohol advertising will target youth.[1] This chapter provides, for the first time, significant data about how industry members allocate their promotional dollars, and information about self-regulatory efforts related to these expenditures. The report also provides comprehensive information about compliance with the voluntary advertising placement standard adopted by the alcohol industry in 2003, and analyzes the status of external review of advertising complaints. Finally, it provides an update on the FTC's "We Don't Serve Teens" campaign to reduce underage access to alcohol from social sources.

This chapter is based on the responses to Special Orders issued to twelve major alcohol suppliers, public comments submitted in response to two Federal Register notices,[2] and discussions with a wide range of stakeholders. Exhibit A is a copy of the Special Order issued to the alcohol suppliers.

B. Scope of the Problem

Underage drinking is a leading public health and social problem in the United States, associated with the three leading causes of death among youth – unintentional injury, homicide, and suicide. A recent study by the Centers for Disease Control and Prevention ("CDC") paints a disturbing picture of the risks associated with youth drinking. These include driving after drinking; riding with a driver who has been drinking; sexual activity and pregnancy of self or partner; tobacco use; interpersonal violence; consideration of or attempt at suicide; and use of marijuana, cocaine, or inhalants.[3] Binge drinkers are even more likely to engage in these risky behaviors.[4] There also is a relationship between academic problems and drinking.[5]

In 2007, about 16 percent of 8th graders, 33 percent of 10th graders, and 44 percent of 12th graders reported drinking in the past thirty days.[6] Although current teen drinking levels are unacceptably high, they have declined substantially over time, as shown in Figure 1.[7]

Once youth start to drink, they are likely to report engaging in drunkenness or binge drinking (defined as the consumption of 5 or more drinks on the same occasion), as shown by Figure 2.[8] Teens drink a wide range of alcohol types, including beer, distilled spirits, wine, and flavored beverages.[9]

Recent federal efforts reinforce the conclusion that underage drinking is an issue of national importance. The Sober Truth About Preventing Underage Drinking Act ("STOP Act"), signed into law in 2006, called for a focused national effort to reduce underage drinking,[10] including a "coordinated approach to prevention, intervention, treatment, enforcement, and research."[11] The Surgeon General's *Call to Action to Prevent and Reduce Underage Drinking* ("*Call to Action*"), issued in 2007, called for reduced societal acceptance of underage drinking, delay of drinking initiation, and reduction of negative consequences related to youth drinking.[12] It emphasized that alcohol use must be understood in the context of adolescent development, taking into account the processes of maturation, the influence of social systems, and individual characteristics.[13]

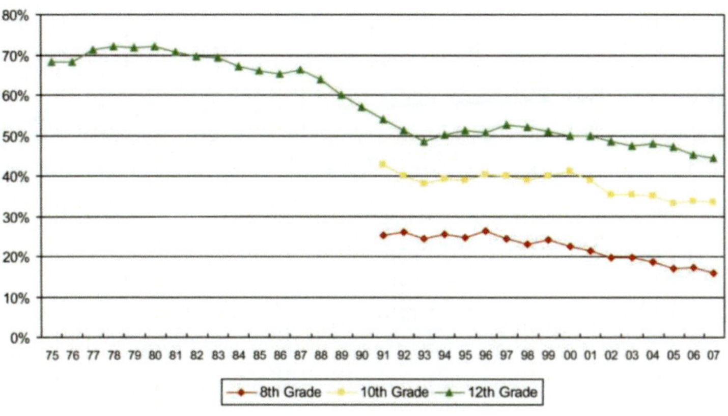

Source: The Monitoring the Future study, the University of Michigan.

Figure 1. Percent of High School Students Reporting Alcohol Use in the Past 30 days, Long-term Trends.

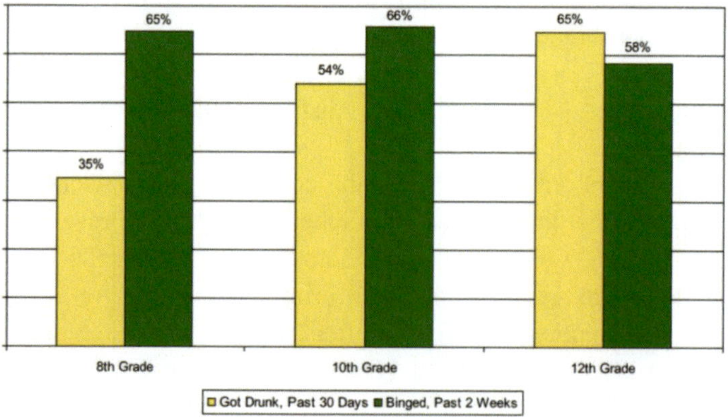

Source: The Monitoring the Future study, the University of Michigan.

Figure 2. Levels of Binging and DrunkennessAmong Teens Who Drink.

C. The FTC and Alcohol Industry Self-Regulation

The three major alcohol supplier trade associations – the Beer Institute ("BI"), the Distilled Spirits Council of the United States ("DISCUS"), and the Wine Institute ("WI") – have adopted voluntary advertising and marketing codes (hereafter referred to collectively as the "codes" and individually as "BI Code," "DISCUS Code," or "WI Code").[14] The codes contain provisions relating to both the content and the placement of marketing efforts. The FTC's two prior alcohol marketing studies, published in 1999 and 2003, evaluated compliance with, and the appropriateness of, alcohol industry voluntary self-regulatory guidelines designed to reduce the likelihood that alcohol advertising will, by its content or placement, target consumers below the legal drinking age. The 1999 Report identified a number of promising practices relating to advertising placement and content and external review of complaints about compliance with code provisions.[15] The 2003 Alcohol Report announced that, at the Commission's recommendation, the industry had adopted improved standards for where advertising could be placed, requiring that at least 70 percent of the audience for each advertisement consist of adults 21 and over, based on reliable data. The 2003 Alcohol Report also noted that one segment of industry had improved external review of code compliance; the Commission encouraged the other industry segments to adopt system for external review of complaints, particularly complaints about underage appeal of alcohol advertising. [16]

After 2003, the Commission continued its active monitoring and review of alcohol advertising and compliance with the self-regulatory guidelines. The FTC staff worked with industry trade associations and individual companies to facilitate compliance with the new 70 percent advertising placement standard and to encourage improvement in external review of compliance. Following media stories about promotions for drinking games, the FTC staff worked with the trade associations to facilitate rapid adoption of code provisions to prohibit such practices.

In March 2006, the agency announced the initiation of this study.[17] In January 2007, following completion of the process set forth by the Paperwork Reduction Act, the Commission issued Special Orders to the twelve alcohol suppliers that were identified by public sources as the top spenders on alcohol advertising in "measured media" (television, radio, print, and outdoor advertising) in 2005.[18] *See* Exhibit A.

The Special Orders required submission of: contact information and other background data (Specification 1); advertising expenditure data (Specification 2); advertisement placement data (Specification 3); and information on external enforcement mechanisms (Specification 4). In addition, the staff requested that the suppliers and the trade associations submit substantial additional information that would "flesh out" the responses to the Special Orders. The Commission's findings are set forth below.

II. Study of Industry Self-Regulation

A. Supplier Background Information[19]

In 2005, the twelve suppliers that received Special Orders sold over 2.4 billion cases of alcohol,[20] representing about 73 percent of U.S. alcohol supplier sales by volume in 2005. Their pre-tax sales revenues were approximately $30.8 billion.[21] They sold 1,133 brands or brand extensions, including 246 wines, 169 beers, 659 distilled spirits, and 59 alternative beverages (such as premixed cocktails and flavored malt beverages).

B. Advertising and Promotional Expenditures

The FTC's 1999 Alcohol Report had estimated, based upon marketing documents provided for a few brands, that measured media expenditures might account for only one-third of alcohol brand promotional budgets. The Special Orders directed the twelve suppliers to report the dollar amount they expended during the calendar year 2005 on the advertising, merchandising, or promotion of beverage alcohol products in the United States in 22 categories.[22]

The purpose of the request was to identify generally what kinds of marketing efforts the suppliers engage in, so that the Commission could evaluate the extent to which current self-regulatory provisions address these efforts. In addition to providing expenditure data, the companies provided examples of programs supported by expenditures, particularly expenditures in lesser-known categories, and described efforts to reduce the likelihood that such expenditures would be targeted to those below the legal drinking age ("LDA").

1. Response Summary

The companies reported just over $3 billion in advertising and promotional expenditures in 2005, presented below in descending order of prevalence:[23]

Table 1. Industry-wide Allocation of Advertising and Promotion Expenditures.

Category	% of Total Industry Expenditure	Amount Spent (in Thousands)	Minimum % of Company Expenditure	Maximum % of Company Expenditure
Television	25.97%	$825,915	1.43%	36.48%
Other Point-of-Sale Advertising and Promotions	18.84%	$599,105	0.00%	53.17%
Sponsorship of Sporting Events, Sports Teams, or Individual Athletes	10.95%	$348,340	0.26%	20.71%
Promotional Allowances	7.49%	$238,200	0.00%	58.87%
Specialty Item Distribution	7.02%	$223,423	0.17%	27.56%
Retail Value-Added	5.99%	$190,481	0.00%	13.43%
Outdoor	5.62%	$178,795	2.99%	12.96%

Table 1. (Continued)

Category	% of Total Industry Expenditure	Amount Spent (in Thousands)	Minimum % of Company Expenditure	Maximum % of Company Expenditure
Public Entertainment: Not Sports Related	5.07%	$161,301	0.73%	13.45%
Radio	5.01%	$159,504	0.00%	12.24%
Magazine	4.36%	$138,784	1.00%	13.47%
Supplier-Sponsored Internet Sites	1.08%	$34,501	0.05%	2.35%
Newspaper	0.91%	$28,815	0.22%	1.96%
Other Internet Sites	0.77%	$24,498	0.00%	2.78%
Transit	0.41%	$13,109	0.00%	1.35%
Direct Mail	0.30%	$9,464	0.00%	2.99%
Product Placements	0.11%	$3,398	0.00%	0.82%
Other Digital	0.06%	$1,797	0.00%	0.17%
Telemarketing	0.02%	$684	0.00%	0.14%
Spring Break Promotions	0.02%	$482	0.00%	0.06%
Total Reportable	**100.00%**	**$3,131 ,130**[24]		
Cross Categories				
Sports and Sporting Events	26.33%	$837,335	0.00%	45.80%
Social Responsibility Programs and Messages	3.50%	$111,219	0.00%	5.31%

2. Traditional Media

Traditional advertising on television and radio and in magazines and newspapers accounted for just over 36 percent of expenditures. The self-regulatory codes of the three trade associations specify that ads should be placed during radio and television programming or in print media only if at least 70 percent of the audience is reasonably expected to consist of persons of legal drinking age and older ("LDA adults").[25] The BI and DISCUS codes – which govern the practices of the twelve suppliers evaluated during this study – include buying guidelines that identify appropriate demographic data to consider when making television, radio, and magazine purchases.[26] Part II.C of this chapter evaluates industry compliance with this standard.

3. Outdoor Advertising

Outdoor advertising (such as billboards) represented about 5.6 percent of expenditures. Transit advertising (such as ads at bus stops and other transportation facilities) represented about 0.4 percent of expenditures. The BI Code and the DISCUS Code specify that outdoor stationary advertising may not be located within 500 feet of elementary and secondary schools or places of worship; the WI Code does not address the placement of outdoor ads.[27]

4. Sponsorships

Sponsorships accounted for 16.3 percent of expenditures. Two-thirds of these funds were directed at sponsoring sports events (e.g., football, baseball, or auto racing), sports teams, and individual athletes.[28] The other third was directed to non-sports events, such as sponsorship of concerts and comedians. The BI Code provides that advertising and marketing is prohibited at any event where "most" of the audience is expected to be below the legal drinking age; the DISCUS Code requires that 70 percent of the audience for sponsored events consist of LDA adults; and the WI Code requires that advertising not "use entertainment or sports celebrities having a particular appeal to persons" below the LDA.[29] If sponsored events are carried on television or radio, the promotions also are subject to the code placement provisions applicable to advertising in those media.

5. Expenditures to Help Others Promote Alcohol Products

Suppliers rarely sell alcohol directly to consumers; instead, they sell to wholesalers (also known as distributors), who in turn sell to retailers. Retailers fall into two categories. They may serve alcohol for immediate use "on premise," as in the case of restaurants, bars, and sports stadiums. Or they can sell product for use "off premise," as in the case of liquor, grocery, and convenience stores. Several of the categories identified in the Special Orders sought information about supplier expenditures to help wholesalers and retailers promote their products to consumers.

Nineteen percent of expenditures were devoted to the other point-of-sale ("POS") category, meaning expenditures by suppliers to produce promotional materials used by retailers engaged in either on-premise or off-premise sales. POS expenditures fell into three general categories. The first was inexpensive items such as temporary signs of all sizes, display racks, table tents, coasters, and napkins. The second was permanent or semi-permanent materials such as neon signs, branded furniture, lighting, and mirrors. The third was promotional events, such as product tastings and bar nights, intended to promote brand trial. In most cases, POS promotional items are installed by a wholesaler, rather than the supplier.

The specialty item and retail value-added categories represented 13.2 percent of expenditures. Specialty items include items other than alcohol that are distributed to consumers at retail; examples are branded clothing or glassware. Retail value-added refers to promotions where a consumer gets a free alcohol or non-alcohol item with a purchase, such as a free bottle of wine or a bottle opener.

Promotional allowances represented 7.5 percent of expenditures. Promotional allowances are funds provided by a supplier to its wholesalers or, infrequently, to retailers. Wholesalers use these funds for a variety of purposes, including the purchase (from the supplier) of POS materials, installation of POS materials at retail, the purchase of local advertising, and the conduct of local marketing programs. Some suppliers provide lump-sum grants to wholesalers in advance; others reimburse the wholesaler for money actually spent.

The suppliers appear to keep self-regulatory provisions in mind when providing assistance to local marketing efforts. One supplier stated:

> We require a distributor to propose . . . a promotional program to our local sales or marketing employees for approval. We require our employees to fully evaluate the program to ensure compliance with local regulations, [the self-regulatory code], as well as compliance with [the supplier's] internal marketing code. Often our local employee will involve the Legal Department if there are any questions or concerns. Similarly, if the local promotion involves media purchases, all purchases must be pre-cleared with [the supplier's director of media services] . . . . In addition, in states where we have contracts with our distributors, we require the distributor to abide by the applicable [self-regulatory codes].

Many of these expenditures are subject to provisions of the Federal Alcohol Administration Act ("FAA Act"), and implementing regulations thereunder, designed to preserve retailer independence from suppliers and wholesalers.[30] In addition, the states heavily regulate retailers' acceptance and use of POS, specialty and retail-value-added items, and promotional allowances from wholesalers and suppliers.[31]

6. Internet

Internet promotions represented only 1.9 percent of expenditures; this likely reflects the relatively low cost of Internet marketing, rather than its potential reach. Just over half of the funds dedicated to Internet marketing supported company-sponsored sites; the remainder was directed to promotions on other sites.

a. Company-Sponsored Sites

In the case of company-sponsored sites, the Commission previously recommended that companies limit access to those users stating that they are over 21, for example, by entering a birth date indicating an age of 21 or older to gain admission.[32] It also recommended that sites featuring content likely to have strong appeal to minors, or that permit alcohol purchases online, consider use of age-verification technologies, *i.e.*, systems that instantly compare the consumer's personal information to electronic databases of government and commercial information, to verify that the identified consumer is 21 or older.[33]

The twelve companies that received the Commission's Special Orders operate 223 websites to promote their brands.[34] Of these, 197 websites require the user to input his or her date of birth to gain entry to the site; if a user indicates an age under 21, the site will prohibit access, often redirecting the browser to a consumer education website.[35] Another ten company-operated websites require the user to certify that he or she is 21 or older (by checking a box). Finally, sixteen company-operated websites do not screen for age in any manner.

One alcohol company uses age-verification technology on a company-owned site. In February 2007, Anheuser-Busch launched an online entertainment network, Bud.TV (www. budtv.com). The company is using an age-verification system to limit entry to the site.[36]

b. Online Alcohol Sales

Four of the suppliers that received the Commission's Special Orders operate websites that offer consumers the ability to purchase alcohol online, either directly from the company, or by linking to a third-party alcohol vendor. In response to Commission recommendations, these companies now all either employ age-verification technologies in connection with online sales or perform a similar check after the potential purchaser has phoned or faxed in his or her personal information.

c. Advertising on Independent Sites

Alcohol suppliers also advertised widely on independent sites. In 2006, the self-regulatory codes applied to Internet advertising but did not specify a 70 percent placement standard or include an Internet buying guideline. Nonetheless, most individual companies advised the Commission that they followed a 70 percent standard for placing advertising on independent sites. They made placement decisions in light of a site's demographic data for the prior two or three months, as measured by one or both of two Internet data measuring services.[37] For websites not so measured, several companies required third-party verification that the target site met the 70 percent placement standard; another assumed that websites based on magazines or television programs shared the demographics of the magazine or program at issue. In addition, some prominent websites used filtering mechanisms to direct alcohol ads only to users whose registration information identified them as being 21 or older.[38]

7. Telemarketing, Mail, and Digital Communications

Three categories of expenditures reflecting communication with individual consumers – telemarketing, direct mail, and other digital advertising – accounted for 0.4 percent of expenditures. Telemarketing, according to suppliers, referred to use of "on hold" messages when consumers call a company, either for general inquiries or in connection with sweepstakes (some states require a 1-800 number for sweepstakes). Direct mail – either U.S. mail or electronic – as reported by suppliers, was used to communicate with consumers who joined a product club. Other digital advertising consisted of email and text messaging communications with customers; only consumers who consented to such messages were included in the promotions.

Suppliers used a variety of means to reduce the likelihood of communicating with those under the legal age. One supplier maintained a database of registered users who opted-in to receive emails; it used an outside contractor to conduct age verification and eliminated from the database those not verified to be 21 or older. Another supplier required that consumers seeking to send text messages "voting" on the appearance of an advertising campaign first enter their date of birth; if the date of birth showed the consumer to be less than 21, the vote was rejected. A third supplier sent emails to website visitors who had entered a date of birth showing that they were LDA adults to gain entry to the site, who thereafter opted-in for email communications. Several companies' forward-to-a-friend campaigns required that the email recipient connect to the company's websites through a gateway page that screened for the recipient's age. Finally, one company's digital marketing policy sought to limit transfer of advertising content to underage users by creating content that could not be copied (*e.g.*, through right-clicking and using the "save as" feature); this company also included statements in close proximity to the downloadable advertising content, prohibiting the sharing of such content with persons under the legal drinking age.

8. Spring Break

Spring break promotions represented 0.02 percent of expenditures. According to the Special Order responses, spring break activities were limited to licensed retail establishments; materials supplied for these activities included special bar signs and branded product give-aways.

9. Product Placement

Product placements accounted for 0.1 percent of expenditures. A product placement most often consists of making product or other branded items available for use as props in movies or television programs. Less often, suppliers have provided cross-promotional support for films, in the form of advertising, website development, and specialty item distribution.

Product placements on television are treated in the same manner as advertising on television, that is, they are appropriate only if the available data supports the conclusion that at least 70 percent or more of audience members will be LDA adults. In the case of films, suppliers advised that product placement decisions have been made on a case-by-case basis, based upon review of the proposed script.[39]

10. Cross-Category Analysis

a. Sports and Sporting Events

Suppliers estimated, from across the previously identified categories, that 27 percent of all promotional expenses were directed to sports and sporting events. This includes expenditures to sponsor teams or events as well as the placement of advertising during sports programming.

Three percent of supplier expenditures were made in connection with college sports. The BI Code permits marketing on college campuses or at college-sponsored events if permitted by the school.[40] DISCUS and WI prohibit marketing on college campuses.[41]

b. Social Responsibility Programs and Messages

The Special Orders required the suppliers to estimate expenditures to support social responsibility programs and messages. The expenditures reported in this category could, but did not necessarily, duplicate expenditures reported in prior categories (such as television and print ads). On average, suppliers reported that an amount equal to about 3.5 percent of 2005 promotional expenditures were dedicated to these efforts.[42]

C. Advertising Placement

The placement provisions of the BI Code and the DISCUS Code include a protocol, as well as a placement standard. They require the companies to check audience composition data before placing an ad, and permit a placement only if specific demographic data identified in the buying guidelines show that 70 percent or more of the audience has, over the past six months to a year (depending on the medium), consisted of LDA adults.[43] The responses to the Special Orders provided information about the extent to which industry adopted procedures consistent with the placement provisions, as well as whether they were successful in attaining an LDA audience composition of 70 percent or higher when the advertisement actually ran.

1. Placement Procedures

It appears that all twelve of the suppliers made good-faith efforts to implement the protocols described in the codes. They directed their media buyers[44] to review the available demographic data before placing ads, and to place ads only if the data showed that the audience historically met the 70 percent standard.[45] Before placing in television, the suppliers directed their buyers to consider the syndicated demographic data for the past six months for the program in which the advertisement would appear, except in the case of small cable networks, where data were available only for three- to six-hour dayparts. Before placing on radio, they directed the buyers to consider the audience composition data for the past six months for the standard daypart in which the advertisement would appear. Before placing in magazines, the suppliers directed the buyers to consider the most recently published syndicated data about the audience for that publication; if the publication was not measured by a syndicated data source, the suppliers relied on other data, as identified in the codes. If a supplier learned that a magazine's readership fell below the 70 percent standard, it would stop advertising in that magazine, or place ads only in a special "21 plus" edition of the publication.[46] Some suppliers also considered other factors when placing ads, to reduce the likelihood of reaching an underage audience. For example, most directed magazines not to place ads in issues that featured underage persons on the cover; others prohibited ads on wrestling or animated programs on television.

Some of the suppliers purchased advertising as much as a full year in advance; in such cases, suppliers and media buyers generally re-reviewed data before the placement actually occurred. If updated data showed that the audience had changed, the outlet was placed on a "no-buy" list until it came into compliance.[47]

2. Placement Results

The preceding paragraphs discussed the procedures that the companies followed, and the data they considered, *before* making a placement. The Special Orders required the companies also to provide data showing the composition of the audience (that is, number and percent of persons below and above the LDA) for each individual television, radio, magazine, and newspaper advertising placement that occurred in the first six months of 2006.[48]

The combined data for the twelve suppliers are summarized in Table 2, below.

Table 2. Summary of Placement Data.

	Column A: Placements That Met Target	Column B: Impressions From Placements That Met Target	Column C: Proportion of Aggregate Audience 21+
All Ads	92.50%	97.12%	86.22%
Television	93.94%	97.45%	85.68%
Radio	92.04%	95.11%	88.12%
Newspapers	99.77%	100.00%	91 .80%
Magazines	98.51%	98.99%	86.34%
Targeted Ads: African American	94.17%	96.86%	87.99%
Targeted Ads: Hispanic	92.85%	94.35%	83.30%

First, the Commission evaluated what percentage of the twelve suppliers' placements met the 70 percent target, industry-wide. As shown in Column A of Table 2, 92.5 percent of all television, radio, and print advertising placements for which data were available hit the 70 percent target, that is, had an LDA audience composition of 70 percent or higher.[49] This included about 94 percent of television advertisements, 92 percent of radio advertisements, 99 percent of newspaper advertisements, and 98 percent of magazine advertisements. Among placements that did not meet the 70 percent target, most (about two-thirds) had an LDA audience of 60 percent or higher.

Second, the Commission evaluated "impressions" data; impressions are the number of persons exposed to an ad. Some programs and print media have large audiences and thus result in many advertising impressions, whereas others have small audiences and result in few impressions. For example, an advertisement on a local radio or special interest cable network generally will result in far fewer impressions than an advertisement shown on national network television.

Column B in Table 2 shows what proportion of the suppliers' advertising impressions results from placements that met the 70 percent target. Overall, about 97 percent of total alcohol advertising impressions were due to advertising placements that met the 70 percent target, including about 97 percent of television impressions, 95 percent of radio impressions, and nearly all newspaper and magazine impressions. Further, less than 0.6 percent of impressions occurred as a result of advertising with less than a 60 percent adult audience.

Column C in Table 2 shows the percentage of the aggregate audience for alcohol ads that was composed of persons 21 and older (as opposed to underage persons) ("aggregate LDA composition"). Overall, about 86 percent of audience members for the measured advertising was 21 or older. Further, among individual suppliers, the aggregate LDA composition ranged from a low of 83.2 percent to a high of 87.8 percent.

The Commission also collected data about advertising targeted to African-American or Hispanic audiences.[50] Among placements targeted to African-American audiences, 94 percent met the 70 percent target, and among placements targeted to Hispanic audiences, 92.8 percent met the 70 percent target, as shown in Column A. More than 87 percent of the audience for African-American-targeted advertising, and more than 83 percent of the audience for advertising targeted to Hispanic audiences, was composed of persons 21 or older, per Column C. Further, among individual suppliers, the aggregate LDA composition ranged from a low of 82.8 percent to a high of

100 percent for ads targeted to an African-American audience, and from a low of 78.8 percent to a high of 89.1 percent for advertising targeted to a Hispanic audience.

3. Motor Sports Promotions

Concerns have been raised about alcohol advertising and promotions related to the National Association of Stock Car Auto Racing, or NASCAR, given recent statements by NASCAR that this sport is highly popular with youth.[51] The Special Order responses confirm that several suppliers sponsor motor sports teams or events, or advertise during motor sports programming. The Commission's study shows that nearly all (98 percent) of motor sports programs on which alcohol advertising appeared in the first half of 2006 had a 70 percent or higher LDA audience; in the aggregate, about 92 percent of the audience for these programs was composed of LDA adults.[52] According to available data, the audience attending NASCAR events is 85 percent above the LDA.[53]

D. External Review of Compliance

1. Background

To increase the effectiveness of self regulation, prior Commission reports recommended supplementing suppliers' internal mechanisms for fostering code compliance with an external system for resolving disputes about whether a particular advertisement violates the code.[54] The Commission recommended that such a system: (1) be impartial and objective; (2) be public; and (3) apply standards consistently.[55] Specification 4 of the Commission's Special Orders directed the companies to provide detailed information about the status of third-party review, including information about complaints reviewed by the BI, DISCUS, or WI review boards in 2006.[56] The Commission considered the responses in light of public comments asking that: (1) the Commission evaluate whether industry members comply with review board recommendations; (2) industry members be barred from the review boards, in order to eliminate bias in industry's favor; and (3) fines be assessed for code violations, in order to increase deterrence.[57]

2. External Review Procedures

The DISCUS review board is made up of senior member company representatives. It also has an Outside Advisory Board that is available to break a tie when the review board cannot reach a majority decision.[58] DISCUS will consider complaints filed by consumers or competitors about advertising of any member's spirits, wine, and beer brands, as well as about advertising for non-members' spirits brands. DISCUS will consider complaints lodged anonymously. The DISCUS website, www.discus.org, contains the DISCUS Code, buying guidelines, information about the outside advisory board, and the decisions of the review board, which are published semi-annually. It does not permit complaints to be filed online, however.

The Wine Institute adopted third-party review in September 2005. The WI requires that complaints about wine advertising be reviewed first by an internal panel of association officers. If this committee finds that an advertisement violates the WI code, the vintner may elect to have the advertisement reviewed by an independent third-party reviewer.[59] The WI website, www. wineinstitute.org, contains the text of the WI Code, a flowchart outlining the complaint review process, and information on how to file a complaint. It also states that findings of the review process will be published on the WI website. The WI considers complaints about WI member products only. The WI will consider complaints by competitors, but it will not take anonymous complaints.

The Beer Institute implemented its external review system in February 2006. The five-member BI review board is comprised wholly of non-industry personnel, drawn from the advocacy, legal, and marketing communities.[60] Under the BI's review process, complaints are first considered by the relevant brewer; complainants who are dissatisfied with the brewer's response may then file a formal complaint with the BI review board. The BI website, www. beerinstitute.org, contains the text of the advertising code and buying guidelines, decisions of the review board, and the review board's annual reports.[61] The site's homepage contains a clearly labeled, prominent link to this information. The BI permits online complaint submissions (the other trade associations do not); the BI's website contains the online form, as well as a downloadable print-and-send complaint form. The BI does not accept anonymous complaints. The BI accepts complaints about non-member company advertising, and sends them to the non-member company for its consideration; to date, no complainant has asked for further consideration of a non-member's advertising by the BI review board. The BI does not accept competitor complaints.[62]

3. Review Board Decisions and Compliance

In 2006, the review boards of the three industry trade associations considered a total of twenty-six complaints alleging that suppliers had violated the placement or content provisions of the codes. The results are shown in Table 3, below:[63]

As shown in Table 3, the review boards agreed with the complainants in 12 of the 26 cases (46 percent). In all cases where the complaint pertained to advertising by a member of the trade association at issue, the member complied with the review board decision. Additionally, in 75 percent of cases involving non-members, DISCUS was able to persuade the advertiser to comply with the findings of the DISCUS review board.

III. YOUTH ALCOHOL ACCESS

Limiting youth access to alcohol is demonstrated to be effective in reducing and preventing underage drinking and drinking-related problems.[66] Experts attribute the substantial long-term reductions in teen drinking depicted in Figure 1 of this chapter to the adoption, in the 1980's, of laws limiting alcohol purchases to persons 21 and older.[67] Indeed, teen drinking rates have declined along with teen perceptions that alcohol is easily available to them.[68]

Table 3. External Review – 2006.

	Complaints Considered	**Decisions Adverse to Advertiser (#, %)**	**Company Compliance with Review Board Decision (#, %)**
DISCUSS			
• Complaints about member ads	12	4 (33%)	4 (100%)
• Complaints about non-member ads	10	8 (80%)	6 (75%)
Beer Institute	4[64]	0	not applicable
Wine Institute	0[65]	not applicable	not applicable
Total	26	12 (46%)	10 (83%)

Today, most teens who drink alcohol obtain it from social sources (from older friends or siblings, at parties where adults are present, or by taking it from their own homes, or those of friends, with or without permission),[69] although older adolescents may also obtain it from commercial sources.[70] In its 2003 Alcohol Report, the Commission stated that the availability of alcohol to teens could only be reduced by changing adult attitudes about teen use.[71] The Institute of Medicine and the Surgeon General also called for increased attention to youth access to alcohol and a change in adult attitudes about youth drinking.[72]

In October 2006, the Commission launched the "We Don't Serve Teens" ("WDST") consumer education program, spreading the message, "Don't serve alcohol to teens. It's unsafe. It's illegal. It's irresponsible." WDST is a government program targeted to parents and other responsible adults. The WDST website, www.dontserveteens.gov, summarizes the available data about teen drinking rates and risks, provides links to state drinking age laws, and describes efforts parents can undertake to protect their children from alcohol-related harm. The site rebuts common assertions about teen drinking – such as the pervasive myth that European teens drink less than American teens.[73] The materials on the website – including public service announcements ("PSAs") for television, radio, and print media – are available in English and Spanish, free of charge. Following the launch, public and private partners identified on the website helped deliver the WDST message to a broad range of constituencies.

In September 2007, the Commission sponsored WDST Week, designed to dramatically heighten awareness of the program by concentrating PSAs and media events in a short period of time. The Commission obtained substantial help in this effort. The alcohol and advertising industries disseminated thousands of WDST PSAs across the nation, on billboards, radio, and television, and in magazines and newspapers.[74] National print media including *Time*, *U.S. News and World Report*, *Newsweek*, *Good Housekeeping*, and *Travel & Leisure* featured WDST ads. On radio, the WDST message was delivered by PSAs featuring state attorneys general and FTC personnel (in both English and in Spanish). On television, the WDST message was delivered via a television ad, also available in both English and Spanish, that can be seen on the WDST website. In seventeen states, state attorneys general participated in WDST press conferences that also featured law enforcement, state alcohol regulators, consumer groups, and industry members; these events generated numerous follow-up articles about the importance of limiting teen access to alcohol in local media.[75] Further, in the weeks and months before the press events, alcohol industry members worked to deliver WDST retail materials (including cold case clings and lapel pins for sales staff) to tens of thousands of retail outlets nationwide.[76] A complete list of 2007's WDST Week participants, and examples of the print and billboard PSAs, are attached as Exhibit B. WDST Week generated more than 1.1 billion advertising impressions for the WDST program, with a market value of over $9 million.

IV. Analysis and Recommendations

A. Placement of Advertising

Alcohol suppliers devote a substantial proportion of promotional expenditures to traditional television, radio, and print media advertising.[77] The suppliers have implemented the placement procedures – including the review of available audience demographic data before making placements and the conduct of periodic post-placement audits–that were added to the codes n 2003. Further, the post-placement data show that more than 92 percent of the placements met the 70 percent target when they ran and more than 97 percent of impressions were due to advertisements that met this target.[78]

Advertising placement relies on historical data to make decisions about the future. Some placement shortfalls – instances when the audience turns out to be different than expected–are likely to be unavoidable, given the nature of the available data.

First, audience composition can change unexpectedly due to programming modifications or competitive factors. In the case of television, national audience demographic data are updated at least monthly and companies can adjust their purchases frequently. Radio data, however, are updated only twice per year, and magazine data are updated only once per year.[79] As a result, advertisements placed on radio and in magazines may run for many months before a company learns of the need to modify a placement.

Second, audience composition data consist of statistical projections from surveys of samples of media users. In the current environment, many media compete for the attention of viewers. In the case of niche media – such as local radio, local television, and small cable networks – the sample from which audience share is projected can be very small.[80] This produces "bounce," which is defined as "a change in station ratings from one [ratings] book to the next that is the result of a sampling error rather than any real change" in audience demographics.[81] Indeed, the study data showed that network television advertisements, where the sample sizes are larger, were far less likely to miss the 70 percent target, as compared to local station advertisements.[82] Bounce appears likely to have contributed to some of the shortfalls seen in the 2006 radio and television data. Upcoming technological improvements in radio[83] and television[84] audience measurements may, over time, produce improvements in the placement process.

The Commission believes, however, that placement management difficulties also contributed to the shortfalls seen in the 2006 data, as described in Part II.C.2, above. In the course of the study, there were instances when data submitted by the suppliers were flawed; the Commission therefore required the submission of corrected and additional data.[85] It appeared that some company personnel did not understand the audience composition data well enough to evaluate the data critically and identify potential problems. These kinds of problems may be avoided in the future with minor improvements in the placement system, as discussed further below.

Some stakeholders have urged the Commission to recommend changes in the placement standard. Two alternative proposals have been put forward. The first proposal calls for limiting advertisements to media where 85 percent of audience members twelve and older are above the legal age (hereafter, the "85 percent baseline standard").[86] Others have recommended that the industry adopt a 75 percent LDA baseline standard for television, radio, and print advertisements, coupled with a minimum aggregate average LDA audience composition of 85 percent per brand and medium ("75 percent baseline/85 percent aggregate" standard), consistent with a commitment made by Beam Global Spirits and Wine ("Beam Global") in 2007.[87] The Surgeon General's *Call to Action* did not call for a change in the placement standard but emphasized that the placement of alcohol advertising, promotions, and other means of marketing should not disproportionately expose youth to messages about alcohol.[88]

A change in the placement standard would require the suppliers to modify their advertising plans. If a 75 percent baseline standard had been in place in 2006, it would have required the suppliers to relocate about 12 percent of their placements.[89] An 85 percent baseline standard would require more significant modifications.[90]

Proponents of the 85 percent baseline standard argue that under the current regime, youth are disproportionately exposed to alcohol advertising – that is, they argue that, per capita, youth see more television, radio, and print alcohol advertising than do adults. In support of their argument, they rely on an analysis that purports to compare alcohol advertising "gross rating points" ("GRPs," a measure of advertising exposure) reaching youth and adults. The proponents' own data, however, appear to show that the primary audience for alcohol advertising is of legal drinking age. For example, under the current 70 percent placement standard, young LDA adults see more alcohol advertising than do youth.[91] Further, as proposed, the 85 percent baseline standard would prohibit alcohol advertisements in media where more than 15 percent of audience is aged 12 to 20, but it would permit an unlimited number of children ages 2 to 11 to be in the audience. Such an approach does not appear sufficiently protective of young children.[92]

Of course, a change in the baseline standard is intended to reduce underage impressions. It is unclear, however, that this is an assured result. Advertising expenditure and placement decisions are a function of numerous factors, including decisions by existing suppliers to introduce new brands or increase their budgets for existing brands, as well as decisions by new entrants to engage in advertising; indeed, each year, several hundred new alcohol brands are introduced in the United States, sometimes accompanied by significant advertising and marketing support.[93] Further, the placement standards apply to individual placements; they do not and cannot control the total level of alcohol advertising and promotional expenditures that occur. If the standard were raised, an advertiser seeking to reach a certain number of young LDA adults[94] could (subject to budget constraints) run advertisements on a greater number of programs. Even if each of the programs met an 85 percent standard, total underage exposure could increase.

An effective alcohol self-regulatory guideline should be designed to prevent industry members from targeting youth without undue restriction of avenues for marketing to the legitimate adult audience.[95] The 70 percent standard is grounded in the 2000 census data (showing that approximately 70 percent of the U.S. population is 21 and older).[96] Despite the placement shortfalls identified previously, when the audience data for television, radio, and magazine advertisements disseminated by the twelve suppliers were aggregated, more than 85 percent of the combined audience during the time period for which data were collected consisted of LDA adults; each individual company's advertising reached at least an 83 percent LDA adult audience. Thus, it appears that the current 70 percent baseline standard has helped to ensure that alcohol advertising is not disproportionately directed to those below the legal drinking age, as recommended by the Surgeon General's *Call to Action*.

Recommendation. Upon consideration of the record – including the comments received during the study, the placement data, the potential costs and benefits of a modified standard, and the risk of unintended adverse consequences – the Commission is not recommending a change in the baseline placement standard at this time. The Commission does, however, recommend that individual suppliers consider aggregate audience composition (that is, what percent of the overall alcohol advertising audience, aggregated across placements, is of legal age) when making placements.[97] Further, the Commission urges the trade associations to consider the results of the 2010 Census, when they become available.[98]

Finally, the Commission has identified practices that will facilitate better management of placements consistent with the self-regulatory codes. These include:

- adoption by the trade associations of consistent and transparent systems for interpretation of the demographic data;[99]
- regular training of company personnel about audience composition data, including training by the trade associations about practices calculated to ensure compliance with the placement standards;
- "hands on" management of media buyers; and
- maintenance of records that reflect actual buys and show the source of post-placement demographic data.

Such changes are essential to facilitate a level playing field, mprove the media buying process, and increase the integrity of self-regulatory codes.

B. Internet Advertising

As discussed in Part II.B. 1, above, Internet promotions represented less than two percent of company marketing expenditures in 2005. Nonetheless, these expenditures may grow substantially over time, as they have for other industries.

1. Supplier Sites

In the 2003 Alcohol Report, the Commission recommended that supplier sites require visitors, at a minimum, to input their date of birth to gain entry to the site, and deny entry if a user indicates an age under 21.[100] The three industry codes require age screening on company- operated Internet sites.[101]

The Commission's survey of sites operated by the twelve suppliers revealed that about 88 percent of the websites promoting the companies' alcohol brands required consumers to enter their birth date, and denied entry to consumers identified as younger than the LDA.[102] Only four percent of the alcohol company websites surveyed included a check-box age certification; seven percent did not screen for age at all.

Recommendation. As the Commission has advised in the children's online privacy arena,[103] website operators should be mindful of the potential for underage consumers to falsify their ages, and take care to install effective age-screening mechanisms. In addition to including a neutral age entry screen on all sites promoting alcohol brands, alcohol companies should consider using tracking tools to prevent minors from back-clicking to change their birth date once they realize that they have been blocked from an alcohol company website based on their age. In addition, the Commission reiterates its admonition that companies avoid online content that is likely to appeal to minors. When such content is unavoidable, companies should consider instituting age-verification, as recently used by Anheuser-Busch, rather than simple screening mechanisms.[104]

2. Online Alcohol Sales

Only a minority of the suppliers in this study engaged in online alcohol sales; the suppliers who engaged in such sales have adopted age-verification technologies. The Commission does not have data showing the extent to which suppliers and other industry members who were not a part of this study engage in direct shipping of alcohol. Online alcohol sales are an important means of competition for small vintners whose brands are not widely distributed by wholesalers, but present special concerns about youth access to alcohol. The WI code recommends, but does not require, that member websites employ third-party age verification, and has an arrangement with a third-party vendor to provide age-verification services to WI members who choose to use it.[105] Major delivery companies have adopted special provisions for shipment of alcohol, including conspicuous labeling and an adult signature requirement to ensure that the recipient of alcohol shipments is an LDA adult;[106] some states mandate use of these systems.[107]

Recommendation. The Commission recommends that companies engaged in online alcohol sales use procedures to ensure that alcohol is not shipped to underage purchasers.[108]

3. Advertising on Third-Party Sites

Alcohol suppliers advertised widely on independent sites and, as previously noted, they have generally applied an informal 70 percent placement standard when making placements on such sites. Further, the WI code already applies a 70 percent standard to Internet placements. With the advent of readily available and apparently reliable Internet audience demographic data, it is appropriate for BI and DISCUS also to adopt a formal self-regulatory guideline for this medium.

Recommendation. In the course of this study, the Commission staff recommended that the BI and DISCUS codes be modified formally to extend the 70 percent baseline placement standards to Internet advertising, and to adopt specific buying guidelines for Internet advertisements.[109] BI and DISCUS adopted such guidelines; they are attached to this chapter as Exhibits C and D.

DISCUS's Internet/Digital Buying Guidelines, effective January 1, 2008, apply to all paid and unpaid advertising placements made by or under the distiller's control. DISCUS's guidelines specify that distillers use a consistent syndicated audience measurement tool as their primary data source; advertisements are to be placed based on a site's most recent three-month unique audience average. For unmeasured sites, distillers must obtain an independent demographic survey based on the most recent three-month unique audience site average. Alternatively, if a site incorporates a registration mechanism, the distillers may limit advertising placements to a site's registered users who are of the legal drinking age. Distillers also may direct advertisements to registered users age twenty-one and above on sites that do not otherwise meet the placement standard. DISCUS's guidelines direct companies to conduct post-placement audits of Internet advertising placements, and to take appropriate corrective measures, as soon as is practicable, when a placement does not meet the placement standard.

BI's new Internet Buying Guidelines, effective for placements made after January 1, 2008, apply to all paid and unpaid placements on third-party websites. When a single purchase is made for advertisements on multiple websites, the placement standard and the buying guidelines apply to each website independently. The BI's guidelines require brewers, in most instances, to use a consistent, recognized, Internet audience measurement source to make advertising placement decisions. Placements are deemed appropriate when the unique audience of monthly visitors for the two most recent consecutive monthly reports prior to placement meets or exceeds the 70 percent standard.

For new or unmeasured websites, brewers may use audience composition data for sites that appear to be in the same category and have similar content. Brewers also may direct advertising placements to websites that are able to restrict dissemination of advertisements to registered users who are of the legal drinking age. Finally, brewers must conduct post- placement audits of actual placements on measured websites at least twice each year.

These new guidelines are flexible, taking into account the evolving nature of the Internet audience measurement services. Because Internet audience data are readily available on an up-to-date basis, the Commission urges companies to monitor their Internet placements frequently, and to take immediate action to pull, or otherwise adjust, advertisements that do not comply with the placement standard.

C. Other Digital Advertising

Other digital advertising, too, will likely grow in importance over the coming years.

Recommendation. As alcohol marketing efforts expand into new digital areas, such as email and mobile marketing, it is important that suppliers continue to expand their age-screening and verification processes, as well. Using currently available technologies, such as directing emails or text messages only to persons who have opted-in to a registered 21+ database, or using third-party age-verification services to eliminate from a company's marketing databases persons not verified to be above the legal drinking age, suppliers can reduce the likelihood that alcohol advertising will be directed to an inappropriate audience.

D. Sponsorships

Sponsorships are a common vehicle for promoting alcohol. Currently, however, the BI and WI codes do not articulate a 70 percent placement standard for events.

Recommendation. The Commission recommends that the BI and WI codes be modified to apply a 70 percent placement standard for sponsorship of events, as well as placements in print and broadcast media.

E. Product Placement in Films

The general standards for placing advertising on television also apply to product placement in television programs. Product placement in movies, however, presents a more difficult subject for self-regulation because it is difficult to predict, when a movie is being produced, what its ultimate audience will be. In 1999, the Commission recommended that companies make product placements only in films that would be rated "R" or "NC- 17" or, if unrated, had a mature theme.[110] This standard has not proved entirely satisfactory. Some companies placed alcohol products in films expected to have an "R" rating, only to learn later that the producer modified the film to obtain a "PG-13" rating. More importantly, movie ratings may not relate well to the age of film attendees.[111] As a result, it does not appear that a film's expected rating is a workable way to gauge the appropriateness of product placements.

The suppliers reported that they consider product placements in film on a case-by-case basis, in light of the proposed script. Some companies considered demographic information about past films as part of this process. Currently, there are three filmgoer demographic databases, including one that surveys audience members ages two and older, and another that surveys audience members twelve and older. Although these data relate to films that have already been released, they may also be informative regarding the likely audience for future, similar films.

Recommendation. The Commission recommends that industry members work with film producers to incorporate available audience demographic data into the case-by-case analysis of prospective product placements, and place only in films that the producer has a good faith basis for believing will have an audience consisting of at least 70 percent LDA adults.

F. Expenditures to Help Others Promote Alcohol to Consumers

The supplier submissions reveal that efforts to assist others to promote alcohol play a significant role in alcohol marketing. Combined expenditures for point-of-sale, retail-value-added, specialty items, and promotional allowances accounted for 26 percent of expenditures by the twelve suppliers included in this study. These expenditures are subject to the existing placement and content provisions of the self-regulatory codes. Moreover, it appears that these efforts are regulated at the federal and state level. While the Commission will continue to monitor this aspect of alcohol marketing, it does not appear that additional self-regulatory provisions are necessary at this time.

G. External Review

Much progress has been made to improve external review since the Commission's 2003 Alcohol Report. By the close of 2006, all three segments of the alcohol industry had established frameworks for consideration of complaints about alcohol advertisements.

Public comments have urged that industry members be barred from the review boards to eliminate a bias in industry's favor, and that fines should be assessed for code violations to increase deterrence.[112] Although the Commission will continue to monitor this issue, it does not appear that such changes are currently necessary. The BI's review system is the only one that is fully comprised of outside experts. It is not clear, however, that the presence of company representatives on the review boards inherently biases the complaint process in industry's favor. DISCUS's review board, composed solely of industry members, rejected alcohol advertisements more often than did the Beer Institute's review board.[113] In 100 percent of cases where the DISCUS review board found that a DISCUS member had committed a code violation, the advertiser took responsive action. The only two instances where the advertiser failed to respond involved non-member companies.

Recommendation. Certain changes are likely to increase the usefulness and reach of the complaint review process. Currently, only BI allows complaints to be submitted online.[114] The Commission recommends that DISCUS and WI also accept online complaints. Active consideration of advertising by non-member companies, as has been done by WI and DISCUS on occasion, substantially increases awareness of and compliance with the self-regulatory codes, particularly by new alcohol marketers. Permitting competitor complaints makes the system more vigorous, as it does not rely solely on consumers to identify problems. Finally, permitting complaints to be submitted anonymously facilitates complaint submission by persons who might otherwise shy away from the process.

H. Youth Alcohol Access

Although legal drinking age laws have substantially reduced teen drinking since their adoption in the 1980s, too many teens still drink, as shown by Figure 1. Reduced teen access to alcohol is essential to further progress on this point. Public education and law enforcement are both critical to this effort. Advertising has undeniable power to shape public opinion and consumer behavior. The Commission's "We Don't Serve Teens" program brings the power of advertising to bear on the issue of teen access to alcohol. It has benefitted from the support of federal government departments, many state regulators, the advertising community, and consumer groups, as well as the alcohol industry.

Recommendation. The Commission continues to encourage all stakeholders concerned about underage alcohol use to support social responsibility efforts, such as WDST, that are designed to reduce youth access to alcohol and the consequent alcohol-related injury.

V. CONCLUSION

The Commission has promoted self-regulation of alcohol marketing to reduce the likelihood that such marketing will, by its content or placement, target those under the LDA. The Commission has recommended self-regulation in a variety of contexts.[115] A well-constructed self-regulatory regime has advantages over government regulation. It conserves limited government resources and is more prompt and flexible than government regulation, given the substantial time required to complete an investigation or to adopt and enforce a regulation. Finally, self-regulation is an appropriate response to concerns about the impact of alcohol advertising on youth, in light of protections provided by the First Amendment to the U.S. Constitution.[116]

The Commission continues to believe, therefore, that alcohol industry self-regulation must play a prominent role in addressing concerns about alcohol marketing and youth. The Commission looks forward to the industry's adoption of its recommendations.

The government also has a role, however. Over the past decade, the Commission has actively monitored self-regulation within the alcohol industry, both formally and informally. Ongoing outreach and studies such as this one have allowed the Commission to evaluate compliance with code provisions and to make recommendations for improvement, when appropriate. These efforts have helped inform the Commission's recommendations, and ultimately resulted in the adoption of code provisions containing an improved placement standard (including a protocol for making placements); a requirement that suppliers conduct periodic internal audits of past placements; and systems for external review of complaints about compliance with code provisions.

Having completed the current study, the Commission will implement a new system for monitoring alcohol advertising self-regulation. Each year, the Commission will send compulsory process orders to between two and four suppliers, seeking information about advertising and marketing practices, systems used to prevent deceptive and unfair marketing, and compliance with self-regulatory guidelines. This procedure will allow the Commission to appraise the industry's response to the recommendations contained in this report. It also will permit the Commission to evaluate alcohol marketing efforts in new media, and to consider efforts to reduce the likelihood that alcohol advertising in such new media will target youth.

In the past, the Commission's alcohol industry monitoring has focused primarily on the practices of the largest suppliers, an approach that may have suggested that smaller companies were immune from scrutiny. Future inquiries will include small as well as large suppliers. The Commission believes that this new monitoring system will support the self-regulatory efforts of the three trade associations.

EXHIBIT A: ORDER TO FILE SPECIAL REPORT

OMB Control No. 3084-0138
Expires: 12/31/09[117]

UNITED STATES OF AMERICA
BEFORE FEDERAL TRADE COMMISSION

COMMISSIONERS: Deborah Platt Majoras, Chairman
Pamela Jones Harbour
Jonathan Leibowitz
William E. Kovacic
J. Thomas Rosch

FTC Matter No. P064505

ORDER TO FILE SPECIAL REPORT

Pursuant to a resolution of the Federal Trade Commission dated [insert], entitled "*Resolution Directing Use of Compulsory Process*," a copy of which is enclosed, [insert target name], hereinafter referred to as "the company," is ordered to file a Special Report with the Commission no later than the dates specified in Appendix A.III. hereto, containing the information and documents specified herein.

The information provided in the Special Report will assist the Commission in preparing a report regarding beverage alcohol advertising expenditures and alcohol industry self-regulatory efforts.

The Special Report should restate each item of this Order with which the corresponding answer is identified. If any specification cannot be answered fully, provide the information that is available and explain in what respects and why the answer is incomplete. **The Special Report and all accompanying documentary responses should be bates-stamped.** For purposes of this Special Report, the term "the company" includes any parent, subsidiary, or affiliated companies located in the United States.

Please supply the information and documents requested in the following Specifications, **consistent with the Definitions and Instructions** contained on Appendix A.

SPECIFICATIONS

1. Provide the following background information:
   D. Identify by full name, business address, telephone number, and official capacity, the officer of the company who has prepared or supervised the preparation of the company's response to this Order.
   E. Fully identify by name, address, and state of incorporation, the company. In addition, identify each subsidiary, joint venture, affiliated company, partnership, or operation under an assumed name that is owned in whole or in part by the company that engages in the manufacturing, labeling, advertising, promoting, offering for sale, or sale of any beverage alcohol product in the United States.
   F. Identify by name each individual beverage alcohol brand or variety sold by the entities identified in subparagraph 1 .B. above, during the calendar year 2005, and for each brand or variety, state total sales for calendar year 2005 in dollars and in number of 9-liter or 2.25 gallon cases sold.
   G. A Produce all documents dated, prepared, or received by the company on or after January 1, 2003 that contain data not otherwise publicly available regarding the demographics of persons under 21 located in the U.S. who have tasted, used, or purchased any brand advertised or sold by the company.
2. Report the dollar amount expended during the calendar year 2005 by the company, including the entities identified in Specification 1.B., above, on the advertising, merchandising, or promotion of beverage alcohol products in the United States in *each* of the categories set forth below (as defined in Appendix A.I.):

   A. Television Advertising
   B. Radio Advertising
   C. Magazine Advertising
   D. Newspaper Advertising
   E. Transit Advertisin
   F. Outdoor Advertising
   G. Direct Mail Advertising
   H. Company-sponsored Internet Sites
   I. Other Internet Site Advertising
   J. Other Digital Advertising

K. Specialty Item Distribution
L. Public Entertainment Events: Not Sports-Related
M. Sponsorship of Sporting Events, Sports Teams, or Individual Athletes
N. Other Point-of-Sale Advertising and Promotions
O. Spring Break Promotions
P. Product Placements
Q. Retail Value-Added Expenditures
R. Telemarketing
S. Promotional Allowances
T. Total Reportable Expenditures
U. Sports and Sporting Events
V. Social Responsibility Programs and Messages

3. Provide the information set forth below with regard to advertising placements
   A. Describe fully the procedures used by the company, including the entities identified in response to Specification 1 .B., above, to facilitate compliance with the guidelines contained in the voluntary advertising codes of the Beer Institute, the Distilled Spirits Council of the United States, and the Wine Institute, providing that television, radio, and print ads should appear only in media where 70% or more of the audience consists of adults 21 and over. In the response, indicate which of the 3 voluntary codes the company follows; whether the company follows another code, such as a company code, that addresses advertising placement; what databases are relied on in making placement decisions; how often post-placement data are reviewed to verify that a placement complied with the guideline and what steps are taken if a compliance shortfall is identified; and, what additional safeguards are in place (such as use of "no buy" lists, use of higher placement standards, media content review, or others) to reduce the likelihood that a non-compliant placement will occur.
   B. With regard to each instance of dissemination by the company, including the entities identified in response to 1.B., above, of an advertisement during the period January 1, 2006 to June 30, 2006, on television, on radio in measured markets, in magazines, and in newspapers, provide the advertisement's name; the brand advertised; the name of the media and location of dissemination; the date and time that the advertisement appeared; the name of the show during, or in conjunction with, which the advertisement

appeared; and the actual demographics of the audience (persons under 21, and persons 21 and over), in absolute numbers and percentages, for that dissemination, consistent with the directions in Appendix A.II. In responding to this Specification 3.B., please mark by use of an asterisk each dissemination that was targeted specifically to Hispanic consumers and mark by the use of a pound sign each dissemination that was targeted specifically to African-Americnan consumers.

C. Based upon the responses to Specification 3.B., provide the following summary information regarding the code compliance of placements made by the company during the period January 1, 2006 to June 30, 2006 in each of the four advertising categories (all television ads; all radio ads in measured markets; all magazine ads; and all newspaper ads)
   ii. The total number of advertisement disseminations;
   iii. The total number of persons reached;
   iv. The number of advertisement disseminations that complied with the 70% guidelines, and, with regard to these compliant disseminations, the total number of persons reached, the number of persons 21 and over reached, and the number of persons under 21 reached; and
   v. The number of advertisement disseminations that did not comply with the 70% guideline and, with regard to these noncompliant disseminations, the total number of persons reached, the number of persons 21 and over reach ed, and the number of persons under 21 reached.

D. Repeat the analysis performed in Specification 3.C.:
   i. With regard to those disseminations identified in Specification 3.B. as targeted specifically to Hispanic consumers; and
   ii. With regard to those disseminations identified in Specification 3.B. as targeted specifically to African-American consumers.

E. Provide copies of all documents relied on to support the company's responses to Specifications 3B., 3C., and 3D., above.

4. Describe in detail the enforcement mechanism(s) available as of December 31, 2006 regarding possible violations of the voluntary advertising code of the industry trade association(s) of which the company is a member (*e.g.*, the Beer Institute, the Distilled Spirits Counsel of the United States, and/or the Wine Institute). With regard to each complaint about the company's advertising, promotion, or marketing forwarded for independent review under the procedures set

forth by the Beer Institute, Distilled Spirits Council of the United States, or Wine Institute at any time between January 1, 2006 and December 31, 2006, provide a copy of the complaint, any document reflecting the recommendation or decision of the reviewer, and describe what action, if any, the company took in response to the recommendation or decision of the reviewer

Penalties may be imposed under applicable provisions of federal law for failure to file Special Reports or for filing false reports.

The Special Report responses called for in this Order are to be filed on or before the dates set forth on Appendix A.III.

By direction of the Commission.

Deborah Platt Majoras
Chairman

SEAL
Date of Order:

The Special Report required by this Order,
or any inquiry concerning it,should
be addressed to the attention of:

Janet M.Evans
Division of Advertising Practices
Federal Trade Commission
NJ-3213
Washington,D.C.20580
(202)326-2125 phone
(202)326-3259 facsimile
jevans@ftc.gov

APPENDIX A: DEFINITIONS AND INSTRUCTIONS

I. Reportable Expenditure Definitions

These definitions of reportable advertising, merchandising, or promotion expenditures track the 22 Categories set forth in Specification 2 of the Order to File Special Report. Please provide information for each Category in thousands of dollars. Expenditures may be rounded to the nearest thousand dollars. In responding to Specification 2, exclude expenditures targeted to the trade, such as expenditures for promotions in trade magazines or password-protected Internet sites targeted to the trade.

A. Television Advertising

Definition: Television advertising on broadcast, cable, or satellite channels, including spot ads, long-form commercials, and sponsored programming (such as televised events bearing the name of, or stated to be sponsored by an alcohol brand or company); **allocate** such expenditures among: (a) advertising placed for national distribution on (i) broadcast, (ii) cable, or (iii) satellite television; and (b) spot advertising placed on (i) broadcast, (ii) cable, or (iii) satellite television. This Category excludes expenditures in connection with product placements (defined in Category P).

B. Radio Advertising

Definition: Radio advertising including spot ads, long-form commercials, and sponsored programing (such as radio broadcast events bearing the name of or stated to be sponsored by an alcohol brand or company); **allocate** such expenditures among: (a) advertising on subscription- based satellite radio channels; (b) advertising in markets where the audience is measured by a syndicated data source (such as Arbitron); and, (c) advertising in unmeasured markets. This Category excludes expenditures in connection with product placements (defined in Category P).

C. Magazine Advertising

Definition: Advertising placed in magazines or other print media; this Category excludes newspaper advertising (defined in Category D) and direct mail advertising (defined in Category G).

D. Newspaper Advertising

Definition: Advertising placed in newspapers, including national, regional, and local papers, and advertising placed in free-standing inserts to newspapers. This Category excludes expenditures for magazine advertising (defined in Category C) and direct mail advertising (defined in Category G).

E. Transit Advertising

Definition: Advertising on or within private or public vehicles and all advertisements placed at, on or within any bus stop, taxi stand, transportation waiting area, train station, airport or any other transportation facility.

F. Outdoor Advertising

Definition: Advertising on billboards; signs, placards or posters placed on outdoor street furniture, kiosks, shopping malls (whether open-air or enclosed), pay telephone booths, parking space bumpers or other advertising in parking lots or garages, or trash receptacles; airplane banners; and, any other advertisements placed outdoors regardless of their size. This Category excludes expenditures in connection with transit advertising (defined in Category E), public entertainment events: not sports-related (defined in Category L), sponsorship of sporting events, sports teams, or individual athletes (defined in Category M), or other point-of-sale advertising and promotions (defined in Category N).

G. Direct Mail Advertising

Definition: Advertising circulars or other printed matter that is sent directly through the mail to consumers. This Category excludes expenditures in connection with magazine advertising (defined in Category C) and newspaper advertising (defined in Category D).

H. Company-sponsored Internet Sites

Definition: Any company-sponsored Internet site that contains information about the company's beverage alcohol brands or beverage alcohol products, and that can be accessed by computers located in the United States, regardless of where the site is located or the Internet address of the site or page.

I. Other Internet Site Advertising

Definition: Advertising on Internet sites other than company-sponsored Internet sites, including, but not limited to, hyperlinks, banner or pop-up advertisements, sponsored-text advertising, search keywords, and advertising in chat rooms, weblogs, bulletin boards, listservs, and on social networking sites.

J. Other Digital Advertising

Definition: Advertising and promotional content visible on personal computers and other digital devices, including PDAs (personal digital assistants) and mobile phones, whether or not Internet-enabled. This Category includes but is not limited to expenditures for electronic mail (email) messages, short message service (SMS or "text") messaging, instant messaging (IM), picture messaging, multimedia messaging, mobile broadcasts, and downloads or podcasts.

K. Specialty Item Distribution

Definition: All net costs (deducting payments by consumers) of distributing items other than beverage alcohol products, whether distributed by sale, redemption of coupons, or otherwise. **Allocate** among expenditures for items that (a) bear the name, logo, or any portion of the package of any brand or variety of beverage alcohol product sold by the company and (b) do not bear the name, logo, or any portion of the package of any brand or variety of beverage alcohol products sold by the company. Exclude costs associated with distributing non-alcohol items in connection with retail value-added programs (defined in Category Q).

L. Public Entertainment Events: Not Sports-Related

Definition: Public entertainment events that are not sports-related, such as appearances by musicians, comedians, celebrities, or other entertainers or public figures, bearing or otherwise displaying the company name or logo, the name, logo, or any portion of the package of any of the company's beverage alcohol brands, or otherwise referring or relating to beverage alcohol, including all expenditures made by the company in promoting and/or sponsoring such events; **allocate** these expenditures among (a) adult-only facilities and (b) general audience facilities. This Category excludes expenditures in connection with television or radio advertising (defined in Categories A and B), Internet or digital programming (defined in Categories H, I, and J), sponsorship of sporting events, sports teams, or individual athletes (defined in Category M), and other point-of-sale advertising and promotions (defined in Category N).

"Adult-only facility" means a facility or restricted area (whether open-air or enclosed) where the operator ensures or has a reasonable basis to believe that no underage person is present and includes company-sponsored private parties and event hospitality tents. A facility or restricted area need not be permanently restricted to adults in order to constitute an adult-only facility, provided that the operator ensures or has a reasonable basis to believe that no underage person is present during the event or time period in question. Furthermore, for purposes of this Order, the term "underage" means younger than twenty-one (21) years of age.

M. Sponsorship of Sporting Events, Sports Teams, or Individual Athletes

Definition: Sponsorship of sporting events, sports teams, or individual athletes. "Sports teams or individual athletes" includes but is not limited to competitors in football, basketball, baseball, soccer, hockey, tennis, wrestling, golf, karate, judo, weight lifting, volleyball, skiing, skating, sailing, boating, equestrian, rodeo, automobile, race car, funny car, motorcycle, bicycle, truck, monster truck, tractor-pull, fishing, and hunting events, competitions, tournaments, and races. This Category excludes expenditures in connection with television and radio advertising (defined in Categories A and B), Internet or digital programming (defined in Categories H, I, and J), public entertainment events: not sports-related (defined in Category L), and other point-of-sale advertising and promotions (defined in Category N).

N. Other Point-of-Sale Advertising and Promotions

Definition: Expenditures for advertising and promotions at on-premise or off-premise locations where beverage alcohol can be purchased. This Category excludes expenditures in connection with specialty item distribution (defined in Category K), public entertainment events: not sports-related (defined in Category L), spring break promotions (defined in Category O), and retail value-added expenditures (defined in Category Q).

O. Spring Break Promotions

Definition: Expenditures for advertising and promotion of college "spring break" events, including vacation trips, cruises, beach or pool parties, and on-premise and off-premise events where beverage alcohol can be purchased. This Category may include expenses reported in response to other categories; if so, indicate which expenses also are reported elsewhere.

P. Product Placements

Definition: The dollar value of consideration provided in connection with permitting, promoting, or procuring the integration of any beverage alcohol product, logo, signage, trade name, or package into a television or radio program, motion picture, music video, music recording, electronic game, or other form of entertainment programming; such expenditures would include, for example, the dollar value of alcohol beverages or logoed items (such as clothing or signage) provided, or expenditures by the company to cross-promote a film or program in which a placement occurs.

Q. Retail Value-Added Expenditures

Definition: Expenditures for promotions involving: (1) free beverage alcohol products (*e.g.,* buy two, get one free), whether or not the free beverage alcohol products are physically bundled together with the purchased beverage alcohol products, including all expenditures and costs associated with the value added to the purchase of beverage alcohol products (*e.g.*, all associated excise taxes paid on the free beverage alcohol products); and (2) free non-alcohol products items (*e.g.,* buy two, get a can opener) including all expenditures and costs associated with the value added to the purchase of beverage alcohol products.

R. Telemarketing

Definition: Expenditures associated with the placement of telephone calls for the purpose of selling a good or service or the maintenance or operation of incoming telephone lines that allow consumers to participate in any promotion or hear pre-recorded product messages, but excluding costs associated with having customer service representatives available for responding to consumer complaints or questions.

S. Promotional Allowances

Definition: Allowances paid to retailers or wholesalers/distributors for development and distribution of consumer-directed advertising and promotional efforts, but excluding expenditures specifically designated to be expended for advertising and promotions in categories A-R above, which expenditures should be reported in the appropriate Category. Allocate such expenditures among payments to (a) retailers and (b) wholesalers/distributors.

T. Total Reportable Expenditures

Definition: The figure provided for total reportable expenditures should equal the sum of the expenses listed in Categories A-S above.

U. Sports and Sporting Events

Definition: "Sports and sporting events" include but are not limited to football, basketball, baseball, soccer, hockey, golf, tennis, wrestling, karate, judo, weight lifting, volleyball, skiing, skating, sailing, boating, equestrian, rodeo, automobile, race car, funny car, motorcycle, bicycle, truck, monster truck, tractor-pull, fishing, and hunting events, competitions, tournaments, and races. Report all items including but not limited to all expenditures connected with or related to the sponsoring, advertising, or promotion of sports or sporting events, including support of an individual or a group sports or racing team, and purchase of, or support for, sports or racing equipment, uniforms, sports or racing facilities and/or training facilities, and all expenditures for advertising including but not limited to print, television, radio, billboards, or banners in the name of the company or any of its beverage alcohol products in a sports or racing facility, on a scoreboard or in conjunction with the reporting of sports or racing results; and all expenditures connected with the production, offer, sale, or provision without fee of all functional promotional items at or in connection with a sporting or racing event, including but not limited to, clothing, hats, bags, posters, sporting or racing goods, and equipment. Allocate among (a) expenditures for college sports and sporting events and (b) all others. The expenditures reported in this Category are intended to be duplicative of expenditures listed above for Categories A-S and totaled in

Category T. For example, televised ball games sponsored by an alcohol brand, reported in Category A, and untelevised events for a sponsored sports teams, reported in Category M, would also be reported in Category U. Do not report any expenditures in this Category that have not also been reported in Categories A-S.

V. Social Responsibility Programs and Messages

Definition: Expenditures for social responsibility programs and messages. The expenditures reported in this Category may be duplicative of expenditures listed for Categories A-S and totaled in Category T.

II. Audience Demographics Definitions

These instructions shall be used in responding to Specification 3.B.'s request for the actual demographics of the audience for an advertisement:

A. Television Ads

Provide, for the program in which or adjacent to which the ad appeared, the quarterly average demographic data for that program in that timeslot; if program-specific data are not available, provide the quarterly average demographic data for the daypart in which the ad appeared.

B. Radio Ads

Provide the quarterly average demographic data for the daypart during which the ad appeared. In responding to this Specification, use Arbitron standard dayparts unless data for a shorter period of time are available.

C. Magazine Ads

Provide average demographic data for the 12-month period during which the ad appeared, if the ad was placed in the standard national edition. If the ad was placed in a 21+ or other specialized edition, identify the edition and explain its demographics.

D. Newspaper Ads

Provide average demographic data for the 12-month period during which the ad appeared. If the demographics of the newspaper are unmeasured, so specify.

III. Due Dates for Responses

Responses to this Order are due on a rolling basis, as follows:

- Response to Specification 1: 30 days after the issuance of this order.
- Response to Specification 2: 45 days after issuance of this order.
- Response to Specification 3.A.: 30 days after issuance of this order.
- Response to Specification 3.B.: 45 days after issuance of this order.
- Response to Specifications 3.C. and 3.D.: 50 days after issuance of this order.
- Response to Specification 3.E.: Within 5 days following receipt from the FTC staff of a written request to provide such documents (but not before timely submission of audience composition data in response to Specification 3.B).
- Response to Specification 4: Within 30 days after issuance of this order, or January 10, 2007, whichever is later.

EXHIBIT B: WE DON'T SERVE TEENS WEEK (2007) PARTICIPANTS AND PROMOTIONAL MATERIALS

Federal Trade Commission

File a Complaint | Order Publications | Privacy Policy | FTC Search

We DON'T SERVE TEENS
WWW.DONTSERVETEENS.GOV

Did you know?
In 2006, 63 percent of eighth graders reported that alcohol is "fairly easy" or "very easy" to get.

Today is June 20, 2008

En Español

Safe summer reminder:
DON'T SERVE ALCOHOL TO TEENS.
It's unsafe. It's illegal. It's irresponsible.

- **21 Is the Legal Drinking Age**
  Learn about laws that reduce teen drinking
- **State Laws**
  Links to state-by-state legislation
- **Dangers of Teen Drinking**
  What can happen to teens who drink
- **Stopping Easy Access**
  Steps you can take to reduce teens' access to alcohol
- **Alcohol Advertising**
  Talk to your kids about alcohol ads
- **Answering Questions About Alcohol**
  What to say to neighbors and friends

How can you help?

Everyone can do something:

- **Individuals & Organizations**
- **Media**
- **Retailers**
- **Law Enforcement**

Get Campaign Materials

Stories from real life

We Don't Serve Teens Week Participants

To the many organizations and individuals who are taking part in We Don't Serve Teens week — thank you! We appreciate the state and local officials identified below, the National Association of Broadcasters, the Outdoor Advertising Association of America, the Magazine Publishers of America, Students Against Destructive Decisions, The Century Council, Distilled Spirits Council, Beer Institute, Wine and Spirits Wholesalers of America, and many others, for contributing their time, effort, and resources. The following is a partial list of We Don't Serve Teens Week participants.

State officials

- Attorney General Troy King, Alabama
- Attorney General Terry Goddard, Arizona
- Congresswoman Lucille Roybal-Allard, California
- Attorney General John Suthers, Colorado
- Lt. Governor Michael Fidele, Connecticut
- Attorney General Thurbert Baker, Georgia
- Attorney General Steve Carter, Indiana
- Attorney General Paul Morrison, Kansas
- Attorney General Greg Stumbo, Kentucky
- Attorney General Charles Foti, Louisiana
- Attorney General Martha Coakley, Massachusetts
- Attorney General Mike Cox, Michigan
- Attorney General Jim Hood, Mississippi
- Attorney General Jay Nixon, Missouri
- Attorney General Catherine Cortez Masto, Nevada
- Attorney General Gary King, New Mexico
- Attorney General Marc Dann, Ohio
- Attorney General Tom Corbett, Pennsylvania
- Attorney General Patrick Lynch, Rhode Island
- Attorney General Henry McMaster, South Carolina
- Attorney General Larry Long, South Dakota

- Attorney General Robert Cooper, Tennessee
- Attorney General Mark Shurtleff, Utah
- Attorney General Bob McDonnell, Virginia
- Attorney General Rob McKenna, Washington
- Attorney General J.B. Van Hollen, Wisconsin

Governors who have issued WDST proclamations to date – and D.C.'s Mayor, too

- Governor Palin, Alaska (PDF)
- Governor Riley, Alabama (PDF)
- Governor Schwarzenegger, California (PDF)
- Governor Ritter, Colorado (PDF)
- Governor Rell, Connecticut (PDF)
- Governor Minner, Delaware (PDF)
- Governor Crist, Florida (PDF)
- Governor Perdue, Georgia (PDF)
- Governor Lingle, Hawaii (PDF)
- Governor Otter, Idaho (PDF)
- Governor Blagojevich, Illinois (PDF)
- Governor Daniels, Indiana (PDF)
- Governor Sebelius, Kansas (PDF)
- Governor Fletcher, Kentucky (PDF)
- Governor Blanco, Louisiana (PDF)
- Governor Baldacci, Maine (PDF)
- Governor O'Malley, Maryland (PDF)
- Governor Patrick, Massachusetts (PDF)
- Governor Granholm, Michigan (PDF)
- Governor Pawlenty, Minnessota (PDF)
- Governor Barbour, Mississippi (PDF)
- Governor Blunt, Missouri (PDF)
- Governor Schweitzer, Montana (PDF)
- Governor Heineman, Nebraska (PDF)
- Governor Gibbons, Nevada (PDF)
- Governor Corzine, New Jersey (PDF)
- Governor Richardson, New Mexico (PDF)
- Governor Spitzer, New York (PDF)
- Governor Henry, Oklahoma (PDF)

- Governor Carcieri, Rhode Island (PDF)
- Governor Sanford, South Carolina (PDF)
- Governor Gregoire, Washington (PDF)
- Governor Doyle, Wisconsin (PDF)
- Mayor Fenty, District of Columbia (PDF)

Television, cable, and radio industry members

- National Association of Broadcasters
- Galavisión
- The Golf Channel
- A&E/History Channel
- Discovery Networks
- Lifetime
- Bravo
- USA Network
- Verizon FiOS
- YES Networks
- Adlink (LA)
- Fox Sports Florida
- Sunshine Network
- Time Warner, Cox, Comcast, and Charter local market cable systems
- National radio networks and over 140 local radio stations across the country

Magazines

- Magazine Publishers of America
- Good Housekeeping
- Newsweek
- PEOPLE
- Time
- US News & World Report
- Gotham
- Travel & Leisure
- THE WEEK
- Ocean Drive
- Boston Dig
- Chicago Reader
- Cleveland Scene

- Denver Westword
- Minneapolis City Pages
- Philadelphia Weekly
- Phoenix New Times
- San Diego Reader
- Seattle Weekly
- Seattle Stranger
- Tuscon Weekly
- Village Voice

News Media

- New York Times
- USA TODAY
- other newspapers across the country

Outdoor advertisers

- Outdoor Advertising Association of America, with over 3,000 outdoor signs across the country

Sports teams

- The Washington Redskins
- The Boston Red Sox
- The Chicago White Sox

Digital media

- Conerstone Entertainment
- MSN
- VH1
- Comcast - E! Networks
- SportsIllustrated.com
- Heavy.com
- Salon.com
- AskMen.com
- Evite
- Gay.com/Planetout
- AOL.com
- Yahoo
- Dennis Digital

- CBS SportsLine

Industry member partners who helped coordinate activities and distribute WDST materials

- The Century Council
- Distilled Spirits Council
- Wine and Spirits Wholesalers of America
- Beer Institute
- many individual alcohol beverage companies

Additional participants who helped coordinate activities and spread the We Don't Serve Teens message

- Students Against Destructive Decisions
- National Consumers League
- U.S. Department of Treasury Alcohol and Tobacco Tax and Trade Bureau
- National Liquor Law Enforcement Administration
- National Association of Beverage Control Authorities
- American Beverage Licensees
- U.S. Department of Labor/Working Partners for an Alcohol- and Drug-Free Workplace
- U.S. Department of Transportation National Highway Traffic Safety Administration
- U.S. Department of Education Office of Safe and Drug Free Schools

Don't serve alcohol to teens.
It's unsafe. It's illegal. It's irresponsible.

Home | About Us | Site Policies and Important Links | Contact Us
We Don't Serve Teens: A National Campaign to Prevent Underage Drinking
www.DontServeTeens.gov

Sample Billboard, Sept. 2007.

Washington Metropolitan Area Transit Authority, Washington, DC, Sept. 2007.

The Washington Post, Page A-13, Sept. 10, 2007.

U.S. News and World Report, Page 52, Sept. 10, 2007.

Time Magazine, Page 8, Sept. 17, 2007.

We Don't Serve Teens

2007 Order Form
30-Sheet

The Federal Trade Commission has designated the week of September 10th as "National We Don't Serve Teens Week" to coincide with back to school activities. A wide array of industry, media, government, and other interested groups are supporting this FTC initiative to put the national spotlight on underage drinking prevention by publicizing the "We Don't Serve Teens" campaign in communities across the country with free campaign media materials. The FTC's "We Don't Serve Teens" campaign addresses the issue of underage access to alcohol, with the message to adults that providing alcohol to teens is unsafe, illegal and irresponsible.

Production and shipping of 30-sheets will be provided and paid for by Century Council. Inner cities and liquor stores are specifically targeted.

Please allow 10-12 business days for delivery after your order has been received.

Quantity

Ship To:

Company: ______________________ Date: ________

Address (street only, no PO Boxes):

____

City: ______________________ State: ____ Zip: ________

Phone: ______________ Ext: ______ Fax: ______________

Attention: ______________________

Email: ______________________

Mail order form to:
Circle Graphics Attn: Order Entry Department
120 Ninth Avenue Longmont, CO 80501

Or Fax: 303-532-2384 Attn: Order Entry Department

oaaa
Outdoor Advertising Association of America

Outdoor Advertising Association of America Order Form, Aug. 2007.

EXHIBIT C: BEER INSTITUTE INTERNET BUYING GUIDELINES

Buying Guidelines for the Implementation of Section 3(c) of the Beer Institute Advertising and Marketing Code—Page 4 of 4

Internet Buying Guidelines

A. The demographic standard in Guideline 3c of the Code applies to all paid and bonus placements by brewers on internet websites operated by others. Where a single purchase is made for placements on multiple websites, the demographic standard and these guidelines apply to each website independently.

B. It is recognized that methodologies for rating internet websites as well as specific measurements of the various forms of Internet advertising are still evolving. Brewers will utilize a consistent internet audience measurement source recognized by the advertising industry (such as, but not limited to, comScore or Nielsen NetRatings) to determine whether advertising placements on websites are reasonably expected to meet the demographic standard in Guideline 3c of the Code. When the source regularly used by a brewer does not measure a particular site, other recognized rating systems may be relied upon.

C. For measured websites, a placement will be considered appropriate if the audience of monthly unique visitors meets or exceeds the demographic standard in Guideline 3c in each of the two most recent, consecutive monthly reports available at the time the placement is purchased.

D. If a placement is made on a website where the dissemination of such placement is restricted only to registered users of that site age 21 or over, such placements will be deemed compliant with the demographic standard, even if the overall audience for the unrestricted content on the website does not meet the standard.

E. For new or unmeasured web sites, placements may be made using audience composition data for measured websites in the same category and with similar content and/or by taking other reasonable measures to predict audience composition. Such steps include, for example, reviewing website content and information on the purpose and target audience of the website prior to purchase of advertising and obtaining confirmation from the website operator that its internal data indicates that the website meets the demographic standard.

F. Downloaded content and content that can be forwarded to others by e-mail directly from brewer websites or from brewer placements on websites operated by others shall include a term of use instructing those downloading or e-mailing such content that they should not forward the content to persons under the legal drinking age.

G. Brewers will conduct post-audits of actual placements on measured web sites at least twice a year to determine whether they met the demographic standard found in Guideline 3c.

EXHIBIT D: DISCUS INTERNET BUYING GUIDELINES

Effective January 1, 2008
Subject to Semi-Annual Post
Audit of Random Placements

INTERNET/DIGITAL BUYING GUIDELINE

In developing this guideline, the DISCUS Code Review Board met with experts in the field, syndicated "internet" demographic data sources and various media companies to obtain their respective best thoughts in devising a "buying guideline" for this medium to implement the 70% 21 years of age and older demographic provisions of the Code. As a result of a host of meetings and discussions, the Board developed the internet/digital buying guideline set forth below that will apply to advertising and marketing materials placed on that medium on and after January 1, 2008. Placements on this medium also will be subject to the Code's provision for semi-annual after-the-fact audits of a random portion of past advertising/marketing placements. To the best of our knowledge, we are the first trade group to issue an internet buying guideline that will be used across an entire industry.

The guideline was designed to anticipate many different scenarios and circumstances for the use of this medium. For example, for new websites not measured by a syndicated data source, the guideline provides that one could use the website's "registered user" database to place advertising or marketing materials to individuals 21 years of age and older viewing the website. Alternatively for new websites, the guideline provides for the option of obtaining from the publisher of the website an independent demographic survey using the most recent three-month site average of available audience data of unique visitors. If those options are not available, the bottom line would be no advertising on that new website. In many ways, the digital guideline is similar to the "unmeasured magazine" initiative whereby maiden/new publications intended for general circulation (even if it is a prototype of another magazine) require a third-party survey of subscribers before an advertisement placement. If there is nothing to measure, then there will be no ad placement pursuant to this Code initiative.

i.) Scope: The internet/digital buying guideline applies to all paid and unpaid (including value-added) placements made by or under the control of the advertiser, including advertising on third-party websites, video advertisements, audio mentions, internet banners, pop-ups, sponsorships, user-generated content (including blogs), and other types of internet/digital advertising or marketing.

ii.) Use of a syndicated data source: Purchase or place using "2 +" syndicated audience composition data, such as comScore or Nielsen//NetRatings, based upon the most recent three-month site average of available audience data of unique visitors (where seasonal fluctuations are evident, prior year data also should be taken into account if available).

(a) An advertiser consistently will use one of these syndicated data sources as its primary demographic measurement by brand and an alternate syndicated data source will be used only when the advertiser's primary source does not measure that particular medium.

(b) Given that the methodologies and measurements of internet/digital media are evolving, this data source guideline will be reviewed as further developments warrant and, if appropriate, revised accordingly.

iii.) Independent measurement of unmeasured medium: If the digital medium is not measured by a syndicated data source, the advertiser prior to purchasing or placing an advertisement or any marketing materials shall obtain from the publisher of the medium an independent demographic survey based upon the most recent three-month site average of available audience data of unique visitors conducted by a third-party research company using established research methods.

iv.) More specific data to meet the demographic standard: Where the average of the syndicated audience composition data or an independent third-party survey over the three-month time period (as described in subsection iii above) does not show a 70% 21 years of age and older (LPA) demographic, the advertiser can use the website's "registered user" database to place their advertising or marketing materials to users 21 years of age and older if the website has that capability.

v.) Unmeasured medium with a "registered user" database: If the digital medium is not measured by a syndicated data source or an independent third-party survey as described in subsection iii above, but has a "registered user" database that can link a user to an age, the advertiser can use the website's "registered user" database to place their advertising or marketing materials to users 21 years of age and older.

vi.) "Limited edition" websites: For "one-time" only, event-specific and/or other similar websites, the advertiser shall review and evaluate comparable websites, the proposed content of the website in question, data provided by the publisher regarding the target audience, and any other relevant factor to project a reasonable expectation of the demographic audience prior to purchasing or placing an advertisement or any marketing materials.

vii.) Compliance standard: A placement will be considered appropriate when the percentage of unique visitors reflected in the above-referenced data show that the placement is in compliance with the Code.

viii.) Post audits: A past placement will be considered appropriate where demographic data for the month(s) in which the placement ran show an LPA audience composition that was in compliance with the Code.

ix.) Post audit corrective measures for future placements: In the event that the post audit indicates that the placement did not meet the LPA demographic standard, the advertiser will, as soon as practicable, make schedule adjustments, cancellations, or other appropriate changes to comply with the standard in future placements.

STATEMENT OF COMMISSIONER PAMELA JONES HARBOUR CONCURRING IN PART AND DISSENTING IN PART

Regarding the 2008 Report on Self-Regulation in the Alcohol Industry
File No. P064505

Today the Commission issues its third report on self-regulation in the alcohol industry. This chapter reflects excellent work by Commission staff, and I concur in the Commission's decision to release it. I dissent in part, however, because I would prefer that the Commission take a tougher stance against alcohol advertising to underage audiences. Specifically, I disagree with the Commission's recommendation that the industry maintain the current 70 percent baseline standard for alcohol advertising.

Underage drinking is a serious public health and safety issue in the United States. Alcohol consumption is the leading drug problem among our youth. According to *The Surgeon General's Call to Action to Prevent and Reduce Underage Drinking*, approximately 50 percent of young people have had an alcoholic drink by age 15, and approximately 90 percent have done so by age 21.[118] Harsh statistics quickly shatter the myth that alcohol is a "safe" drug for young people. Each year, more than 5,000 youths die of alcohol-related injuries involving underage drinking.[119] Beyond this startling death toll, underage drinking also is associated with an increased risk of physical and sexual assault, academic failure, and illicit use of other drugs.[120] The consequences of underage drinking can be devastating for young people, their parents, and their communities.

Popular culture – especially consumer advertising – idealizes the effects of alcohol and increases the pressure on young people to engage in underage drinking. To counteract this powerful influence, the alcohol industry must shoulder some responsibility for reducing youth exposure to alcohol advertising.

The industry has taken important steps in the right direction. In 2003, at the Commission's recommendation, the three major alcohol industry trade associations adopted improved self- regulatory standards for the placement of alcohol advertising in print, radio, and television media. According to these standards, at least 70 percent of the audience for each advertisement must consist of adults of legal drinking age. Since 2003, the Commission staff has been actively monitoring the alcohol advertising, working with industry trade associations as well as individual companies, to facilitate compliance with the 70 percent standard.

End Notes

[1] The prior two studies are: FTC, *Alcohol Marketing and Advertising* (Sept. 2003), *available at* http://www. ftc.gov/os/2003/09/alcohol08report.pdf ("2003 Alcohol Report"), and FTC, *Self-Regulation in the Alcohol Industry* (Sept. 1999), *available at* http://www.ftc.gov/ reports/alcohol ("1999 Alcohol Report").

[2] The Federal Register notices were published in March and October 2006. *See* Federal Trade Commission, Agency Information Collection Activities, 71 Fed. Reg. 11,659 (Mar. 8, 2006), *available at* http://www. ftc.gov/os/2006/03/P064505ProposedInfoRequeststo BeverageAlcoholManufacturers.pdf; and Federal Trade Commission, Agency Information Collection Activities, 71 Fed. Reg. 62,261 (Oct. 24, 2006), *available at* http://www. ftc.gov/os/2006/10/P064505frnotice_inforeqalcoholads.pdf. The public comments, submitted in response to the notices, are posted on the FTC website http://www. ftc.gov/os/comments/ beveragealcoholadvertise/index.shtm *http://www.ftc .gov/ os/ comments/ alcoholmanufacadstudy/index.shtm.*

[3] J.W. Miller et al., *Binge Drinking and Associated Health Risk Behaviors Among High School Students*, 119 Pediatrics 76-85 (2007), http://www.pediatrics.org/ cgi/content/ full/119/1/76.

[4] *Id.*

[5] Experts disagree, however, whether it is youth drinking that leads to academic failure, or academic failure that increases youth drinking. CDC's study concludes that drinking increases the likelihood of academic failure, citing data showing that students who report receiving "mostly A's" are three times more likely to be nondrinkers than binge drinkers; those who report receiving "mostly D's or F's" are more likely to be binge drinkers than nondrinkers. *Id.*, Table 3. On the other hand, researchers with the Monitoring the Future ("MTF") project at the University of Michigan looked at long-term data and concluded that academic failure occurs prior to and predicts teen drinking. *See* J.G. Bachman et al.,*The Education-Drug Use Connection: How Successes and Failures in School Relate to Adolescent Smoking, Drinking, Drug Use, and Delinquency* (2007); Press release, University of Michigan, Early School Success Protects Against Teen and Young Adult Drug Use (Oct. 4, 2007), http://monitoringthefuture.org/ pressreleases/jgbpr04oct07.pdf.

[6] L.D. Johnston et al., *Monitoring the Future National Results on Adolescent Drug Use: Overview of Key Findings* (2007) ("*2007 MTF Results*"), at Table 3, *available at* http://www.monitoringthefuture.org/ data/07data/pr07t3.pdf.

[7] *2007 MTF Results, supra note* 6, at Figure 14, *available at http://www.monitoringthefuture.org/ data/07data/* fig07_14.pdf. The 2007 MTF Results show that, as compared to 1996, alcohol use by 8th graders has declined by 39 percent; use by 10th graders has declined by 17 percent; and use by 12th graders has declined by 12 percent. *2007 MTF Results*, Table 3, *available at* http://www.monitoringthefuture.org/data/07data/pr07t3.pdf. Some have suggested that this decrease is due only to changes in drinking by boys, but data show that drinking by teen girls has also decreased. Specifically, between 1996 and 2007, drinking rates for 8th grade girls dropped from 25.8 percent to 16 percent; for 10th grade girls, the rate dropped from 38.3 percent to 33.3 percent; and for 12th grade girls, the rate dropped from 46.9 percent to 41.4 percent. *See* L.D. Johnston, P.M. O'Malley et al., *Demographic Subgroup Trends for Various Licit and Illicit drugs, 1975-2006* (Monitoring the Future Occasional Paper No. 60), at Tables D-64-66, *available at* http://monitoringthefuture.org/ pubs/occpapers/ occ67.pdf; L.D. Johnston et al., *Monitoring the Future National Survey*

Results on Drug Use, 1975–2007, Volume I: Secondary School Students (2008, forthcoming) (NIH Publication No. to be determined), Table 4-7.

[8] *2007 MTF Results*, *supra* note 6, Tables 3 and 4, available at http://www. monitoringthefuture.org/data/07data/pr07t3.pdf and http://www.monitoringthefuture.org //data/07data/pr07t4.pdf.

[9] Teens reported using the following kinds of alcohol in the 30 days prior to participating in the 2007 MTF survey:

Grade	Beer %	Spirits %	Wine %	Wine Coolers %	Flavored Alcohol %
8	12.2	n/c	n/c	n/c	12.2
10	24.4	n/c	n/c	n/c	21.8
12	36.6	34.1	14.1	12.7	29.1

n/c= information not collected

L.D. Johnston et al., *Monitoring the Future National Survey Results on Drug Use, 1975–2007, Volume I: Secondary School Students* (2008, forthcoming) (NIH Publication No. to be determined), Tables D-75, D-76, D-77, D-81, D-83, D-85, D-86, D-87, D-89.

MTF also surveys alcohol use by older teens and adults. It reported that in 2006 (the most recent year for which data are available), 24 percent of study participants ages 19-30 reported drinking flavored alcohol beverages in the past 30 days and 56.8 percent reported drinking them in the past year. L.D. Johnston et al., *Monitoring the Future National Survey Results on Drug Use, 1975–2006, Volume II, College students and adults ages 19–45* (NIH Publication No. 07-6206) (2007), Figure 4-1, *available at* http://monitoringthefuture.org/pubs/monographs/vol2_2006.pdf (page 103 of 326).

[10] Sober Truth On Preventing Underage Drinking Act, Pub. L. No. 109-422, 120 Stat. 2890 (Dec. 20, 2006), *available at* http://frwebgate.access.gpo.gov/cgi-bin/getdoc.cgi?dbname=109_cong_public_laws&docid=f:publ422.109. Among other things, the STOP Act directs the Secretary of the Department of Health and Human Services to issue two reports to Congress each year. The first is a report on federal efforts to reduce underage drinking, including identification of evidence-based best practices to prevent underage drinking and treat those who need help as a result of youth drinking. Id. at Section 2(c)(1)(F). The second is a report on state laws and programs to prevent youth access to alcohol. Id. at Section 2(c)(2).

[11] *Id.* at Section 2(b)(1).

[12] Department of Health and Human Services, *The Surgeon General's Call to Action to Prevent and Reduce Underage Drinking* (2007) at 1-27, available at http://www.surgeon general.gov/topics/underagedrinking/ calltoaction.pdf.

[13] *Id.* at 75.

[14] Wine Institute Code of Advertising Standards, available at http://www.wineinstitute. org/initiatives/ issuesandpolicy/adcode/details; Beer Institute Advertising and Marketing Code, *available at* http://www. beerinstitute.org/BeerInstitute/files/ccLibraryFiles/Filename/000000000384/2006ADCODE.pdf; Distilled Spirits Council of the United States Code of Responsible Practices for Beverage Alcohol Advertising and Marketing Guideline, *available at* http://www.discus.org/responsibility/code/read.asp.

[15] 1999 Alcohol Report, *supra* note 1.

[16] 2003 Alcohol Report, *supra* note 1, at 11, 13.

[17] *See supra,* note 2.

[18] The Commission identified the companies based on publicly available data regarding measured media spending by alcohol companies in 2005. See Adams Beverage Group, *Adams Beer Handbook 2006*, at 126 (2006); Adams Beverage Group, *Adams Liquor Handbook 2006*, at 233 (2006); Adams Beverage Group, *Adams Wine Handbook 2007*, at 122-30 (2007). The companies that received the Special Orders (and examples of their brands) are:

Anheuser-Busch Companies, Inc. (Budweiser, Busch, Michelob, and Rolling Rock beers, Bacardi Silver flavored malt beverage)
Miller Brewing Co., Inc. (Miller, Icehouse, and Foster's beers)
Heineken USA, Inc. (Heineken and Amstel Light beers)
Diageo North America (Smirnoff vodka, Jose Cuervo tequila, Guinness beer, Beaulieu Vineyards and Sterling wines, Smirnoff Twist flavored malt beverages)
Bacardi U.S.A., Inc. (Bacardi rums, Bacardi pre-mixed cocktails, Grey Goose vodka)
Pernod Ricard USA (Chivas Regal, Beefeater, Mumm and Perrier-Jouët wines)
Brown-Forman Corp. (Jack Daniels, Southern Comfort, Fetzer and Bolla wines)
Constellation Brands (Corona and St. Pauli Girl beers, Robert Mondavi and Inglenook wines, Black Velvet whiskey, ChiChi's pre-mixed cocktails)
InBev USA (Stella Artois, Bass, and Beck's beers)
Absolut Spirits Company, Inc. (Absolut vodka)
Beam Global Spirits & Wine, Inc. (Jim Beam bourbon, Sauza tequila, Gilbey's gin, and DeKuyper cordials; at the time the study commenced, Beam also owned several wine brands, since sold).

[19] In response to comments, Specification 1(d) required the suppliers to provide data regarding the demographics of persons under 21 located in the U.S. who have tasted, used, or purchased the company's brands. See Exhibit A, Specification 1(d). The request called for data prepared or received by them on or after January 1, 2003 and excluded publicly available data, such as data published by the government or advocacy groups. One of the twelve suppliers possessed data that technically fell within the scope of the request; it was in the form of summary survey data on behaviors and habits of panels of 26,000 to 78,000 consumers, in which fewer than 3 percent and more often less than .01 percent of participants (depending on the survey company and the year) were under 21. All data were provided in an anonymous aggregate form; the company received no information on individual consumers. In some cases, the company received data sets that included information on consumers aged "18-24" or "18-34," as well as older age breaks; it was not possible, however, to extract from this information any data that were specific to alcohol purchase, tasting, or use by 18-20 year olds. As of 2007, data on consumers under 21 will no longer be provided to the company at issue. None of the other suppliers that received Special Orders had information responsive to this specification.

[20] For the purposes of this report, a "case" is 9 liters or 2.25 gallons.

[21] Consumer expenditures to purchase alcohol are substantially more than this, given price mark-ups at the wholesale and retail levels, as well as taxes. Retail sales in 2005 were $92.5 billion for beer, $58 billion for distilled spirits, and $26 billion for wine. Adams Beverage Group, *Adams Beer Handbook 2007* (2007) at 189.

[22] *See* Exhibit A, Specification 2 and Appendix A.

[23] It was not always possible for suppliers to precisely allocate expenditures as set forth in Specification 2. For example, differences in company accounting systems and promotional item labeling sometimes meant that items destined for retail outlets could be classified as non-sports public entertainment events, other point of sale, or specialty items. In addition, expenditure data were often incomplete for brands that had changed ownership.

[24] Because some expenditures were reported in more than one category, the sum of the categories is higher than actual total expenditures ($3.18 billion versus $3.13 billion).

[25] BI Code, ¶ 3(c); DISCUS Code, Responsible Placement, ¶ 3; WI Code, ¶ 3.4.

[26] BI Code, Buying Guidelines, available at http://www.beerinstitute.org/ BeerInstitute/files/ ccLibraryFiles/FILENAME/000000000441/ ADCODEBUYINGGUIDELINES2006.pdf; DISCUS Code, Demographic Data/ Advertising Placement Guidelines, *http://www. discus.org/pdf/ DemographicGuidelines Revised3- 06.pdf.*

[27] BI Code, ¶ 11; DISCUS Code, Responsible Placement ¶ 7.

[28] Part II.B.10.a of this report provides additional information about sports sponsorships.

[29] BI Code ¶ 3(e); DISCUS Code, Responsible Placement ¶¶ 4, 5; WI Code, ¶ 3.8.

[30] *See* FAA Act, 27 U.S.C. §§ 205(b) (tied house provision) and (c) (commercial bribery provision), *available at* http://www.ttb.gov/trade and http://www.ttb.gov/trade_practices/commercial_ bribery.shtml and 16 C.F.R. §§ 6.8 1-84, 91-93, 95, 98, 99, 101(b) & 102.

[31] A partial list of such state laws and regulations follows; the laws or regulations may also be complemented by other advisory information such as opinion letters or decisions. *Alabama*: Ala. Admin Code r.20-X-6.12, -7.01(f) & (g), -7.03(c) & (d), -7.11, -8.03, -8.04, -8.06, -8.07. *Alaska:* Alaska Stat. § 04.16.015. *Arizona*: Ariz. Stat. § 4-243(B)(2) & (3); Ariz. Comp. R. & Regs. 19-1-206, -210, 19-1-226(A)(1), (B)(3) & (M). *Arkansas*: Ark. Code § 3-5-104; *Ark.* ABC Reg. §§ 1.79(1), 2.28(4), (6), (10), & (13), 3.17. *California*: Cal. Bus. & Prof. Code §§ 23363.1 & .2, 23386, 23790.5, 25503.2, .5, .6, .8, & .27, 25611.1, 25612.5; Cal. Code Reg. tit. 4, div. 1, § § 52 & 106(c), (d), (e), (i), & (j). *Colorado*: Col. Rev. Stat. § 12-47-901; Col. Liq. Reg. §§ 47-100, -316, -320, -322(B), & -416. Connecticut: Conn. Gen. Stat. § 30-20; Conn. Agencies. Reg. § § 3 0-6- A32a, -A33, -A40, & 30-6-B21. Delaware: Del. ABCC Rules 2, 15, 27. *District of Columbia*: D.C. Code § 25-735(c), -736(c) & (d); D.C. Mun. Regs. tit. 23, §§ 903, 904. *Florida*: Fla. Stat. §§ 561.42(1), (11), (12), & 565.17; Fla. Admin. Code § 61A-1.010, -4.018; Ind. Bull. 97-09 & 99-05. *Georgia*: Ga. Comp. R. & Regs. r. 560-2-2.06, .16, .28, .45, .48, .55, & .58, r.560-2-3.36. Hawaii: Haw. Rev. Stat. §§ 281-42(a)(3), (4), & (8), 281-42(c), 281-85; Hon. Liq. Reg. § 3-84-85.1; Maui Liq. Reg. § 08-101-109. *Idaho*: Idaho Code §§ 23-313, -1033; Idaho Liq. Reg. 15.10.01 at §§ 004.17, 004.19, 021.8; 021.11 to 021.15; 022.02. *Illinois*: 235 ILCS Ch. 5, para. 6-6; see also ILCC Trade Practice Policies 2, 3, 9, 10 & 25. *Indiana*: Ind. Code § 7.1-1-3-16(f); Ind. Admin. Code tit. 905, r.1-5.2-1 to r.1-5.2-10, -12, -14, -15, & -17. *Iowa*: Iowa Code § 123.186; Iowa Admin. Code r.185-16.1; 16.3 to 16.5, 16.9(123), 16.10(123), 16.11(123) to 16.16(123). *Kansas*: Kan. Stat. § 41- 709(b); Kan. Admin. Regs. §§ 14-10-1(a), 14-10-6, 14-10-8, -10, -11(b), -12 to -14. *Kentucky*: Ky. Rev. Stat. §§ 244.240, .250, .260, 244.461, .590, & .804, Ky. Admin. Reg. §§ 1:070; 1:090; 1:100, 2:005. *Louisiana*: La. Admin. Code tit. 55: VII, § 3 17(B), (C). Maine: 28-A M.R.S.A. §§ 708(5), 708-A; Me. Liq. Regs. §§ 3.3, 4.13(A), 7.10 to 7.14, & 15.3, .4. *Maryland*: Md. Code [Alc. Bev.] Art. 2B, §12-104; Md. Code Regs. §§ 03.02.05.04, .05, .08, .10, & .13. *Massachusetts*: Mass. Liq. Reg. §§ 2.03, .06(8), .08, & 4.03(h). *Michigan*: Mich. Admin Code r. 436.1035, .1313, .1315, .1317, .1319, .1321, .1323, .1325, & .1329. *Minnesota*: Minn. Stat. §340A.308, 340A.5071; Minn. R. 7515.0300(5)-(7), 7515.0760(2), (3). *Mississippi*: Miss. Code § 67- 1-77; Miss. Liq. Reg. Subpart 01, Ch. 12 §§ 101-03. *Missouri*: Mo. Rev. Stat. §§ 311.070.3 to 311.070.5, 311.070.7 to 311.070.9, and 311.355. *Montana*: Mont. Code § 16-3-241, 16-3-244; Mont. Admin. R. §§ 42.11.205, 42.11.243 to 42.11.245, 42.11.111, 42.11.251, 42.13.211, and 42.13.221. *Nebraska*: Neb. Rev. Stat. §§ 53-123.02, 53-168; Neb. Admin. R. & Regs. §§ 237-6-001, -002, -016. *Nevada*: Nev. Rev. Stat. §§ 369.485, 597.225. New Hampshire: N.H. Rev. Stat. §§ 179:28-:31(II), 179:44; N.H. Code (Admin. R.) (Liq. Comm.) §§ 402.02 -.04, 405.0 -.05, 508.09, 508.10. *New Jersey*: N.J. Rev. Stat. §§ 33:1 to 43(b); N.J. Admin. Code tit. 13, §§ 2-24.2, .5-.7, .11, 2-23.16, 2-24.5, 2-24.11. *New Mexico*: N.M. Stat. § 60-8A-1(B) (3); 15 NMAC 10.5.1 at § 11.3.4 to 11.3.6; 11.3.7; N.M. Rev. Stat. §§ 60-6A-4 to -7. New York: NYCCRR, tit. 9, 83.1 to 83.4, 85.15, 86.1 to 86.5, 86.8, .9, .12-.16, and .17; N.Y. [Alco. Bev. Cont.] Law § 101-b(3)(a). *North Carolina*: 4 N.C. Admin. Code 2S.1006, .2S.1010 to 2S.1012, 2S.1020, 2T.0101(2), .2T.0712, 2T.0713, 2T.0716. *North Dakota*: N.D. Cent. Code § 5-01-11; N.D. Reg. §§ 81-12-01-10, -11. Ohio: Ohio Rev. Code § 4301.22; Ohio Admin. Code §§ 4301:1–32, -43(A), (B), -44, -45, & -46(D). *Oklahoma:* Okla. Stat. tit. 37, §§ 534-36, 537(B)(3); Okla. Liq. Reg. §§ 45:10-3-24, -25. *Oregon*: Or. Code §§ 471.398, .400-01, & .750(2); Or. Admin. R. 845-006-0350, 845-013-0001 (3), (4), (5), 845-013-0010, -0025, -0030, -0040, -0050, -0060, -0075, -0090(3)(c), 845-015-0165(3)(a), -0175, -0177. *Pennsylvania*: 47 Pa. Stat. §§ 4-305(a), 4-493, 4-498; 40 Pa. Admin. Code §§ 5.30, 5.32(h), 13.42, 13.43, 13.51-.53, 13.81, 13.201, & 13.211. *Rhode Island*: R.I. Gen. Laws § 3-7-4.1; R.I. Liq. Regs. 1(d), 13, 29, 36. *South Carolina*: S.C.

Code §§ 61-6-1035, -1540, -1560, -1640, -2980, 61-9-940. *South Dakota*: S.D. Regs. §§ 64:75:04:10, 11, 13, 14. *Tennessee*: Tenn. Code §§ 57-3-404, 57-3-406; Tenn. Comp. R. & Regs. §§ 0100-3-.06, -3-.14, 0100-6-.03. Texas: Tex. [Alc. Bev.] Code §§ 52.01, 102.02, 102.07; Tex. Admin. Code tit. 16, §§ 45.101; 45.106, 45.109, 45.112, 45.113, 45.117, 45.120. Utah: Utah Code § 32A-12-603(4). *Vermont*: Vt. Liq. Regs.: Advertising, §§ 1, 5, 7; Wholesale Dealers and Certificate Holders and Vt. Manufacturers §§ 9, 15. *Virginia*: 3 VAC 5-20-20, -30, -60 -90. *Washington*: Wash. Rev. Code §§ 66.28.010(2), 66.28.040, 66.28.045, 66.28.155; Wash. Admin. Code §§ 314-52-040, -080, -085, -090, & -113. *West Virginia*: W.Va. Reg. §§ 175-1-2.19, -2.21, -5.1.3, -5.4.1, -5.4.5, -5.4.6, & 176-1-7. *Wisconsin*: Wis. Stat. § 125.33. *Wyoming*: Wyo. Stat. § 12-5-403; Wyo. Admin. Code Ch. 20, § 8.

[32] 2003 Alcohol Report at 17.

[33] *Id.* at 18. These systems rely on data in electronic records containing consumer information (including date of birth), such as voter registrations, court filings, license applications, auto and property transaction records, motor vehicle violation header records, and credit headers.

[34] The companies operate an additional six websites providing corporate information (*e.g.*, financial information, annual reports, and corporate contact information) that were not considered for the purpose of this analysis.

[35] However, if the user subsequently attempts to re-enter the site by providing a birth date showing him to be of legal age, the websites generally do allow entry; most websites neither permanently nor temporarily barred (e.g., through use of a "cookie") underage users from entering a different, older, age.

[36] Further, users may not back-button during that web session in order to attempt to reenter the Bud.TV site with a different, older, age.

[37] Currently, two primary services measure Internet audience demographics, Nielsen/NetRatings (NNR), and comScore Media Metrix (comScore). They use differing data collection technology and different sampling approaches. In some cases, one will report that a website has a 70 percent or greater legal age audience, but the other will not. The Media Rating Council, a media and advertising industry trade association responsible for accrediting audience measurement services, is auditing the NNR and comScore systems.

[38] Concerns have been raised about alcohol ads on social networking sites, given the popularity of these sites with teenagers. MySpace carries alcohol ads, but under a long-standing policy, now codified in a January 14, 2008 agreement with 49 state attorneys general, the site does not deliver them to registered users who have stated that they are under 21 years of age. *See Joint Statement on Key Principles of Social Networking Sites' Safety,* appendix A, at 2, ago.mo.gov/newsreleases/2008/pdf/MySpace-JointStatement0108.pdf. Unregistered users are assumed to be below the LDA and alcohol ads are not delivered to them. MySpace does not independently verify age information; however, the MySpace/Attorney General agreement calls upon the site to organize an industry-wide Internet Safety Technical Task Force aimed at finding and developing online identity authentication tools. *Id.* The social networking site Facebook currently does not accept advertising from alcohol companies in the United States. *See* Facebook Advertising Guidelines, Part 7 ("Content Restrictions") ("We do not accept advertising referencing, facilitating or promoting . . . Liquor, beer, or wine. . ."), *available at* http://www.facebook. com/ad_guidelines. The site does accept such advertising in other countries.

[39] The BI Code specifically provides that product placement should not be made where the primary characters are under the legal drinking age or the primary themes are, because of their content or presentation, especially attractive to persons below the legal drinking age beyond the general attractiveness such themes have for persons above the legal drinking age. BI Code, ¶ 12.

[40] BI Code, ¶ 10.

[41] DISCUS Code, Responsible Placement, ¶ 6; WI Code, ¶ 3.5.

[42] The 2003 Alcohol Report provides information about some of these responsibility efforts, at notes 69-72.

[43] BI Code, Buying Guidelines, *available at* http://www.beerinstitute.org/BeerInstitute/files/ccLibraryFiles/ FILENAME/000000000441/ADCODEBUYINGGUIDELINES2006.pdf; DISCUS Code, Demographic Data/ Advertising Placement Guidelines, *available at* http://www.discus.org/pdf/DemographicGuidelinesRevised3- 06.pdf.

[44] One company owns its media buyer.

[45] The available television demographic data provide information about viewers ages two and older. Currently, the available radio data provide information about listeners age 12 and older, although the service that provides such measurements is in the process of introducing a new technology that will measure listeners six and older in some markets. *See* note 83, *infra*. Newspaper demographic data are available for readers 18 and older. Finally, two syndicated sources, Mediamark Research, Inc. ("MRI") and Simmons Research, provide magazine demographic data. Syndicated audience composition data are available only for magazines that are willing to pay to be included in the audience measuring survey. Data on the composition of audience members ages 12 and older are available for only 80 national magazines; these data are updated once per year. Data on the composition of the audience 18 and older are available for many more magazines, but these data are of limited utility for the purpose of measuring what percentage of a magazine's audience is below the legal age, unless they show in a convincing manner that the magazine skews to an older (for example, predominantly 30+) audience. The companies did not advertise in teen-targeted magazines, such as *Teen Vogue and Cosmo Girl*.

[46] These special editions, not available on newsstands, typically are sent only to subscribers 21 and above. In addition, DISCUS member ads do not appear in school library subscription editions of *Newsweek, People, Sports Illustrated, Time*, and *U.S. News & World Report.* DISCUS, *Magazine Special Binding Initiative, available at* http://www.discus.org/pdf/MAGAZINE_SPECIAL_BINDING_INITIATIVE_description.pdf.

[47] The suppliers also conducted periodic, after-the-fact audits of a random portion of past placements to verify that they met the 70 percent target; if not, they took corrective action as required by the BI Code at ¶ 3(c) and the DISCUS Code, Responsible Placement ¶ 3.

[48] Special Orders, Section 3(B) and Appendix A.II (instructions). The order required submission of quarterly average data for television and radio, and annual average data for magazines and newspapers. For example, for a television placement made in February 2006, the companies were ordered to provide data showing the average audience composition data for that program, in that time slot, for the quarter that spanned January 1-March 31, 2006.

[49] The Commission's analysis is based on placements for which complete demographic data (including both the absolute numbers of audience members younger than 21 and 21 and older, plus audience composition percentages) were provided. The syndicated data services cover only major media; they do not, for example, measure the audiences for radio stations in numerous small markets, for local magazines, or for small cable networks such as hotel television. Further, even for television and radio markets that are measured, the syndicated data sources will not provide an audience estimate if the number of apparent viewers falls below a particular threshold. If impressions data were not provided, the Commission could not include the placement in its analysis.

[50] This analysis was conducted in response to comments asking whether the suppliers' minority-targeted advertising complied with the 70 percent placement standard. See the Commission's October 24, 2006 Federal Register notice, *supra* note 2, at 62,263 and 62,265.

[51] Letter to Deborah Platt Majoras from George A. Hacker, Alcohol Policies Project, Center for Science in the Public Interest ("CSPI") (July 13, 2005).

[52] Data provided are for advertising on NASCAR, CASCAR (NASCAR's Canadian counterpart), Craftsman Truck, and Formula 1 racing television programs.

[53] Data provided by ESPN Sports Poll, a service of TNS Sport.

[54] 1999 Aohol Report at 14-15; 2003 Alcohol Report at 9.

[55] 2003 Alcohol Report at 9.

[56] *See* Exhibit A, Specification 4.

[57] *See* comments of the Center on Alcohol Marketing and Youth ("CAMY"), the National Association of Attorneys General Youth Access Committee, and Ziming Xuan, *available at* http://www.ftc.gov/os/comments/ alcoholmanufacadstudy.

[58] DISCUS's Outside Advisory Board currently is comprised of Joan Z. Bernstein, former Director of the FTC's Bureau of Consumer Protection; Constantine W. Curris, President of the American Association of State Colleges and Universities; and Richard Glitter, former Vice President of Advertising Standards and Program Compliance for NBC. In addition to serving as a tie-breaker for code review deliberations, the outside advisory board also provides guidance about Code implementation and, if requested, provides confidential non-binding guidance to DISCUS members about draft advertising copy.

[59] If the internal committee cannot agree on whether a violation has occurred, the committee may refer the question to a separate and independent third-party reviewer.

[60] The current BI review board members are Rory Davis, former Executive Vice President, National Association of Broadcasters; William Cunningham, PhD, Professor of Marketing, University of Texas at Austin; Gloria Rodriguez, President and CEO, Comunicad, and past chairwoman, National Hispana Leadership Institute; and Paul G. Summers, former Attorney General, State of Tennessee.

[61] The BI review board published its first annual report, detailing advertising complaints considered in calendar year 2006, on January 31, 2007. *See* Beer Institute's 2006 Annual Report, *available at* www.beerinstitute.org/ tier.asp?bid=284.

[62] In addition to participating in the BI review process, Heineken USA has an independent complaint review process. Established in December 2004, Heineken's independent review board is comprised of three members with experience in advertising, alcohol regulation and policy, and adolescent behavior. Complaints about Heineken's marketing activities are first forwarded to this review board, each member of which independently considers the matter. In 2006, Heineken referred complaints about two advertisements to its review board, which recommended that no action be taken in either instance. Heineken communicated the board's decision in writing to both complainants, informing them that if they were dissatisfied with the decision, they were free to submit a formal complaint to the Beer Institute's review board.

[63] In July 2007, the WI wrote to the Walt Disney Company regarding its plans to market a wine with the name *Ratatouille*, in connection with the release of the company's G-rated animated film of the same name. Although Disney was not a member of the WI, the organization cited provisions of its Code prohibiting advertising with a particular appeal to persons below the legal drinking age and the use of cartoon characters that are predominantly popular with children. Disney decided not to distribute the product. *See* "Costco Pulls Ratatouille Wine: Plans for Cartoon-character-inspired Wine Label Shelved After Suggestions That the Wine Could Be Attractive to Minors" (July 31, 2007), *available at* http://www.winespectator.com/Wine/ Features/0,1 197,3921 ,00.html.

[64] In March 2006, an advocacy organization submitted a complaint to the BI about a brewer's ad that ran during the 2006 Super Bowl. Because the advertiser had ceased running the ad by the time the complaint was received, the BI review board declined to consider the complaint. At the recommendation of the Commission staff, BI subsequently modified its complaint process so that complaints about discontinued advertisements are not automatically barred from review board consideration. Under the modified procedures, complaints about discontinued advertisements will be considered unless the brewer notifies the BI review board that it had permanently discontinued dissemination of the ad more than 30 days prior to receipt of the complaint and took all reasonable steps to withdraw the ad from the marketplace.

[65] The WI received two complaints about wine advertising in early 2007 but no review occurred because the complaints related to non-member brands.

[66] National Research Council, Institute of Medicine, *Reducing Underage Drinking: A Collective Responsibility 163 (2003) ("IOM Study").*

[67] *See*, e.g., A.C. Wagenaar, *Effects of Minimum Drinking Age Laws: Review and Analysis of the Literature from 1960 to 2000*, J. Stud. Alcohol, Supplement No. 14, 206, at 219 (2002); H.D. Holder, *Supply Side Approaches to Underage Drinking: An Assessment of the Scientific Evidence* (2003); *IOM Study, supra* note 66, at 45 8-89.

[68] See 2007 MTF Results, *supra* note 6, at Figure 14, *available at* http://monitoring thefuture.org/data/07data/ fig07_14.pdf. The press release accompanying the 2007 MTF Results noted that reported alcohol availability rates have declined most significantly among 8th graders. In 1996, 75 percent of 8th graders thought they could get alcohol if they wanted some, but by 2007 the number had fallen to 62 percent. MTF, *Overall, Illicit Drug Use by American Teens Continues Gradual Decline in 2007* (Dec. 11, 2007), at 5, *available at* http:// monitoringthefuture.org/pressreleases/07drugpr.pdf.

[69] *See* M.O. Hearst et al., "*Who needs liquor stores when parents will do? The importance of social sources of alcohol among young urban teens*," 44 Prev. Med. 471 (2007) (sixth to eighth graders who drank alcohol reported getting it from parents, older teens, other adults, or by taking it from a home without permission); American Medical Association, *Teen Drinking Key Findings* (2005), http://www.alcoholpolicymd. com/pdf/poll_080805.pdf (reporting that in survey by Teenage Research Unlimited of youth 13 to 18, two out of three said it was easy to get alcohol from their own home without a parent being aware of it; one out of four teens reported that they had been at a party where teens were drinking in front of a parent); DISCUS, *Underage Alcohol Access* (2003) (reporting that survey by Teenage Research Unlimited showed that 65 percent of 10- to 18-year-olds who drank in the past year got alcohol from family and friends). S*ee also IOM Study, supra* note 66 at 168 (according to the IOM, parties, friends, and adult strangers are the most frequent sources of alcohol among college students and older adolescents).

Given that teens most often obtain alcohol from an intermediary source (rather than directly from a retail outlet), it is unclear the extent to which they have the ability to choose a particular type or brand. Their alcohol use may be based on availability.

[70] The IOM reported that use of commercial sources appears to be much higher among college students, in urban settings, and where possession and purchase laws are relatively weak or unenforced. *IOM Study, supra* note 66, at 169.

[71] 2003 Alcohol Report at 23-24.

[72] *IOM Study, supra* note 66, at 116-17, 170; *Call to Action, supra* note 12, at 39. The STOP Act requires an annual survey of state efforts to reduce underage alcohol access, including underage alcohol access from commercial and social sources. STOP Act, *supra* note 10, Section 2(c)(1)(F).

[73] Data show that European teens have high levels of alcohol use and intoxication. See National Institute on Alcohol Abuse and Alcoholism, Alcohol Research and Health, Vol. 28, No. 3 (2004/2005) "Scope of the Problem," at Figure 2, *t http://pubs.niaaa. nih.gov/ publications/arh283/111-120.htm.*

[74] Press events were coordinated by The Century Council in sixteen states, and by Students Against Destructive Decisions in one state. No entity has provided funds to the FTC in connection with the WDST program.

[75] *See, e.g., AG Launches "We Don't Serve Teens Week,"* WFMZ-TV News, Sept. 18, 2007, *available at* http://wfmz.com/view/?id Editorial, "Don't Serve Teens Week" Emphasizes Responsibility, Sept. 13, 2007, *available at* www.battlecreekenquirer.com (in "archives" for "2007" search "We Don't Serve Teens"); *AG Hood Spot Tells Adults to Stop Giving Minors Alcohol,* SunHerald.com, Sept. 11, 2007, *http://www. sunherald. com/news/breaking_news/story/139706.html;* S. Israelsen, *Letting Teens Drink is Illegal, Parents Warned, Deseret Morning News*, Sept. 8, 2007, *available at* http://deseretnews.

com/article/1,5143,695210966,00.html; *State: NC Wine Distributors Launch Statewide Campaign Against Underage Drinking*, Lincoln Tribune, Oct. 20, 2007, *available at* http://www.lincolntribune.com/modules news/article.php?storyid=7262.

[76] The Century Council, Wine and Spirits Wholesalers of America, and American Beverage Licensees, and their members, were involved in delivery of program materials to retail outlets.

[77] *See*, supra, Part II.

[78] Again, this analysis addresses only the placements for which complete data were provided, as described in note 49, *supra*.

[79] Magazine data for the portion of the audience that is eighteen or older are updated twice per year, but the critical data on magazine readers ages twelve to seventeen are updated only annually.

[80] According to Alan Wurtzel of NBC Universal, "The sample sizes now are so small for some of the niche cable networks that if only one regular viewer happens to go on vacation, it could significantly affect the ratings." See D. Bauder, "*Nielsen to Triple TV Sample*," Sept. 27, 2007, quoting Alan Wurtzel of NBC Universal, available at http://www.huffington post.com/huff-wires. Changes in consumer use of media, including use of TiVo and other time-delay technologies, have resulted in disputes about the proper way to measure audiences. D. Leonhardt, "*Bar the Door. TV Ads Want Your TiVo*," N.Y. Times, May 17, 2006, available at http://www.nytimes. com/2006/05/17/ business/media/17leonhardt.html?ex=1305518400&en=e0ce9a4bad830abd&ei=5090&part ner=rssuserland&emc=rss<br%20/>. The syndicated measuring services are working to adopt improvements in radio and television survey technology, including movements away from the diary system of audience measurement, and toward electronic systems, that are calculated to address these problems. These changes include tripling the size of the national TV sample and use of electronic people meters in additional local TV markets. *See* D. Bauder, *supra*. For additional information about audience composition measurements, see notes 82 and 83, below.

[81] J.G. Webster, *Ratings Analysis: The Theory and Practice of Audience Research* (2005), at 217.

[82] About 2.4 percent of advertisements shown on national television missed the 70 percent target; by contrast, 6.5 percent of advertisements shown on local television missed the target. Currently, the national television audience projections, as well as projections for audiences in the top 20 percent of local markets, are based on data from electronic "people meters" that are kept on top of television sets. In most local televison markets, however, audiences are estimated based on paper diaries sent out four times a year during "sweeps" periods that usually occur around February, May, July, and November. The diary system relies on consumers' recollections about media use and has been criticized as unreliable. Further, the diary surveys do not measure the local audience for programs (such as specific sports events) that appear only outside the sweeps periods. It is for this reason that the DISCUS and BI buying guidelines previously have recommended that suppliers refer to national audience composition data, where available, when making decisions on the placement of local television advertising. In the course of this study, it was clear that some companies nonetheless had relied on local data when national data were available. This likely contributed to the number of local placements that appeared to miss the 70 percent target.
For additional information regarding audience samples, see Nielsen Media, *Products and Services*, "National Audience Sample" and "Local Audience Samples," *available at* http://www.nielsenmedia.com/nc/ portal/site/Public/menuitem.4f84194d341befbc3a81e810d8a0 62a0/?vgnextoid=e3f6da86b0715010VgnVCM1 00000880a260aRCRD.

[83] The company that measures radio audience composition is in the process of replacing a diary-based measuring system with portable "people meters" that will permit monthly radio demographic data on audience members ages six and older in major markets. Radio audience demographics traditionally have been calculated based on responses to written

diaries that rely on consumer recollections about media use. A new portable people meter (PPM) system will use a passive device to track consumer exposure to inaudible codes embedded in radio signals. Carried throughout the day by participants, the PPM device can track when and where they are exposed to radio signals, and are expected to be more reliable. *See* Arbitron, *The Portable People Meter*, http://www.arbitron.com/portable_people_meters/home.htm. In addition to providing previously unavailable information on the presence of younger audience members (which may, as a practical matter, reduce the number of radio dayparts and stations that meet the 70 percent standard), these new data will allow advertisers to make more rapid adjustments when a change in audience occurs.

[84] The company that measures television audience demographics is tripling the size of the sample on which it makes its projections. This change is likely to increase the stability of the television audience data, including cable audience data. For information about the planned increase in the sample size, see K. Bachman, MediaWeek, *Nielsen Nat'l PM TV Panel to Triple In Size* (Sept. 26, 2007), http://www.mediaweek. com/mw 003646903.

[85] For example, some suppliers provided radio audience data for eight- to twelve-hour time segments, rather than for Arbitron's standard three- to six-hour time segments (dayparts). The Commission has previously cautioned that longer dayparts may obscure time segments when the audience is unusually young. *See* 1999 Alcohol Report at note 15. The Commission required suppliers that made this kind of error to submit data pertaining to the standard daypart in which the advertisement ran, or, if a company was not certain precisely when during the eight- to twelve-hour segment the advertisement ran, it was required to provide "worst case scenario" data (that is, data for the period of time when the audience composition was at its youngest). Also as part of the study, the Commission requested backup data for a sample of advertisements from each company. At that juncture, some companies learned for the first time that advertisements had not been placed as reported by a media buyer, or had been placed at a different time than reported; they were required to supplement their responses with corrected data. Additional data problems that had to be addressed in the course of the study are discussed in note 96, *infra*.

[86] *See, e.g.*, CAMY, *Striking A Balance: Protecting Youth from Overexposure to Alcohol Ads and Allowing Alcohol Companies to Reach the Adult Market* (July 2005), at 5-5, *available at* http://camy.org/research/ striking/striking.pdf; Comment, National Association of Attorneys General, Youth Access to Alcohol Committee (Nov. 22, 2006), *available at* http://www. ftc.gov/os/comments/beveragealcoholadvertise/526363- 00061 .pdf.

[87] In April 2007, Beam Global issued a public letter to the state attorneys general stating that effective January 1, 2008, it would implement a 75 percent baseline/85 percent aggregate standard for advertising. *See* Letter to Attorneys General from Thomas J. Flocco, Beam Global (Apr. 23, 2007). The state attorneys general and the CSPI have applauded these commitments. *See* Letter to Thomas J. Flocco, Beam Global, from National Association of Attorneys General (May 7, 2007); Letter to Deborah Platt Majoras, Chairman, from George A. Hacker, Alcohol Policies Project, CSPI (May 9, 2007).

[88] The *Call to Action* noted that the FTC was conducting a study to evaluate this issue. *Call to Action, supra* note 12, at 44.

[89] This represents the total of the placements that had a legal age composition lower than 70 percent (about 7.5 percent of placements) plus the placements that had a legal age audience composition of between 70 and 75 percent (about 4.7 percent of placements).

[90] The proposed 85 percent standard excludes audience members 2 to 11 from the analysis. In the case of advertisements on television, the data obtained by the Commission showed the number and percentage of audience members ages 2 to 20, but it did not show what proportion of these persons were ages 2 to 11 as opposed to ages 12 to 20. If one assumes that *all* of the underage audience members for the television ads were ages 12 to 20, the suppliers would have had to relocate about 35 percent of their placements. This represents the total of the placements that had a legal age composition lower than 70 percent (about 7.5

percent of placements) plus the placements that had a legal age audience composition of between 70 and 85 percent (about 28 percent of placements).

[91] The argument that GRP data prove that youth are overexposed to alcohol advertising has been set forth in numerous studies published by CAMY over the past several years. *See, e.g.,* CAMY, *Radio Daze: Alcohol Ads Tune in Underage Youth* (Apr. 2003), *available at* http://camy.org/research/files/radio0303.pdf; *see also* 2003 Alcohol Report at note 47.

Gross rating points measure the total volume of delivery of a media message to a target audience. They are calculated by multiplying the percentage of an audience reached by the number of times reached (known as frequency). Thus, for example, 100 GRPs could be the result of reaching 100 percent of the target audience one time, one percent of the target audience 100 times, or any other combination equaling 100. *See, e.g.*, A. Cherney, Strategic Marketing Analysis (2nd Ed.), at 120.

Comparing GRPs works only if the "audience" reached by advertising is correctly identified. Alcohol marketing documents reviewed by the Commission in the course of its investigations and studies very often identified campaign targets as being "adults 21-25," "adults 21-29," or "men 21-34." CAMY's data have repeatedly shown that youth per capita alcohol advertising exposure is *lower* than young LDA adult per capita exposure. *See, e.g.*, CAMY, *Youth Exposure to Alcohol Advertising on Television and in National Magazines,* 2001 to 2006 (Dec. 2007), at 19, 20 (Tables 6 and 7) (compare GRPs for "Youth Ages 12-20" with "Young Adults Ages 21-34"), http://camy.org/research/ tvmag1207/ tvmag1207.pdf; CAMY, *Is "Spillover"* Exposure of Youth to Alcohol Advertising an Inevitable Consequence? (Working Paper, Sept. 20, 2007). Calculations that purport to compare per capita alcohol advertising exposure of all adults 21+ and older, e.g., that include even adults 50+, are unpersuasive because they rely on including, in the calculation of the average, those who are far outside the intended target.

[92] CAMY states that children under twelve should be excluded from the placement analysis because they "generally do not drink alcohol, have a low level of awareness of alcohol advertising, and are not being overexposed to alcohol advertising." *Id.* At least one study, however, suggests that young children are attuned to the presence of alcohol in the environment at an early age. M.A. Dalton, *Use of Cigarettes and Alcohol by Preschoolers While Role-playing as Adults*, Arch. Pediatr. Adolesc. Med., Vol 159, 854 (Sept. 2005) (concluding that "preschoolers have already begun to develop behavioral expectations regarding the use of cigarettes and alcohol"). Indeed, ten percent of children have drunk alcohol at least once by age ten. *Call to Action, supra* note 12, at 3, Figure 1.

[93] *See* Adams Beverage Group, *Handbook Advance* (2007), at 20, 92, and 125 (showing 200 new spirits introductions, 257 new wine introductions, and 42 new beer introductions in 2006). New entrants can engage in substantial advertising. *See, e.g.*, K.W. Bieler, *Behind the [yellow tail] phenomenon, How it happened and what's next?* (Mar. 2006), *http://www.bevnetwork.com/monthly_issue_article.asp?ID=152* (discussing the introduction of [yellow tail] wines into the United States).

[94] Acohol brands often are targeted to adults in a narrow age range, such as "adults 21-29." *See* note 91, *supra.*

[95] As the Commission previously has stated:

> Restrictions in advertising self-regulatory codes that are reasonably designed to prevent the targeting of advertising to underage persons are unlikely to violate the antitrust laws. First, the conduct targeted by the restrictions – advertising of alcohol to underage persons – is not the kind of activity the antitrust laws were designed to protect. While advertising is an important part of the competitive process, selling alcohol to underage persons is not; it is unlawful and thus not a legitimate form of competitive activity. Second, there are many means by which advertising messages can reach persons who are of legal age. So long as the means available for marketing to adults is not unduly restricted, legal age consumers will continue to have access to product information, and sellers can continue to compete for their patronage.

See 1999 Alcohol Report, at Appendix H.

[96] U.S. Census Bureau, Census 2000, Sex by Single Years of Age (PCT12), http://factfinder.census. gov/servlet/DTTable?_bm=y&-geo_id 000US&-ds_name= DEC_2000_SF1_U&-mt_name=DEC_2000_ SF1_U_PCT012.

[97] In the course of future monitoring, the Commission will consider whether it is appropriate to recommend formal adoption of an 85 percent aggregate annual average standard. Such a requirement may be unnecessary, as many of the major companies already appear to operate at this level. At the same time, it is unclear what effect such a standard would have on small suppliers that engage in only occasional advertising.

[98] Although the U.S. Census Bureau issues estimated population data annually based upon projections from the Census 2000 data, the next official census will not be conducted until 2010.

[99] In some instances, suppliers appear to have relied on out-of-date audience composition estimates, until the Commission alerted them to the fact that newer data were available. If the trade associations obtained the estimates, and promptly shared them with members, erroneous placements could better be avoided. Additionally, there is a need to develop common systems for evaluating data. For example, data originally provided by one audience measurement service purported to show audience figures in the negative numbers, or cumulative audience composition (that is, underage plus 21+ percentages) of more than 100 percent. The trade associations should work with the audience measurement services to resolve these kinds of issues.

[100] 2003 Alcohol Report at 18.

[101] *See* BI code, ¶ 3.g; DISCUS code, Responsible Content, ¶ 9 ("Websites"); WI code, ¶ 5.2.

[102] *See supra*, Part II.B.6.a.

[103] See FTC, *Implementing the Children's Online Privacy Protection Act: A Report to Congress* (Feb. 2007), *available at* http://www.ftc.gov/reports/coppa/07COPPA_ Report_to_ Congress.pdf ("2007 COPPA Report to Congress").

[104] In its 2007 COPPA Report to Congress, the Commission noted the absence of age-verification technologies that might be used to prevent children under age 13 from accessing websites that are not intended for their use or viewing. *See id.* at 1, 12. The Commission's assessment of the age-verification technology landscape was directed at the current inability to accurately verify the identities of young children, given the lack of available public records information on them. Indeed, the agreement entered into between MySpace and 49 state attorneys general in January 2008 recognizes this fact, and envisions the creation of a task force, comprised of Internet businesses, identity authentication experts, non-profit organizations, and technology companies charged with "finding and developing online identity authentication tools." *See Joint Statement on Key Principles of Social Networking Sites' Safety*, at 1, *available at* ago.mo.gov/newsreleases/2008/pdf/MySpace-JointStatement0108.pdf. By contrast, adult age-verification tools, such as the one used by Anheuser-Busch to verify the LDA status of visitors to the BudTV website, rely upon information about U.S. adults contained in databases of government and commercial information, and have long been in use.

[105] WI code, ¶ 5.3.

[106] *See* FedEx Alcohol Shipping (Wine) Requirements, *available at* www.fedex. com/us/wine/requirements. html?link=4; UPS Wine Program, available at *http://www.ups. com/wine* (all wine shipments must be shipped using UPS's "delivery confirmation adult signature required" service). While it does not appear to have a formal alcohol shipment program, DHL will only accept shipment of beverage alcohol from licensed distributors and requires an adult signature upon delivery. See List of Prohibited & Restricted Commodities, available at http://www.dhl-usa.com/resources

[107] See FTC Staff, Letter to the Hon. Paula Dockery (Florida State Legislature) (Apr. 10, 2006), *available at* *http://www.ftc.gov/os/2006/04/V060013FTCStaff CommentReFlorida SenateBill282.pdf* (commenting in support of proposed Florida legislation, SB 282)

("Dockery Letter"); see also Letter to the Hon. Eric D. Fingerhut (Ohio Senate) (Mar. 22, 2006), available at http://www.ftc.gov/os/2006/03/ V060010CommentReOhioSB 179DirectShipmentofWine.pdf (commenting in support of proposed Ohio legislation, SB 179, and noting that, under the bill, the individual ordering the wine to be delivered must be at least 21 and must personally sign a document acknowledging the wine's receipt at time of delivery).

[108] In a recent letter on proposed state legislation, the FTC staff stated that a requirement that the vendor use an approved age-verification process at the time of purchase, plus conspicuous package labeling requiring that an adult sign for delivery of alcohol, was an effective safeguard against the direct shipping of alcohol to minors. *See* Dockery Letter, *supra* note 107.

[109] The issue required significant consideration of the quality and reliability of the data provided by the two primary sources of Internet demographic data, Nielsen/NetRatings and comScore Media Metrix. *See supra* note 37.

[110] 1999 Alcohol Report at 17.

[111] The Commission obtained data about the audience composition of six popular films in theaters during the month of October 2006. These data showed that three films with a PG-13 rating (*Flyboys, The Guardian*, and *The Illusionist)* had LDA audiences composition rates of between 70 and 90 percent, whereas only 60 percent of the R-rated film J*ackass Number Two* was above the LDA. The remaining two films, which were R-rated, did have a 21+ audience composition that exceeded 70 percent (*Little Miss Sunshine* and *The Departed*).

[112] *See* comments of CAMY, the National Association of Attorneys General Youth Access Committee, and Ziming Xuan, *available at http://www.ftc.gov/os/ comments/alcohol manufacadstudy.*

[113] No complaints were submitted to the Wine Institute's review board in 2006.

[114] *See* http://www.beerinstitute.org/tier.asp?bid=258 (BI online complaint submission form).

[115] For more information about FTC promotion of self-regulation to address consumer economic, health, and safety issues, see, for example, FTC Staff of the Bureau of Consumer Protection, *Comment to NACHA – The Electronic Payments Association*, Apr. 2007, *available at* http://www.ftc.gov/os/opinions/070423staffcomme nttonacha.pdf; FTC, *Prepared Statement of the FTC on Marketing Violent Entertainment to Children: Self-Regulation and Industry Practices in the Video Game Industry*, June 2006, *available at* http://www.ftc.gov/ os/2006/06/P994511MarketingViolentEntertainmenttoChildren-TheVideoGameIndustry06142006.pdf; FTC and DHHS, *Perspectives on Marketing, Self-regulation and Child Obesity: A Report on a Joint Workshop of the Federal Trade Commission and the Department of Health and Human Services*, Apr. 2006, *available at* http://www.ftc.gov/os/2006/05/PerspectivesOnMarketingSelf-Regulation&ChildhoodObesityFTCandHHSRep ortonJointWorkshop.pdf; *see also* Deborah Platt Majoras, Chairman, *Food for Thought: The FTC and Market* Influences on Consumer Health, Apr. 2007, available at http://www.ftc.gov/speeches/majoras/070412FDL_ DK.pdf; Deborah Platt Majoras, Chairman, *Self-Regulation in the Infomercial Industry: Moving Forward*, Apr. 2006, available at http://www.ftc.gov/speeches/ majoras/060503 eraspeech.pdf.

[116] There is undoubtedly a compelling national and state interest in reducing underage alcohol use, given the substantial risks associated with youth drinking. Further, the Commission has jurisdiction to challenge specific alcohol marketing practices, if there is reason to believe that they are deceptive or unfair pursuant to 15 U.S.C. § 45(a)(1) and (n).

Nonetheless, applicable case law suggests that regulation of alcohol advertising to address underage appeal could face significant challenges in court. The Supreme Court has ruled that alcohol advertising and marketing receive the same protections as advertising for other products. *See 44 Liquormart Inc. v. Rhode Island*, 517 U.S. 484, 514 (1996) (striking down a state ban on alcohol price advertising); *Rubin v. Coors Brewing Co.*, 514 U.S. 476, 497-98 (1995) (striking down a federal law that prevented alcohol content claims on beer labels).

The Court also has ruled that non-deceptive commercial speech enjoys substantial First Amendment protections. *See, e.g.*, *Lorillard Tobacco Co. v. Reilly*, 533 U.S. 525, 553-66 (2001) (striking down state restrictions on tobacco advertising despite arguments that they were needed to protect children); Bolger *v. Youngs Drug Prods. Corp.*, 463 U.S. 60, 73 (1983) (striking down federal law prohibiting mailing of unsolicited contraceptive advertisements); *Virginia State Bd. of Pharmacy v. Virginia Citizens Consumer* Council, 425 U.S. 748, 770 (1976) (invalidating a state ban on price advertising of prescription drugs).

Subsequent to the Court's decision in Lorillard, federal and state courts have struck down statutory limits on alcohol advertising. *See Pitt News v. Pappert*, 379 F.3d 96, 111 (3d Cir. 2004) (striking down a state law banning payment for alcohol advertisements in communications media affiliated with an educational institution, such as a college paper or college football program); *Eller Media Co. v. City of Cleveland*, 326 F.3d 720 (6th Cir. 2003) (striking down a city ban on most billboard advertising for alcohol); Utah Licensed *Bev. Assoc. v. Leavitt*, 256 F.3d 1061, 1074 (10th Cir. 2001) (striking down restrictions on wine and spirits advertising because the regulatory scheme failed to materially advance the asserted government interest); *Educ. Media Co. at Virginia Tech., Inc. v. Swecker*, No. 3 :06CV396, slip op. at 31 (E.D. Va. Mar. 31, 2008) (striking down state regulations prohibiting alcohol advertising in college papers); see also Fulsom v. City of *Jasper*, 279 Ga. 260, 262-63 (2005) (striking down regulations that prohibited advertising of alcohol prices and brand names, noting that the regulations were more extensive than necessary, given the availability of other means to reduce alcohol consumption).

[117] For your information, under the Paperwork Reduction Act, as amended, an agency may not conduct or sponsor, and a person is not required to respond to, a collection of information unless it displays a currently valid OMB control number. For this information request, that number is 3084-0138.

[118] U.S. DEP'T OF HEALTH AND HUMAN SERVS., THE SURGEON GENERAL'S CALL TO ACTION TO PREVENT AND REDUCE UNDERAGE DRINKING 3 (2007), *http://www.surgeongeneral.gov/topics/underagedrinking/calltoaction.pdf.*

[119] *Id.* at 10.

[120] *Id.* at 10-11.

[121] Janet Maslin, *Between Drinks, A Coming of Age*, N.Y. TIMES, Feb. 7, 2005, at E1 (quoting KOREN ZAILCKAS, SMASHED: STORY OF A DRUNKEN GIRLHOOD (2005)), *available* at 2005 WLNR 1682157.

[122] *Id.*

In: Underage Drinking
Ed: David Edvin and Samuel Harald
ISBN: 978-1-60876-141-8

Chapter 5

UNDERAGE ALCOHOL USE: FINDINGS FROM THE 2002-2006 NATIONAL SURVEYS ON DRUG USE AND HEALTH*

Michael R. Pemberton, James D. Colliver, Tania M. Robbins and Joseph C. Gfroerer

ACKNOWLEDGMENTS

This chapter was prepared by the Division of Population Surveys, Office of Applied Studies, Substance Abuse and Mental Health Services Administration (SAMHSA), and by RTI International, a trade name of Research Triangle Institute, Research Triangle Park, North Carolina. Work by RTI was performed under Contract No. 283-2004-00022. At RTI, the report was authored by Michael R. Pemberton, and all statistical analyses were conducted by Tania M. Robbins. Other contributors and reviewers at RTI listed alphabetically include Jeremy Aldworth, Justine Allpress, Teresa R. Davis, David C. Heller, Larry A. Kroutil, Mary Ellen Marsden, Lisa Packer, and Kathryn Spagnola. At SAMHSA, the report was coauthored by James D. Colliver, conceptualized by Joseph C. Gfroerer, and reviewed by Joel Kennet. Also at RTI, report and web production staff listed alphabetically include

* This is an edited, reformatted and augmented version of a Department of Health and Human Services publication dated June 2008.

Teresa G. Bass, Wendy Broome, Cassandra M. Carter, Joyce Clay-Brooks, Diane G. Eckard, Shari B. Lambert, Danny Occoquan, Brenda K. Porter, Pamela Couch Prevatt, and Richard S. Straw. Final report production was provided by Beatrice Rouse, Coleen Sanderson, and Jane Feldmann at SAMHSA.

HIGHLIGHTS

Alcohol is the drug of choice among young people in the United States, and alcohol use constitutes one of the principal public health issues for this population. Approximately 5,000 persons under 21 years of age lose their lives each year as a result of underage drinking, and early initiation of alcohol use is associated with increased risk of subsequent alcohol use disorders and increased risk of involvement in violent behaviors, suicide attempts, and a variety of other problematic activities. In response to this issue, this study presents findings from the 2002 to 2006 National Surveys on Drug Use and Health (NSDUHs) on the use of alcohol by persons aged 12 to 20.

NSDUH is an annual survey of the civilian, noninstitutionalized population of the United States aged 12 or older. The survey is sponsored by the Substance Abuse and Mental Health Services Administration (SAMHSA) of the U.S. Department of Health and Human Services and is planned and managed by SAMHSA's Office of Applied Studies (OAS). Data collection is conducted under contract with RTI International, Research Triangle Park, North Carolina.[1] Selected key findings from this study are described below.

Prevalence of Underage Drinking Behaviors in 2006

- In 2006, more than half (53.9 percent) of persons aged 12 to 20 (20.6 million persons) had used alcohol in their lifetime, almost half (46.1 percent, 17.6 million) had used it in the past year, and more than a quarter (28.3 percent, 10.8 million) had used it in the past month (current use). One in five persons in this age group (19.0 percent, 7.2 million) engaged in binge alcohol use, meaning they had consumed five or more drinks of alcohol on at least one occasion in the past month. This includes 2.4 million (6.2 percent of persons aged 12 to

20) who drank heavily, defined as 5 or more days of binge alcohol use in the past month.

Trends in Underage Current and Binge Drinking

- Between 2002 and 2006, rates of current and binge drinking among those aged 12 to 20 remained stable. Current use among underage persons was 28.8 percent in 2002 and 28.3 percent in 2006, while binge use was 19.3 percent in 2002 and 19.0 percent in 2006.
- There were varying trends by age. Among youths aged 12 to 14, there was no change in current or binge alcohol use between 2002 and 2006, but past year use declined from 17.6 to 16.2 percent. Among 15 to 17 year olds, the rates declined from 2002 to 2006 for past year use (from 52.3 to 48.7 percent) and current use (from 28.3 to 26.1 percent), but binge use remained stable. There were no changes for 18 to 20 year olds in any of these alcohol use measures from 2002 to 2006.

Sociodemographic and Geographic Differences in Underage Drinking

- Combined data from 2002 to 2006 indicated that rates of current (past month) alcohol use were 7.0 percent for youths aged 12 to 14, 27.5 percent for youths aged 15 to 17, and 51.3 percent for 18 to 20 year olds. Binge alcohol use rates for these age groups were 3.3, 17.8, and 36.3 percent, respectively.
- Underage males were more likely than underage females to be current alcohol users (29.4 percent for males, 27.8 percent for females) and binge drinkers (21.6 percent for males, 16.5 percent for females). Among youths aged 12 to 14, the rate of current drinking was higher for females (7.7 percent) than males (6.3 percent), but there was no gender difference in the rate of binge drinking. For those aged 15 to 17, males and females did not differ in the rate of current alcohol use, but binge drinking was higher for males than females (19.0 vs. 16.5 percent). Among those aged 18 to 20, males had higher rates of current and binge drinking than females.

- Past month underage alcohol use was higher among non-Hispanic whites (32.6 percent) than Hispanics (25.7 percent), who in turn had a higher rate than blacks (18.8 percent). Underage current drinking rates were 27.2 percent among American Indians or Alaska Natives and 17.1 percent among Asians.
- One third (33.9 percent) of persons aged 12 to 20 whose family income was less than $20,000 consumed alcohol in the past month, higher than the rate among those with a family income in any category over $20,000. The rate of current alcohol use among underage persons in the highest income category ($75,000 or more) was 28.6 percent, higher than the rate for those with a family income of $20,000 to $49,999 (26.0 percent) and $50,000 to $74,999 (26.4 percent). A similar pattern was found for binge drinking.
- Underage persons who lived in nonmetropolitan areas were more likely than those who lived in metropolitan areas to engage in binge drinking (20.8 percent in nonmetropolitan areas, 18.8 percent in metropolitan areas). The rate of current drinking among underage persons was 29.4 percent among those who lived in nonmetropolitan areas and 28.5 percent among those who lived in metropolitan areas, though this difference was not statistically significant.
- Among underage persons who lived in metropolitan areas, the prevalence of current drinking was higher for non-Hispanic whites (33.2 percent) than for Hispanics (25.3 percent). Among those who lived in rural areas, however, Hispanics had a higher prevalence of current drinking (32.4 percent) than whites (28.9 percent).
- Rates of current and binge alcohol use among 12 to 20 year olds were higher in the Northeast and Midwest than in the South or West. For example, 21.4 percent of those in the Northeast and 21.8 percent of those in the Midwest engaged in binge drinking compared with 17.3 percent of those in the South and 17.8 percent of those in the West. Among the 10 States with the highest rates of binge drinking, 4 were in the Midwest (Iowa, North Dakota, South Dakota, and Wisconsin), and 4 were in the Northeast (Massachusetts, New Hampshire, Rhode Island, and Vermont).

Alcohol Use Disorders among Persons Aged 12 to 20

- Combined data from 2002 to 2006 indicated that an annual average of 9.4 percent of persons aged 12 to 20 (3.5 million persons in that age range) met the diagnostic criteria for an alcohol use disorder (dependence or abuse) in the past year.
- Among all persons aged 12 to 20, a higher percentage of males (10.3 percent) than females (8.5 percent) had an alcohol use disorder, though this pattern varied by age group. Among youths aged 12 to 14, a higher percentage of females (2.2 percent) than males (1.6 percent) were classified with an alcohol use disorder. In contrast, among 18 to 20 year olds, a higher percentage of males (19.6 percent) than females (13.4 percent) were classified with an alcohol use disorder.
- The rate of past year alcohol use disorder among persons aged 12 to 20 was higher for American Indians or Alaska Natives (14.9 percent) than for whites (10.9 percent), blacks (4.6 percent), Hispanics (8.7 percent), and Asians (4.9 percent). One in eight Native Hawaiians or Other Pacific Islanders (12.7 percent) met the criteria for an alcohol use disorder.

Association of Underage Drinking with Parental Alcohol Use

- Rates of current and binge alcohol use among underage persons were higher among persons aged 12 to 20 who lived with a mother or father who had consumed alcohol in the past year compared with those who lived with a mother or father who had not consumed alcohol in the past year. For example, rates of binge drinking among underage persons were 17.6 percent for those whose mother was a past year drinker versus 9.3 percent for those whose mother was not a past year drinker, and 16.5 percent for those whose father was a past year drinker versus 10.2 percent for those whose father was not a past year drinker. Rates of underage binge drinking were also higher among those aged 12 to 20 who lived with a mother (21.3 percent) or father (19.5 percent) who was a binge drinker than among those whose mother (17.5 percent) or father (15.4 percent) was a current drinker but not a binge drinker.

Social Context of Last Alcohol Use

- In 2006, 80.9 percent of persons aged 12 to 20 who had consumed alcohol in the past month were with two or more people the last time they drank alcohol, 14.3 percent were with one other person the last time they drank, and 4.9 percent were alone. Underage persons who drank with two or more other people on the last occasion in the past month had more drinks on the last occasion on average (4.9 drinks) than those who drank with one other person (3.1 drinks) or those who drank alone (2.9 drinks).
- Among current drinkers, youths aged 12 to 14 were more likely to have been alone (9.0 percent) or with one other person (21.9 percent) the last time they drank compared with youths aged 15 to 17 (5.2 percent alone and 14.6 percent with one other person) or 18 to 20 year olds (4.2 percent alone and 13.2 percent with one other person).

Location of Last Alcohol Use

- A majority of underage current drinkers in 2006 reported that when they last used alcohol they were either in someone else's home (53.4 percent) or their own home (30.3 percent).
- Drinkers aged 12 to 14 were more likely to have been in their own home the last time they drank (38.8 percent) and less likely to have been in someone else's home (45.0 percent) compared with underage drinkers in older age groups (26.0 and 60.9 percent, respectively, for those aged 15 to 17, and 31.4 and 50.7 percent, respectively, for those aged 18 to 20). Drinkers aged 18 to 20 were more likely than those in younger age groups to have been in a restaurant, bar, or club on their last drinking occasion (12.9 percent for those aged 18 to 20 vs. 4.6 percent for those aged 12 to 14 and 3.7 percent for those aged 15 to 17).

Sources of Alcohol

- Among all underage current drinkers, 31.0 percent paid for the alcohol the last time they drank, including 9.3 percent who purchased the alcohol themselves and 21.6 percent who gave money to someone else to purchase it. Underage persons who paid for alcohol themselves consumed more drinks on their last drinking occasion (average of 5.9 drinks) than did those who did not pay for the alcohol themselves (average of 3.9 drinks).

- More than one in four underage drinkers (25.8 percent) indicated that on their last drinking occasion they were given alcohol for free by an unrelated person aged 21 or older. One in sixteen (6.4 percent) got the alcohol from a parent or guardian, 8.3 percent got it from another family member aged 21 or older, and 3.9 percent took it from their own home.
- Underage persons in older age groups were more likely to have paid for alcohol themselves on their last drinking occasion, with 37.6 percent of 18 to 20 year olds paying for it themselves compared with 23.5 percent of 15 to 17 year olds and 6.6 percent of 12 to 14 year olds. Among underage drinkers, males were more likely to have paid for alcohol themselves on their last drinking occasion (36.7 percent) than were females (24.5 percent).

Underage Drinking and Illicit Drug Use

- In 2006, more than one third (35.8 percent) of persons aged 12 to 20 who used alcohol in the past month also had used an illicit drug in the past month, and 16.0 percent of underage drinkers used an illicit drug within 2 hours of using alcohol on their last occasion of alcohol use.
- Marijuana was the illicit drug most used by underage drinkers, with nearly one third (30.0 percent) having used marijuana in the past month, and 15.0 percent having used marijuana within 2 hours of their last alcohol use.

1. Introduction

This chapter presents findings from the 2002 to 2006 National Surveys on Drug Use and Health (NSDUHs) on the use of alcohol by persons aged 12 to 20, that is, those who are under the minimum legal age for alcohol use. NSDUH is an annual survey of the civilian, noninstitutionalized population of the United States aged 12 or older and is conducted by the Substance Abuse and Mental Health Services Administration (SAMHSA). This chapterexamines trends in alcohol use from 2002 to 2006 among underage persons and variations in underage drinking and alcohol use disorders across demographic groups and geographic areas. The discussion is based on measures of alcohol use in the past month, past year, and lifetime included in NSDUH, as well as questions that allow for the classification of past year dependence on or abuse of alcohol. Findings also are presented from items added to the 2006 NSDUH regarding the social context and location of underage drinking, the sources for alcohol among underage drinkers, and the co-occurrence of underage alcohol use and illicit drug use.

1.1. Background

Alcohol is the drug of choice among young people in the United States, and alcohol use constitutes one of the principal public health issues for this population (National Institute on Alcohol Abuse and Alcoholism [NIAAA], 2006). Each year, approximately 5,000 young people under the age of 21 die as a result of underage drinking, including about 1,900 deaths from motor vehicle crashes (Hingson & Kenkel, 2004). Drinking drivers under age 21 are involved in fatal crashes at twice the rate of adult drivers (National Highway Traffic Safety Administration [NHTSA], 2002). Early initiation of alcohol use is associated with higher likelihood of involvement in violent behaviors, suicide attempts, unprotected sexual intercourse, and multiple sex partners (Stueve & O'Donnell, 2005; Swahn, Bossarte, & Sullivent, 2008).

In addition, early initiation of alcohol use has been linked to higher rates of alcohol dependence or abuse in later life (Grant & Dawson, 1997). In the 2006 NSDUH, for example, the rate of alcohol abuse or dependence among adults aged 21 or older was 2.4 percent for those who first used alcohol at age 21 or older compared with 9.6 percent among those who initiated alcohol use prior to age 21 and 16.3 percent among those who first used alcohol before age 15 (Office of Applied Studies [OAS], 2007a). An estimated 38.7 percent of adults age 21 or older with past year alcohol dependence or abuse initiated alcohol use before age 15 (OAS, 2007b).

Information from several national sources indicates that underage alcohol use is widespread. According to the 2006 NSDUH, about 10.8 million persons aged 12 to 20 (28.3 percent of this age group) reported drinking in the past month (OAS, 2007a). Approximately 7.2 million (19.0 percent) were binge drinkers (consumed five or more drinks at the same time or within a couple of hours of each other on at least 1 day in the past 30 days), and 2.4 million (6.2 percent) were heavy drinkers (five or more drinks on the same occasion on each of 5 or more days in the past 30 days). The percentage of underage persons reporting past month alcohol use was similar from 2002 to 2006, according to the 2006 NSDUH. The 2006 Monitoring the Future (MTF), a survey of 8th, 10th, and 12th graders that also includes a follow-up of persons who had participated in the survey as high school seniors, indicated that 17.2 percent of 8th graders, 33.8 percent of 10th graders, 45.3 percent of 12th graders, and 57.6 percent of those aged 19 or 20 had consumed alcohol in the past month (Johnston, O'Malley, Bachman, & Schulenberg, 2007a, 2007b). Furthermore, 6.2 percent of 8th graders indicated that they had been drunk in the past month, as did 18.8 percent of 10th graders, 30.0 percent of 12 graders, and 42.5 percent of those aged 19 or 20. Data from the Treatment Episode Data Set (TEDS) indicate that in 2006 there were over 61,000 admissions to substance abuse treatment among persons aged 12 to 20 in which alcohol was the primary substance of abuse, a number that represented 24.1 percent of all substance abuse treatment admissions for this age group (Substance Abuse and Mental Health Data Archive [SAMHDA], 2008).

Reduction of underage alcohol use has been highlighted as a top health priority of the Federal Government. In 2007, the Surgeon General issued a *Call to Action to Prevent and Reduce Underage Drinking* to highlight the nature and extent of underage drinking and to focus the attention of the public on this enduring problem (U.S. Department of Health and Human Services [DHHS], 2007). As part of SAMHSA's leadership role to coordinate the Federal effort to address this problem, the agency has issued *A Comprehensive Plan for Preventing and Reducing Underage Drinking* that outlines a detailed, goal-driven plan to reduce underage drinking (DHHS, 2006). Currently, SAMHSA sponsors two workgroups that address the underage drinking problem, one internal to SAMHSA and the other involving other agencies. SAMHSA's internal workgroup coordinates the agency's activities with regard to the prevention and treatment of alcohol-related problems and addresses such topics as the prevention of underage drinking, adolescent treatment, the prevention of excessive drinking by those of legal age, and alcohol treatment in general. The Interagency Coordinating Committee on the Prevention of Underage Drinking, which includes members from NIAAA, NHTSA, and other agencies in addition to SAMHSA, was responsible for developing SAMHSA's *Report to Congress on the Prevention and Reduction of Underage Drinking*.

This analytic series report, the first full-length NSDUH report to focus solely on underage drinking, complements these recent and ongoing efforts. NSDUH's large sample of the population aged 12 to 20 (more than 158,000 respondents in this age range from 2002 to 2006 combined), its inclusion of items to measure alcohol use and alcohol use disorders, and the added items on the context, location, and co-occurrence of alcohol use and illicit drug use make the survey a unique source of data to address the issue of underage alcohol use. NSDUH provides estimates that are representative at both the national level and within each State. It has sufficient sample size to examine the prevalence of rare drug use patterns, to study trends from 2002 to 2006, and to investigate differences in prevalence and other indicators across demographic groups, socioeconomic circumstances, and geographic areas.

1.2. General Information about NSDUH

NSDUH is the primary source of statistical information on the use of alcohol and illicit drug use by the U.S. civilian, noninstitutionalized population aged 12 or older. Conducted by the Federal Government since 1971, the survey collects data by administering questionnaires to a representative sample of the population through face-to-face interviews at their places of residence. The survey, which has been repeated annually since 1990, is sponsored by SAMHSA, an operating division of the DHHS, and is planned and managed by OAS within SAMHSA. Data collection is conducted under contract with RTI International, Research Triangle Park, North Carolina.[1] This section briefly describes the survey methodology; a more complete description is provided in Appendices A and B.

Prior to 2002, the survey was called the National Household Survey on Drug Abuse (NHSDA). Because of improvements to the survey in 2002, the 2002 data constitute a new baseline for tracking trends in substance use and other measures. Estimates from 2002 to 2006 included in this chapter should not be compared with estimates from the 2001 or earlier versions of the survey to examine changes in underage alcohol use over time.

Particular strengths of the NSDUH data for reporting on underage alcohol use in the United States include, but are not limited to, the probability sampling design and large sample sizes (see below). Data are weighted to allow inferences to be made for the civilian, noninstitutionalized population aged 12 or older in the United States and for specific demographic subgroups (such as those aged 12 to 20) and geographic subgroups within the United

States. Large sample sizes and probability sampling yielding representative estimates in each of the 50 States and the District of Columbia ensure coverage of even relatively rare behaviors and provide a high level of precision in the national estimates, particularly when survey data are pooled across multiple years.

NSDUH collects information from residents of households, noninstitutional group quarters (e.g., shelters, rooming houses, dormitories), and civilians living on military bases. The survey does not include homeless persons who do not use shelters, military personnel on active duty, and residents of institutional group quarters, such as jails and hospitals.

Since 1999, the NSDUH interview has been carried out using computer-assisted interviewing (CAI). Most of the questions are administered with audio computer-assisted self- interviewing (ACASI). ACASI is designed to provide the respondent with a highly private and confidential means of responding to questions to increase the level of honest reporting of illicit drug use and other sensitive behaviors. Less sensitive items are administered by interviewers using computer-assisted personal interviewing (CAPI).

The 2002 to 2006 NSDUHs employed a State-based design with an independent, multistage area probability sample within each State and the District of Columbia. The eight States with the largest population (California, Florida, Illinois, Michigan, New York, Ohio, Pennsylvania, and Texas), which together account for 48 percent of the total U.S. population aged 12 or older) were designated as large sample States. For the remaining 42 States and the District of Columbia, smaller, but adequate, samples were selected. In this report, State variations are studied using direct, weighted, and design-based estimates from the sample. For these estimates, 5 years of data (2002 to 2006) were combined to obtain sample sizes sufficient to produce State estimates and estimates for small demographic groups that met the precision criteria for publication (see Appendix A). The NSDUH design also oversampled persons aged 12 to 17 and those aged 18 to 25, so that each State's sample was approximately equally distributed among three major age groups: 12 to 17 years, 18 to 25 years, and 26 years or older.

Each year's survey was conducted from January through December of that calendar year (e.g., January through December 2006 for the 2006 NSDUH). Sampled dwelling units were screened to identify eligible residents aged 12 or older. Up to two persons per dwelling unit were selected to be interviewed. In each year, respondents were given an incentive payment of $30 for completing the interview.

Weighted response rates for household screening ranged from 90.6 to 91.3 percent for these 5 survey years. Weighted response rates for interviewing ranged from 74.2 to 78.9 percent. Sample sizes were 68,126 in 2002, 67,784 in 2003, 67,760 in 2004, 68,308 in 2005, and 67,802 in 2006, for a total of 339,780 completed interviews for all those aged 12 or older across the 5 years. Sample sizes just for those aged 12 to 20 were 32,787 in 2002, 31,475 in 2003, 31,235 in 2004, 31,282 in 2005, and 31,320 in 2006, for a total of 158,099 completed interviews for those aged 12 to 20 across the 5 years. The weighted response rates for interviewing among those aged 12 to 20 were 89.2 percent in 2002, 88.5 percent in 2003, 88.0 percent in 2004, 86.8 percent in 2005, and 84.9 percent in 2006.

1.3. Measures of Alcohol Use and Disorders

NSDUH includes questions about the recency and frequency of consumption of alcoholic beverages, such as beer, wine, whiskey, brandy, and mixed drinks. An extensive list of examples of the kinds of beverages covered is given to respondents prior to the question administration. A "drink" is defined as a can or bottle of beer, a glass of wine or a wine cooler, a shot of liquor, or a mixed drink with liquor in it. Times when the respondent only had a sip or two from a drink are not considered to be consumption.

For this report, estimates for the prevalence of alcohol use are reported primarily at five levels defined for both males and females and for all ages as follows:

- *Lifetime use* – Use of alcohol at least once in the respondent's lifetime. This measure includes respondents who also reported last using alcohol in the past 30 days or past 12 months.

- *Past year use* – Use of alcohol in the 12 months prior to the interview. This definition includes those respondents who last used alcohol in the 30 days prior to the interview. Respondents who indicated past year use of alcohol also were classified as lifetime users.

- *Current (past month) use* – At least one drink in the past 30 days (includes binge and heavy use).

- *Binge use* – Five or more drinks on the same occasion (i.e., at the same time or within a couple of hours of each other) on at least 1 day in the past 30 days (includes heavy use).

- *Heavy use* – Five or more drinks on the same occasion on each of 5 or more days in the past 30 days.

NSDUH includes questions designed to measure dependence on and abuse of alcohol based on the criteria in the *Diagnostic and Statistical Manual of Mental Disorders,* 4th edition (DSM-IV) (American Psychiatric Association [APA], 1994). A respondent was defined as having dependence on alcohol if he or she met three or more of the following seven dependence criteria:

1. Spent a great deal of time over a period of a month getting, using, or getting over the effects of alcohol.
2. Used alcohol more often than intended or was unable to keep set limits on the alcohol use.
3. Needed to use alcohol more than before to get desired effects or noticed that the same amount of alcohol had less effect than before.
4. Inability to cut down or stop using alcohol every time tried or wanted to.
5. Continued to use alcohol even though it was causing problems with emotions, nerves, mental health, or physical problems.
6. Alcohol use reduced or eliminated involvement or participation in important activities.
7. Experienced withdrawal symptoms (e.g., having trouble sleeping, cramps, hands tremble).

A respondent was defined as having abused alcohol if he or she met one or more of the following four abuse criteria and was determined not to be dependent on alcohol in the past year:

1. Serious problems at home, work, or school caused by alcohol, such as neglecting your children, missing work or school, doing a poor job at work or school, or losing a job or dropping out of school.
2. Used alcohol regularly and then did something that might have put you in physical danger.
3. Use of alcohol caused you to do things that repeatedly got you in trouble with the law.

4. Had problems with family or friends that were probably caused by using alcohol and continued to use alcohol even though you thought alcohol use caused these problems.

Criteria used to determine whether a respondent was asked the dependence and abuse questions included responses from the core alcohol use questions and the frequency of alcohol use questions, as well as the noncore alcohol use questions. Missing or incomplete responses in the core alcohol use and frequency of use questions were imputed. However, the imputation process did not take into account reported data in the noncore questions, including those on dependence and abuse. Respondents with missing information on dependence or abuse (3.5 percent of past year users aged 12 to 20) were included in the analyses, but they were not counted as having dependence or abuse.

1.4. New Alcohol Use Items in the 2006 NSDUH

The 2006 NSDUH included a new module on consumption of alcohol that asked for additional information about respondents' last use of alcohol for those who indicated that they had consumed alcohol at least once in the past month. In this module, past month drinkers were asked to think about the last time they used alcohol and then were asked to provide the following information about their last drinking occasion:

- the number of drinks they had when they last drank;
- their use of illicit drugs while using alcohol or within 2 hours of using alcohol the last time they drank;
- for those aged 12 to 20, the social context of their last drinking occasion (i.e., whether they were alone, with one other person, or with two or more other people when they last drank);
- for those aged 12 to 20, the location of their last drinking occasion (in a car or other vehicle; at home; at someone else's home; at a park, on a beach, or in a parking lot; at a restaurant, bar, or club; at a concert or sports game; at school; or at some other place); and
- for those aged 12 to 20, their source for obtaining the alcohol the last time they drank (e.g., whether or not they paid for the alcohol; if they paid for it, whether they purchased it themselves or gave money to

somebody else to purchase the alcohol for them; and if they did not pay for it, who it was who gave them the alcohol).

In addition, respondents of all ages who indicated that they had binged on alcohol at least once in their life also were asked about their age when they first binged on alcohol. Respondents who indicated an age of first binge episode that was the same as their current age or 1 year younger than their current age were then asked to give the month and year when they first binged, which enabled a measure of initiation of binge alcohol use in the year prior to the survey.

Moreover, females who were lifetime drinkers were asked whether they had ever had four or more drinks on the same occasion, as well as their age when they first had four or more drinks on the same occasion. These two questions enable a comparison of binge drinking rates based on the definition used previously by NSDUH, which was five or more drinks on the same occasion for both males and females, and an alternative definition used by the NIAAA (2004), which is five or more drinks on the same occasion for males and four or more drinks on the same occasion for females.

Findings based on most of the items in the new consumption of alcohol module are presented in Chapter 4 and the tables in Appendix C. Section B.4 of Appendix B presents additional technical information and findings from items in this module.

1.5. Measures of Demographic and Geographic Characteristics

Data are presented for racial/ethnic groups in several categorizations, based on current standards for collecting and reporting race and ethnicity data (Office of Management and Budget [OMB], 1997) and on the level of detail permitted by the sample. Because respondents were allowed to choose more than one racial group, a "two or more races" category is presented that includes persons who reported more than one category among the seven basic groups listed in the survey question (white, black or African American, American Indian or Alaska Native, Native Hawaiian, Other Pacific Islander, Asian, Other). It should be noted that, except for the "Hispanic or Latino" group, the racial/ethnic groups discussed in this chapter include only non-Hispanics. The category "Hispanic or Latino" includes Hispanics of any race. Also, more detailed categories describing specific subgroups were obtained from survey respondents if they reported either Asian race or Hispanic ethnicity. Data on Native Hawaiians and Other Pacific Islanders are combined in this report.

Data also are presented for four U.S. geographic regions in this report. These regions and the nine geographic divisions within those regions, as defined by the U.S. Census Bureau, consist of the following groups of States:

Northeast Region - *New England Division:* Connecticut, Maine, Massachusetts, New Hampshire, Rhode Island, Vermont; *Middle Atlantic Division:* New Jersey, New York, Pennsylvania.

Midwest Region - *East North Central Division:* Illinois, Indiana, Michigan, Ohio, Wisconsin; *West North Central Division:* Iowa, Kansas, Minnesota, Missouri, Nebraska, North Dakota, South Dakota.

South Region - *South Atlantic Division:* Delaware, District of Columbia, Florida, Georgia, Maryland, North Carolina, South Carolina, Virginia, West Virginia; East South Central Division: Alabama, Kentucky, Mississippi, Tennessee; *West South Central Division:* Arkansas, Louisiana, Oklahoma, Texas.

West Region - *Mountain Division:* Arizona, Colorado, Idaho, Montana, Nevada, New Mexico, Utah, Wyoming; *Pacific Division:* Alaska, California, Hawaii, Oregon, Washington.

Geographic comparisons also are made based on county type, which reflects different levels of urbanicity and metropolitan area inclusion of counties, based on metropolitan area definitions issued by the OMB in June 2003 (OMB, 2003). For this purpose, counties are grouped based on the 2003 rural-urban continuum codes. These codes were originally developed by the U.S. Department of Agriculture (Butler & Beale, 1994). Each county is either inside or outside a metropolitan statistical area (MSA), as defined by the OMB.

Large metropolitan areas have a population of 1 million or more. Small metropolitan areas have a population of fewer than 1 million. Small metropolitan areas are further classified based on whether they have a population of 250,000 or more. Nonmetropolitan areas are areas outside MSAs. Counties in nonmetropolitan areas are further classified based on the number of people in the county who live in an urbanized area, as defined by the U.S. Census Bureau at the subcounty level. "Urbanized" counties have 20,000 or more population in urbanized areas, "less urbanized" counties have at least 2,500 but fewer than 20,000 population in urbanized areas, and "completely rural" counties have fewer than 2,500 population in urbanized areas.

1.6. Organization of This Report

This chapter contains separate chapters that discuss the following topics related to the use of alcohol by persons aged 12 to 20: trends in underage alcohol use and disorders from 2002 to 2006 (Chapter 2); patterns of underage alcohol use and alcohol use disorders by demographic and geographic groups (Chapter 3); and the social context and location of underage drinking, the sources of alcohol for underage drinkers, and the co-occurrence of underage drinking and illicit drug use (Chapter 4). Most analyses are presented for all underage persons aged 12 to 20 and by gender and age group (12 to 14, 15 to 17, 18 to 20). Technical appendices describe NSDUH (Appendix A) and its statistical methods and measurement (Appendix B). Appendix C contains the tables of estimates referenced in Chapters 2 through 4. Tables showing standard errors for the estimated numbers and percentages in the tables in Appendix C are available on the SAMHSA/OAS website at http://oas.samhsa.gov/WebOnly.htm.

Tables, text, and figures present prevalence measures for the population in terms of both the number of alcohol users and the rate of alcohol use for those aged 12 to 20. The tables and figures for Chapter 2 include trend data that are based on comparisons of single-year estimates between 2002 to 2006. In these tables and figures showing trend data, significant differences between estimates from 2006 and previous years of the survey are indicated. The tables and figures for Chapter 3 are based on averages for 2002 to 2006; combining data from these 5 survey years increases the sample sizes to support detailed estimates. The tables and figures for Chapter 4 are based on new items added to NSDUH in 2006.

Statistical tests have been conducted for all statements appearing in the text of the report that compare estimates between years or subgroups of the population. Unless explicitly stated that a difference is not statistically significant, all statements that describe differences are significant at the .05 level. Statistically significant differences are described using terms such as "higher," "lower," "increased," and "decreased." Statements that use terms such as "similar," "no difference," "same," or "remained steady" to describe the relationship between estimates denote that a difference is not statistically significant. In addition, a set of estimates for survey years or population subgroups may be presented without a statement of comparison, in which case a statistically significant difference between these estimates is not implied and testing was not conducted.

All estimates presented in the report have met the criteria for statistical reliability (see Appendix B). Estimates that do not meet these criteria are suppressed and do not appear in tables, figures, or text. Also, subgroups with suppressed estimates are not included in statistical tests of comparisons. For example, a statement that "whites had the highest prevalence" means that the rate among whites was higher than the rate among all nonsuppressed racial/ethnic subgroups, but not necessarily higher than the rate among a subgroup for which the estimate was suppressed.

2. Trends in Underage Drinking: 2002-2006

This chapter presents 2002 to 2006 data on the prevalence of alcohol use and alcohol dependence and abuse among persons aged 12 to 20. Findings are presented overall and by age group and gender. The trends are based on single years of data from the 2002 to 2006 National Surveys on Drug Use and Health (NSDUHs). This chapter includes estimates of lifetime, past year, and current (past month) alcohol use, binge alcohol use, heavy alcohol use, and alcohol dependence or abuse in the past year.

2.1. Overall Trends

In each year from 2002 to 2006, more than half of all persons aged 12 to 20 had consumed at least one drink of alcohol in their lifetime. In 2006, an estimated 53.9 percent of underage persons (20.6 million persons) had used alcohol in their lifetime, which was lower than the percentage in 2003 (55.8 percent) or 2002 (56.2 percent) (Figure 2.1; also see Table 2.1 in Appendix C). Lifetime alcohol use among underage persons was stable from 2004 to 2006.

In 2006, about 17.6 million (46.1 percent) underage persons used alcohol in the past year, 10.8 million (28.3 percent) used in the past month, 7.2 million (19.0 percent) engaged in binge alcohol use, and 2.4 million (6.2 percent) engaged in heavy alcohol use. Also in 2006, about 3.5 million (9.1 percent) underage persons were classified with alcohol dependence or abuse in the past year. In this overall age group, rates of past year use, current use, binge use, heavy use, or past year dependence or abuse remained stable from 2002 to 2006. For example, current use among underage persons was 28.8 percent in 2002 and 28.3 percent in 2006, while binge use was 19.3 percent in 2002 and 19.0 percent in 2006.

2.2. Trends, by Age

Among youths aged 12 to 14 and youths aged 15 to 17, the prevalence of lifetime alcohol use was lower in 2006 compared with 2002, 2003, or 2004 (Table 2.2). For example, the rate of lifetime alcohol use for 12 to 14 year olds declined from 24.9 percent in 2002 to 22.1 percent in 2006, and the rate of lifetime use for 15 to 17 year olds declined from 62.7 percent in 2002 to 57.7 percent in 2006. The prevalence of past year drinking was lower in 2006 (16.2 percent) than in 2002 (17.6 percent) for youths aged 12 to 14, and it was lower in 2006 (48.7 percent) compared with 2002 (52.3 percent), 2003 (51.6 percent), or 2004 (50.9 percent) for youths aged 15 to 17 (Figure 2.2). Among 15 to 17 year olds, the prevalence of past month alcohol use was lower in 2006 (26.1 percent) compared with 2002 (28.3 percent), 2003 (28.2 percent), or 2004 (28.3 percent). Among 15 to 17 year olds, the rates of binge drinking and alcohol use disorders in 2006 were not different from the rates in 2002. However, the rate of binge drinking among 15 to 17 year olds was lower in 2006 (17.1 percent) than in 2004 (19.1 percent), and past year dependence or abuse also decreased from 10.1 percent in 2004 to 8.8 percent in 2006. There were no changes in any measures of alcohol use from 2002 to 2006 for 18 to 20 year olds.

2.3. Trends, by Gender

Among both males and females aged 12 to 20, rates of lifetime alcohol use decreased between 2002 and 2006 (Figure 2.1 and Table 2.1). Rates of lifetime alcohol use decreased from 56.5 percent in 2002 to 54.0 percent in 2006 for underage males and from 56.0 to 53.7 percent for underage females. Among underage males, the prevalence of past year dependence or abuse was lower in 2006 (9.6 percent) than in 2004 (10.8 percent) or 2002 (10.9 percent). Among underage females, the prevalence of past year alcohol use was lower in 2006

(46.2 percent) than in 2003 (48.0 percent). There were no differences between 2006 and the previous 4 years of the survey for either males or females on past month alcohol use, binge use, or heavy use.

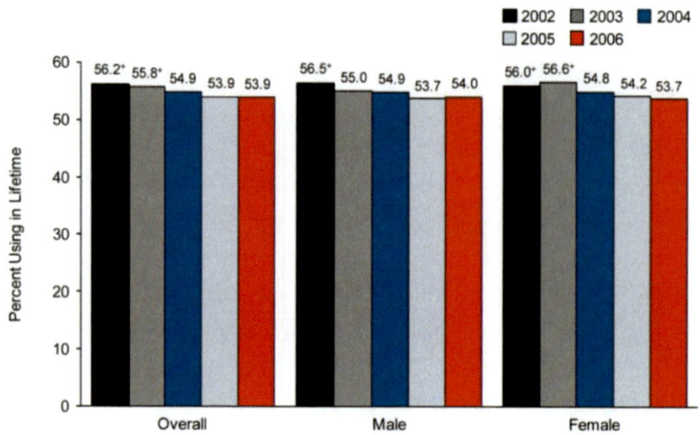

+Difference between estimate and 2006 estimate is statistically significant at the 0.05 level.

Figure 2.1. Lifetime Alcohol Use among Persons Aged 12 to 20, by Gender: 2002-2006.

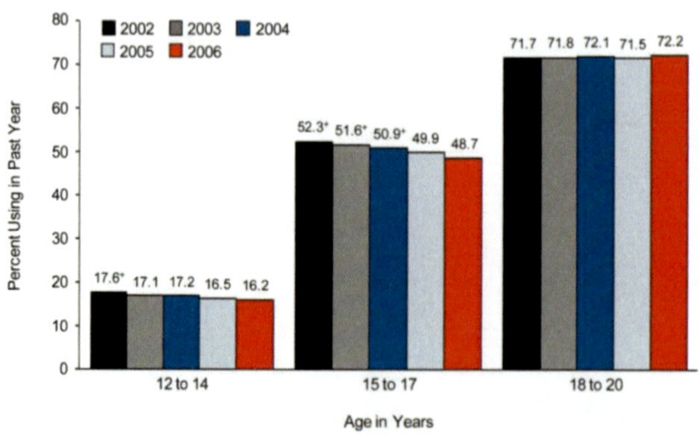

+Difference between estimate and 2006 estimate is statistically significant at the 0.05 level.

Figure 2.2. Past Year Alcohol Use among Persons Aged 12 to 20, by Age: 2002-2006.

3. Patterns of Underage Alcohol Use and Disorders: 2002-2006

This chapter presents estimates of alcohol use and alcohol dependence or abuse among persons aged 12 to 20 based on annual averages for the combined 2002 to 2006 National Surveys on Drug Use and Health (NSDUHs). Combining data from these 5 survey years increases the sample size to support detailed estimates and is particularly useful for examining demographic and geographic correlates of alcohol use and alcohol use disorders.

The first section in this chapter presents estimates of alcohol use by demographic group, including age group, gender, race/ethnicity, income level, county type, and geographic area. Variations by State also are presented. The alcohol use measures include current (i.e., past month) use, binge use, and heavy use. The second section presents estimates of alcohol use disorders, defined as alcohol dependence or abuse in the past year, by demographic group and geographic area. The third section presents associations between underage drinking and parent alcohol use using data from households in which both a person aged 12 to 20 and his or her mother or father was interviewed.

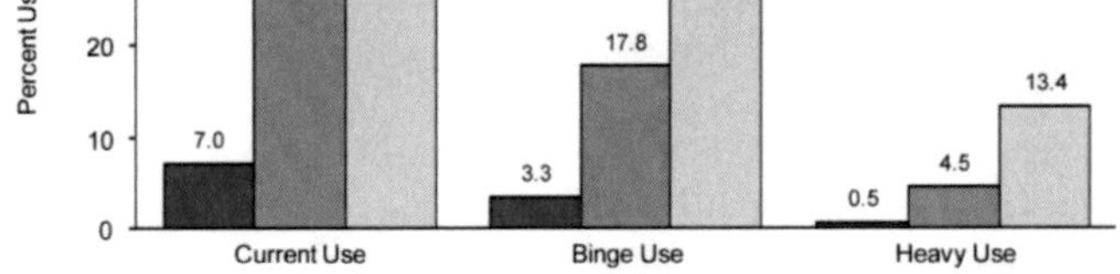

Figure 3.1. Current, Binge, and Heavy Alcohol Use among Persons Aged 12 to 20, by Age: Annual Averages, 2002-2006.

3.1. Alcohol Use

In 2002 to 2006, more than one in four persons aged 12 to 20 (28.6 percent) had consumed alcohol in the past month, corresponding to an estimated 10.8 million underage current alcohol users (see Table 3.1 in Appendix C). Within this age group, 7.2 million (19.2 percent) engaged in binge alcohol use, and 2.3 million (6.2 percent) were heavy drinkers.

3.1.1. Age

The prevalence of current, binge, and heavy alcohol use among persons aged 12 to 20 was higher for older age groups than for younger age groups (Figure 3.1). For example, current drinking was reported by 7.0 percent of youths aged 12 to 14 (Table 3.3), 27.5 percent of youths aged 15 to 17 (Table 3.4), and 51.3 percent of 18 to 20 year olds (Table 3.5). In addition, 3.3 percent of persons aged 12 to 14, 17.8 percent of persons aged 15 to 17, and 36.3 percent of persons aged 18 to 20 were binge alcohol users. The prevalence of heavy drinking was 0.5 percent for 12 to 14 year olds, 4.5 percent for 15 to 17 year olds, and 13.4 percent for 18 to 20 year olds. Thus, more than one in three persons aged 18 to 20 was a binge drinker, and more than one in eight was a heavy drinker.

3.1.2. Gender

Among all underage persons, males were more likely than females to be current alcohol users (29.4 percent for males, 27.8 percent for females), binge drinkers, (21.6 percent for males, 16.5 percent for females), and heavy drinkers (7.9 percent for males, 4.3 percent for females) (Table 3.1).

3.1.3. Race/Ethnicity

Among persons aged 12 to 20, non-Hispanic whites had higher rates of current and heavy alcohol use than any other racial/ethnic group, and they had a higher rate of binge use than non- Hispanic blacks, Asians, or Hispanics (Table 3.2). For example, approximately one third (32.6 percent) of whites were current users compared with 27.2 percent of American Indians or Alaska Natives, 25.7 percent of Hispanics, 24.3 percent of Native Hawaiians or Other Pacific Islanders, 18.8 percent of blacks, and 17.1 percent of Asians (Figure 3.2). Blacks had lower rates of current, binge, and heavy drinking compared with whites or Hispanics.

Among underage Hispanics, Cubans had a higher rate of current alcohol use (32.0 percent) than Central or South Americans (26.0 percent), Puerto Ricans (25.0 percent), or Mexicans (24.9 percent) (Table 3.2). There were no differences between Hispanic groups for binge or heavy alcohol use. Among underage Asians, rates of binge alcohol use were higher among Japanese (12.9 percent), Koreans (12.9 percent), and Filipinos (12.0 percent) than among Chinese (7.2 percent) or Vietnamese (5.2 percent). Koreans and Filipinos also had higher rates of binge alcohol use than Asian Indians (7.1 percent).

3.1.4. Gender, by Age Group

The pattern of differences between males and females in the prevalence of current drinking differed by age group. Among youths aged 12 to 14, the rate of current drinking was higher for females (7.7 percent) than for males (6.3 percent) (Table 3.3 and Figure 3.3). For those aged 18 to 20, however, the rate of current drinking was higher for males (54.4 percent) than for females (47.9 percent) (Table 3.5). There was no difference in the rate of current drinking for males and females among persons aged 15 to 17 (Table 3.4). For binge and heavy drinking, there were no gender differences for those aged 12 to 14, whereas for those aged 15 to 17 or 18 to 20, males had higher rates than females. For example, the rates of binge drinking were higher for males than for females for those aged 15 to 17 (19.0 percent for males, 16.5 percent for females) and those aged 18 to 20 (42.6 percent for males, 29.7 percent for females).

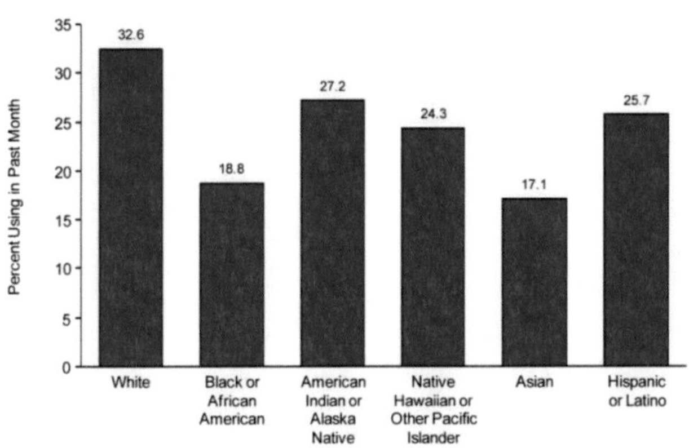

Figure 3.2. Current Alcohol Use among Persons Aged 12 to 20, by Race/Ethnicity: Annual Averages, 2002-2006.

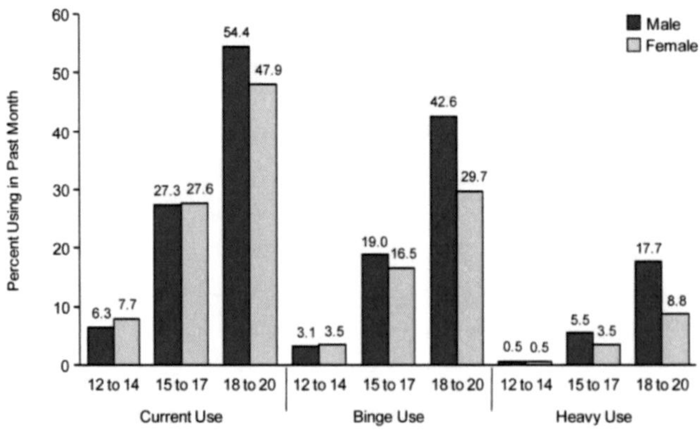

Figure 3.3. Current, Binge, and Heavy Alcohol Use among Persons Aged 12 to 20, by Age Group and Gender: Annual Averages, 2002-2006.

3.1.5. Race/Ethnicity, by Age Group

Among youths aged 12 to 14, non-Hispanic whites had a higher prevalence of current, binge, and heavy alcohol use compared with blacks or Asians (Table 3.3). For example, 7.5 percent of whites in this age group had consumed alcohol in the past month compared with 4.7 percent of blacks and 3.2 percent of Asians. However, rates of binge drinking for those aged 12 to 14 were lower for whites (3.4 percent) than for American Indians or Alaska Natives (8.1 percent) or for Hispanics (4.3 percent).

The pattern of racial/ethnic differences for those aged 15 to 17 was similar to that for those aged 12 to 14, with a higher percentage of non-Hispanic whites engaging in current, binge, and heavy alcohol use than blacks or Asians (Table 3.4). In contrast to the findings for those 12 to 14, a higher percentage of whites than Hispanics aged 15 to 17 engaged in current alcohol use (31.4 percent for whites, 26.0 percent for Hispanics), binge alcohol use (21.0 percent for whites, 17.1 percent for Hispanics), and heavy alcohol use (5.8 percent for whites, 3.7 percent for Hispanics). Within this age group, rates of current and binge alcohol use were also higher among whites (31.4 percent current users, 21.0 percent binge users) compared with Native Hawaiians or Other Pacific Islanders (17.4 percent current users, 9.1 percent binge users).

There were also differences between non-Hispanic whites and other racial/ethnic groups in alcohol consumption among persons aged 18 to 20. A higher percentage of whites in this age group were current or heavy drinkers compared with those in any other racial/ethnic group, though this difference was not statistically significant for those who reported being two or more races

(Table 3.5). For example, 17.4 percent of whites in this age group were heavy drinkers compared with 8.8 percent of Hispanics, 7.9 percent of American Indians or Alaska Natives, 7.4 percent of Native Hawaiians or Other Pacific Islanders, 4.3 percent of Asians, and 4.1 percent of blacks. A similar pattern was found for binge drinking, which was more prevalent among whites (42.9 percent) than among American Indians or Alaska Natives (35.4 percent), Hispanics (31.3 percent), blacks (18.6 percent), or Asians (18.4 percent).

3.1.6. Income Level

As shown in Table 3.6 and Figure 3.4, persons aged 12 to 20 whose family income was less than $20,000 had higher rates of current (33.9 percent), binge (23.7 percent), and heavy drinking (8.7 percent) compared with those whose family income was $20,000 or higher. In addition, persons in this age group whose family income was $75,000 or higher were more likely to have engaged in current, binge, and heavy alcohol use than those whose family income was $20,000 to $49,000 or those whose family income was $50,000 to $74,999. For example, 28.6 percent of persons aged 12 to 20 whose family income was $75,000 or higher were current drinkers compared with 26.0 percent for those with a family income of $20,000 to $49,999 and 26.4 percent for those with a family income of $50,000 to $74,999.

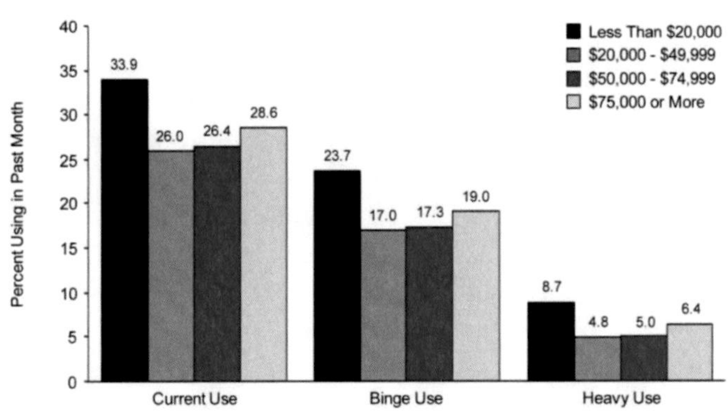

Figure 3.4. Current, Binge, and Heavy Alcohol Use among Persons Aged 12 to 20, by Family Income: Annual Averages, 2002-2006.

3.1.7. County Type

There was considerable variation in the rates of alcohol use among persons aged 12 to 20 by county type. Underage persons who lived in counties in nonmetropolitan areas were more likely than those who lived in counties in metropolitan areas to engage in binge drinking (20.8 percent in nonmetropolitan areas, 18.8 percent in metropolitan areas) and heavy drinking (6.9 percent in nonmetropolitan areas, 6.0 percent in metropolitan areas) (Table 3.6 and Figure 3.5). The rate of current drinking among underage persons was 29.4 percent among those who lived in nonmetropolitan areas and 28.5 percent among those who lived in metropolitan areas, though this difference was not statistically significant. Underage persons who lived in counties in small metropolitan areas (population less than 1 million) had higher rates of current, binge, and heavy drinking than those who lived in counties in large metropolitan areas (population of 1 million or more). Furthermore, persons aged 12 to 20 who lived in urbanized nonmetropolitan counties had higher rates of current, binge, and heavy drinking than those who lived in counties in large metropolitan areas, counties in small metropolitan areas, or rural counties. For example, 22.2 percent of underage persons who lived in urbanized nonmetropolitan counties were binge drinkers compared with 17.7 percent of those who lived in counties in large metropolitan areas, 20.8 percent in small metropolitan areas, and 19.8 percent in rural counties.

3.1.8. Demographic Differences within County Type

Across county types, underage persons in younger age groups had lower rates of current, binge, and heavy alcohol use compared with older age groups. For example, the prevalence of current drinking in counties in metropolitan areas was 6.7 percent for 12 to 14 year olds, 27.1 percent for 15 to 17 year olds, and 51.5 percent for 18 to 20 year olds (Table 3.7). Within rural counties, the prevalence of current drinking was 8.7 percent for 12 to 14 year olds, 30.0 percent for 15 to 17 year olds, and 46.1 percent for 18 to 20 year olds (Table 3.9).

There was little variation in the pattern of alcohol use among males and females by county type. For example, the rate of current alcohol use among those who lived in counties in metropolitan areas was higher for males (29.1 percent) than females (27.8 percent), and current drinking was also more prevalent among males in rural counties (30.0 percent) than among females (26.0 percent).

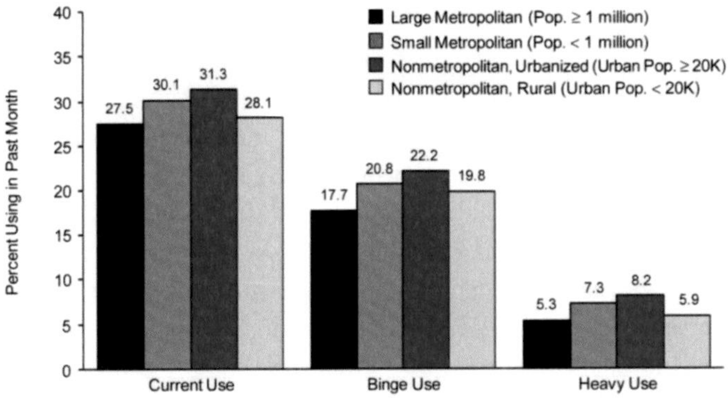

Figure 3.5. Current, Binge, and Heavy Alcohol Use among Persons Aged 12 to 20, by County Type: Annual Averages, 2002-2006.

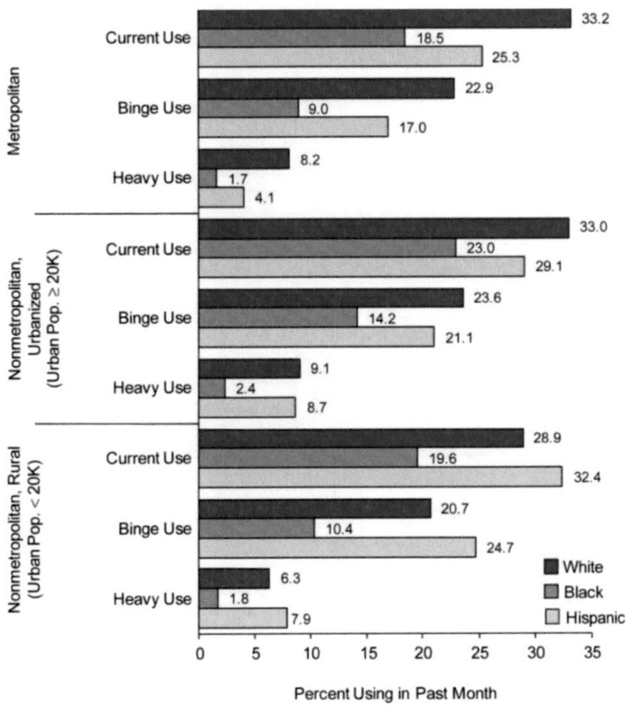

Figure 3.6. Current, Binge, and Heavy Alcohol Use among Persons Aged 12 to 20, by Race/Ethnicity and County Type: Annual Averages, 2002-2006.

There was considerable variation in the pattern of alcohol use by race/ethnicity between counties in metropolitan areas and rural counties. For example, among persons aged 12 to 20 who lived in counties in metropolitan areas, the prevalence of current drinking was higher for non-Hispanic whites (33.2 percent in metropolitan areas) than for Hispanics (25.3 percent) (Table 3.7 and Figure 3.6). In rural counties, however, underage Hispanics had a higher prevalence of current drinking (32.4 percent) than underage whites (28.9 percent) (Table 3.9). This pattern was similar for binge drinking, with a higher percentage of whites (22.9 percent) than Hispanics (17.0 percent) who lived in metropolitan areas reporting binge drinking, and a higher percentage of Hispanics (24.7 percent) than whites (20.7 percent) in rural counties reporting binge drinking. Whites aged 12 to 20 who lived in counties in metropolitan areas also were more likely to drink heavily (8.2 percent) than were Hispanics (4.1 percent), though there was no difference in the prevalence of heavy drinking between whites and Hispanics in rural counties. Within each county type, blacks were less likely to be current, binge, or heavy drinkers than either whites or Hispanics.

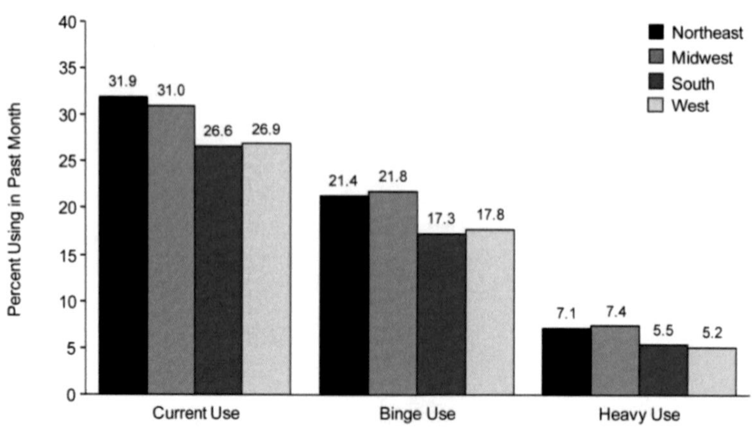

Figure 3.7. Current, Binge, and Heavy Alcohol Use among Persons Aged 12 to 20, by Geographic Region: Annual Averages, 2002-2006.

3.1.9. Geographic Regions

For each of the three measures of past month alcohol use, rates among 12 to 20 year olds were higher in the Northeast and Midwest than in the South or West (Table 3.6 and Figure 3.7). For example, 21.4 percent of those in the Northeast and 21.8 percent of those in the Midwest engaged in binge drinking compared with 17.3 percent of those in the South and 17.8 percent of those in the West.

3.1.10. States

There was substantial variation among States in the prevalence of underage alcohol consumption. In 2002 to 2006, the rate of current alcohol use among those aged 12 to 20 ranged from a high of 41.2 percent in North Dakota to a low of 19.3 percent in Utah (Table 3.10 and Figure 3.8). Among the States in the highest fifth for current drinking, four were in the Midwest (Nebraska, North Dakota, South Dakota, and Wisconsin), four were in the Northeast (Massachusetts, New Hampshire, Rhode Island, and Vermont), and two were in the West (Montana and Wyoming). Among the States in the lowest fifth for current drinking, six were in the South (Alabama, Georgia, Mississippi, North Carolina, South Carolina, and Tennessee), three were in the West (California, Idaho, and Utah), and one was in the Midwest (Indiana).

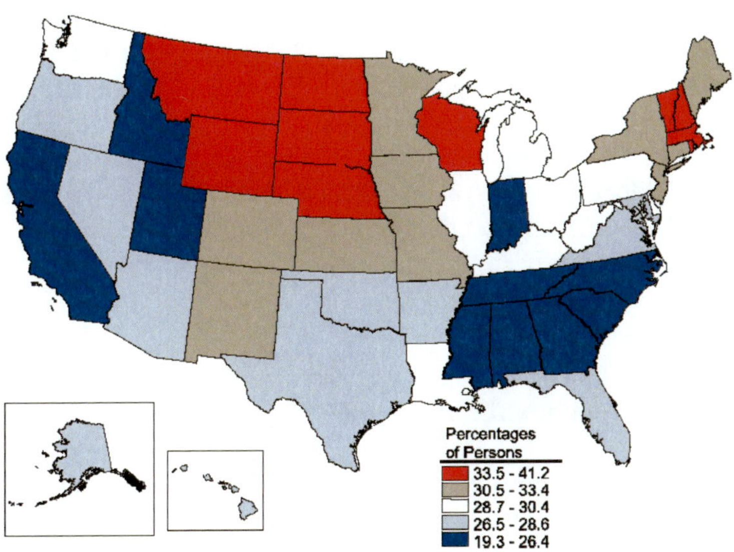

Figure 3.8. Current Alcohol Use among Persons Aged 12 to 20, by State: Annual Averages, 2002-2006.

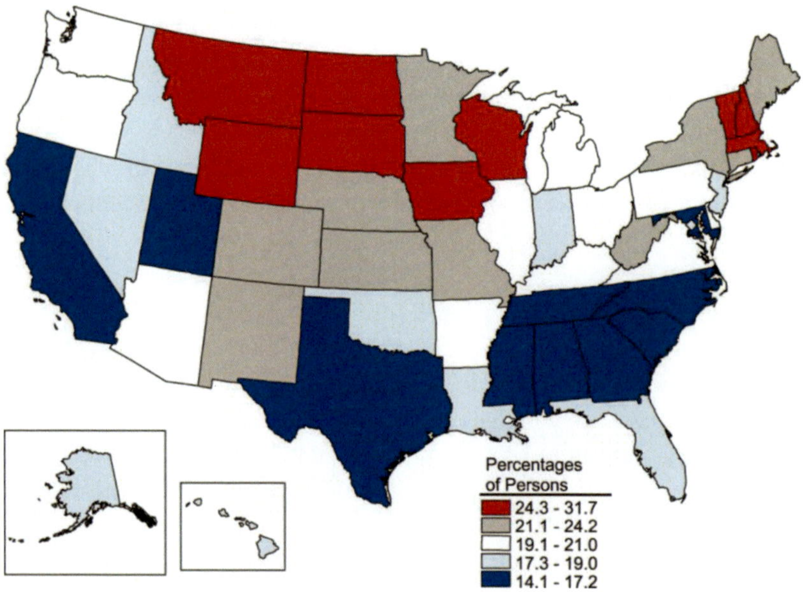

Figure 3.9. Binge Alcohol Use among Persons Aged 12 to 20, by State: Annual Averages, 2002-2006.

The distribution of underage binge drinking by State was similar to the pattern of current use, ranging from a high of 31.7 percent in North Dakota to a low of 14.1 percent in Utah (Table 3.10 and Figure 3.9). Among the States in the highest fifth for binge drinking, four were in the Midwest (Iowa, North Dakota, South Dakota, and Wisconsin), four were in the Northeast (Massachusetts, New Hampshire, Rhode Island, and Vermont), and two were in the West (Montana and Wyoming). Among the States in the lowest fifth for binge drinking, eight were in the South (Alabama, Georgia, Maryland, Mississippi, North Carolina, South Carolina, Tennessee, and Texas), and two were in the West (California and Utah).

3.2. Alcohol Dependence or Abuse

This section presents differences by demographic group and geographic area in the prevalence of underage persons who met the criteria for alcohol use disorders, defined as alcohol dependence or abuse in the past year. The prevalence rates cited are averages based on combined data from the 2002 to 2006 NSDUHs. In 2002 to 2006, an annual average of 3.5 million persons aged 12 to 20 met the criteria for alcohol dependence or abuse in the past year (9.4 percent of all persons in this age range) (Table 3.1).

3.2.1. Age

As was the case with the prevalence of alcohol use, the prevalence of past year alcohol dependence or abuse among persons aged 12 to 20 was higher for older persons than for younger persons. Only 0.5 percent of 12 year olds were classified with alcohol use disorders compared with 10.0 percent of those aged 16 and 17.7 percent of those aged 19 or 20 (Table 3.1).

3.2.2. Gender

Among all 12 to 20 year olds, a higher percentage of males (10.3 percent) than females (8.5 percent) met the criteria for past year alcohol dependence or abuse (Table 3.1).

3.2.3. Race/Ethnicity

Dependence or abuse among underage persons varied considerably by race/ethnicity. Among underage persons, more than one in seven American Indians or Alaska Natives (14.9 percent) and one in eight Native Hawaiians or other Pacific Islanders (12.7 percent) met the criteria for an alcohol use disorder (Table 3.2 and Figure 3.10). This rate of alcohol use disorders for underage American Indians or Alaska Natives was higher than the rate for whites (10.9 percent), blacks (4.6 percent), Hispanics (8.7 percent), or Asians (4.9 percent). Furthermore, Native Hawaiians or Other Pacific Islanders had a higher prevalence of alcohol use disorders than non-Hispanic blacks or Asians, and whites had a higher prevalence of alcohol use disorders than non-Hispanic blacks, Hispanics, or Asians.

Among Hispanics, the rate of alcohol use disorders among 12 to 20 year olds was lower among Puerto Ricans (6.8 percent) than among Mexicans (8.9 percent) (Table 3.2). Among Asians, the rate of alcohol use disorders was higher among Koreans (9.3 percent) than among any other Asian subgroup except for Filipinos.

3.2.4. Gender, by Age Group

Differences between males and females in the percentage of underage persons who met the criteria for alcohol use disorders in the past year varied considerably by age group. Among youths aged 12 to 14, a higher percentage of females (2.2 percent) than males (1.6 percent) were classified with an alcohol use disorder (Table 3.3 and Figure 3.11). In contrast, among those aged 18 to 20, a higher percentage of males (19.6 percent) than females (13.4 percent) was classified with an alcohol use disorder (Table 3.5). For youths aged 15 to 17, there was no difference between males and females in alcohol dependence or abuse.

3.2.5. Race/Ethnicity, by Age Group

The pattern of alcohol dependence or abuse in the past year among racial/ethnic groups was similar for those aged 12 to 14 or aged 15 to 17. Among youths aged 12 to 14, the percentage of American Indians or Alaska Natives classified with alcohol dependence or abuse (4.2 percent) was higher than among non-Hispanic whites, blacks, or Asians (Table 3.3). Among youths aged 15 to 17, the percentage of American Indians or Alaska Natives classified with alcohol dependence or abuse (19.0 percent) was higher than among whites, blacks, Native Hawaiians or Other Pacific Islanders, Asians, or Hispanics (Table 3.4). Blacks and Asians aged 12 to 14 or 15 to 17 had a similar prevalence of alcohol use disorders as Native Hawaiians or Other Pacific Islanders, but they had a lower prevalence than any other racial/ethnic group. Similarly, for persons aged 18 to 20, the prevalence of alcohol use disorders was lower among blacks (9.2 percent) and Asians (9.6 percent) than among whites (19.2 percent), American Indians or Alaska Natives (22.1 percent), Native Hawaiians or Other Pacific Islanders (24.5 percent), persons reporting two or more races (22.4 percent), or Hispanics (14.5 percent) (Table 3.5). These data indicate that nearly one out of four American Indians or Alaska Natives, Native Hawaiians or Other Pacific Islanders, or persons aged 18 to 20 reporting two or more races met the criteria for an alcohol use disorder.

3.2.6. Income Level

As shown in Table 3.6, persons aged 12 to 20 whose family income was less than $20,000 had higher rates of past year alcohol dependence or abuse (11.6 percent) compared with those whose family income was $20,000 to $49,999 (8.4 percent), $50,000 to $74,999 (8.5 percent), or $75,000 or higher (9.2 percent).

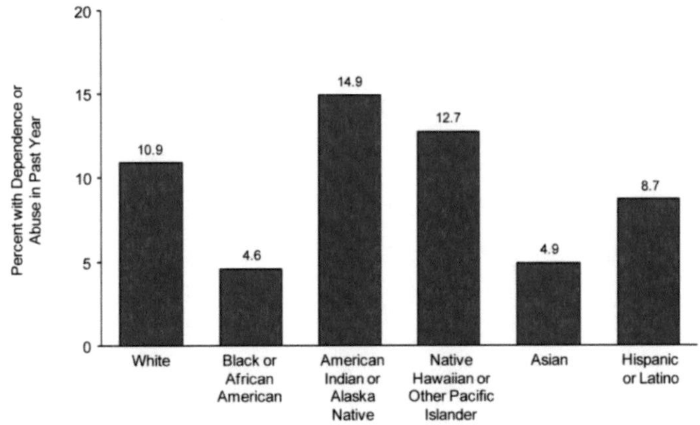

Figure 3.10. Alcohol Dependence or Abuse in the Past Year among Persons Aged 12 to 20, by Race/Ethnicity: Annual Averages, 2002-2006.

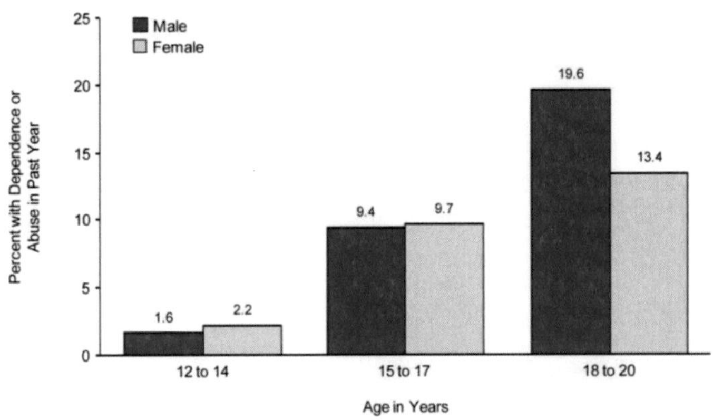

Figure 3.11. Alcohol Dependence or Abuse in the Past Year among Persons Aged 12 to 20, by Gender and Age: Annual Averages, 2002-2006.

3.2.7. County Type

Among underage persons, those who lived in counties in nonmetropolitan areas were more likely than those who lived in counties in metropolitan areas to meet the criteria for alcohol dependence or abuse in the past year (10.6 percent in nonmetropolitan areas, 9.1 percent in metropolitan areas) (Table 3.6). Underage persons who lived in small metropolitan areas had higher rates of alcohol use disorder (10.3 percent) than those who lived in large metropolitan areas (8.5 percent). Furthermore, persons aged 12 to 20 who lived in urbanized nonmetropolitan counties had higher rates of alcohol use disorders (11.7 percent) than those who lived in counties in large metropolitan areas (8.5 percent), small metropolitan areas (10.3 percent), or rural counties (9.8 percent).

3.2.8. Demographic Differences within County Type

As was the case with the prevalence of alcohol use, the pattern of alcohol use disorder by age group and gender was similar across county types. In each county type, those in older age groups were more likely to be classified with alcohol dependence or abuse than younger age groups, and males were more likely to be classified with alcohol dependence or abuse than females (Tables 3.7 to 3.9). However, there was considerable variation in the pattern of alcohol use disorders by race/ethnicity between counties in metropolitan areas and rural counties. Among persons aged 12 to 20 who lived in counties in metropolitan areas, the prevalence of alcohol dependence or abuse in the past year was higher for non-Hispanic whites (10.9 percent in metropolitan areas) than for Hispanics (8.4 percent) (Table 3.7 and Figure 3.12). In contrast, there were no statistically significant differences in the prevalence of alcohol use disorders among underage whites and Hispanics who lived in either urbanized nonmetropolitan counties or in rural counties. Within each county type, blacks were less likely to be classified with alcohol dependence or abuse in the past year than either whites or Hispanics, though this difference did not reach statistical significance for those who lived in urbanized nonmetropolitan counties.

3.2.9. Geographic Regions

Persons aged 12 to 20 who lived in the Midwest had higher rates of alcohol dependence or abuse (10.7 percent) than those who lived in the Northeast (9.5 percent), West (9.5 percent), or South (8.4 percent) (Table 3.6). The prevalence of alcohol use disorders among underage persons in the South was lower than for any other region.

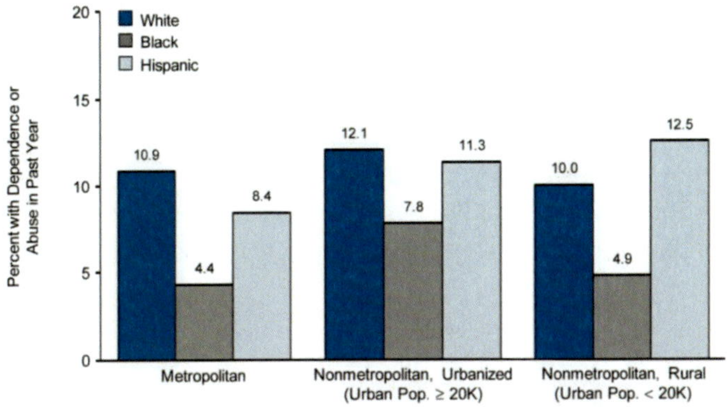

Figure 3.12. Alcohol Dependence or Abuse in the Past Year among Persons Aged 12 to 20, by Race/Ethnicity and County Type: Annual Averages, 2002-2006.

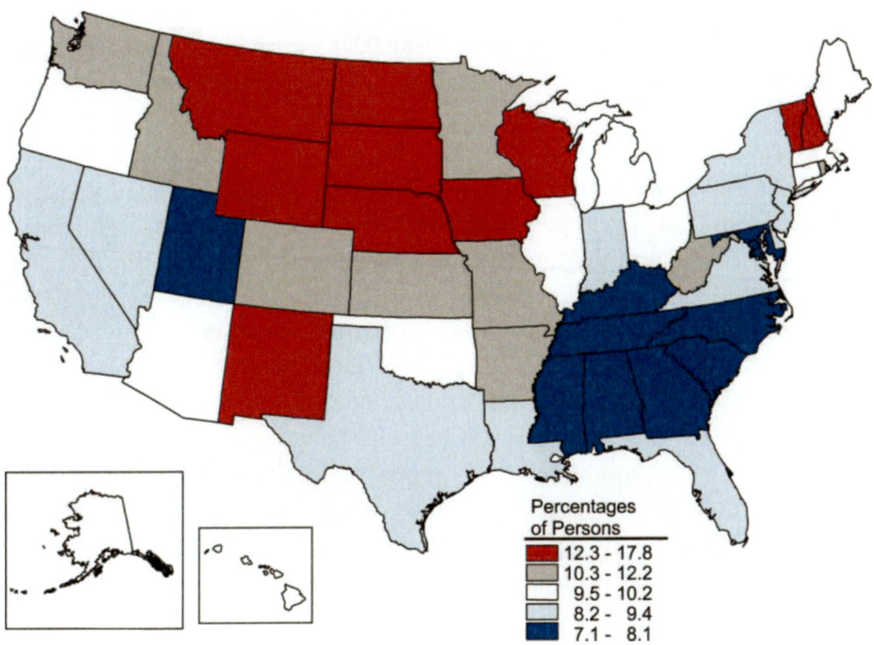

Figure 3.13. Alcohol Dependence or Abuse in the Past Year among Persons Aged 12 to 20, by State: Annual Averages, 2002-2006.

3.2.10. States

In 2002 to 2006, the rates of alcohol dependence or abuse in the past year among those aged 12 to 20 ranged from a high of 17.8 percent in Montana to a low of 7.1 percent in Mississippi (Table 3.10 and Figure 3.13). Of the States in the top fifth in the prevalence of alcohol use disorders, five were in the Midwest (Iowa, Nebraska, North Dakota, South Dakota, and Wisconsin), three were in the West (Montana, New Mexico, and Wyoming), and two were in the Northeast (New Hampshire and Vermont). Of the States in the bottom fifth, nine were in the South (Alabama, District of Columbia, Georgia, Kentucky, Maryland, Mississippi, North Carolina, South Carolina, and Tennessee), and one was in the West (Utah).

3.3. Association of Underage Drinking and Parental Alcohol Use

This section presents information on the association between drinking by persons aged 12 to 20 and drinking by their parents. The prevalence rates cited are averages from the 2002 to 2006 NSDUHs, utilizing data from households in which both a person aged 12 to 20 and his or her mother or father was interviewed.

3.3.1. Alcohol Use

In 2002 to 2006, there was a clear association between current drinking by persons aged 12 to 20 and past year drinking by their parents. Rates of current alcohol use, binge use, and heavy use among underage persons were considerably higher among persons aged 12 to 20 who lived with a parent who had consumed alcohol in the past year compared with those who lived with a parent who had not consumed alcohol in the past year (Table 3.11). For example, rates of binge drinking among underage persons were higher for those who lived with a parent who had consumed alcohol in the past year, whether that parent was a mother (17.6 percent for those whose mother was a past year drinker vs. 9.3 percent for those whose mother was not a past year drinker) or a father (16.5 percent for those whose father was a past year drinker vs. 10.2 percent for those whose father was not a past year drinker) (Figure 3.14). Furthermore, rates of underage binge drinking were higher among those who lived with a mother who was a binge drinker (21.3 percent) than among those whose mother had used alcohol in the past month but had not binged (17.5 percent). Similarly, 19.5 percent of underage persons whose father had binged in the past month were binge drinkers compared with 15.4 percent among those whose fathers had used alcohol in the past month but had not binged.

Household Structure

The comparisons of drinking patterns of underage persons and their parents can be further examined by the number of parents living in the household. Mother-child pairs are more likely than father-child pairs to come from single-parent households (22.3 vs. 5.3 percent). For both one-parent and two-parent households, rates of binge and heavy alcohol use were higher among underage persons who lived with a mother or father who had consumed alcohol in the past year compared with those who lived with a mother or father who did not drink in the past year (Table 3.12). In addition, for underage persons who lived in two-parent households, rates of binge drinking were higher among those who lived with a mother who had binged on alcohol in the past month compared with those who lived with a mother who had consumed alcohol in the past month but had not binged. Rates of heavy drinking were higher among those who lived with a father who had binged on alcohol in the past month compared with those who lived with a father who was a current drinker but was not a binge drinker.

3.3.2. Dependence or Abuse in the Past Year

As was the case for alcohol use, there was a clear association between the prevalence of alcohol use disorders among 12 to 20 year olds and drinking by their parents. Underage persons whose parents had consumed alcohol in the past year had a higher prevalence of alcohol use disorders in the past year whether that parent was a mother (7.9 percent for those whose mother was a past year drinker vs. 5.2 percent for those whose mother was not a past year drinker) or a father (8.0 percent for those whose father was a past year drinker vs. 5.2 percent for those whose father was not a past year drinker) (Table 3.11 and Figure 3.15). A similar pattern was found for fathers who binged on alcohol during the past month, with higher rates of alcohol use disorders among underage persons whose fathers were binge drinkers versus those whose fathers were past month users but were not binge drinkers (10.2 and 7.1 percent, respectively). There was no significant difference in alcohol use disorders between underage persons whose mothers were binge drinkers and those whose mothers were past month drinkers but were not binge drinkers.

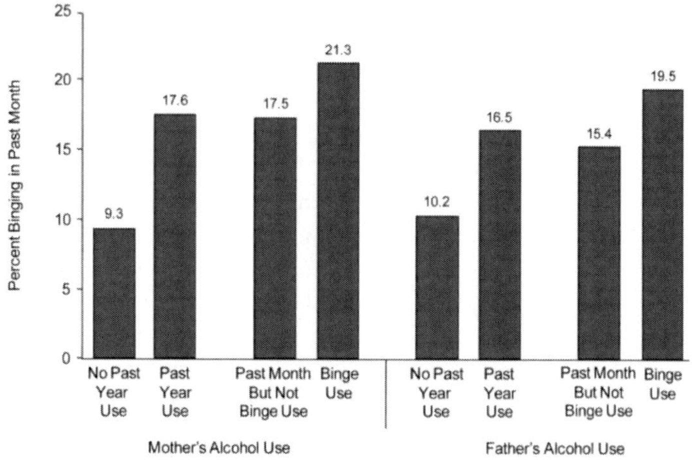

Figure 3.14. Binge Alcohol Use among Persons Aged 12 to 20, by Parental Alcohol Use: Annual Averages, 2002-2006.

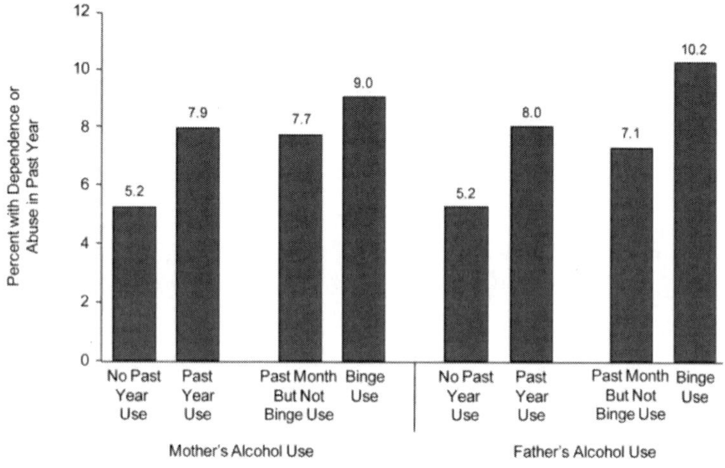

Figure 3.15. Dependence or Abuse in the Past Year among Persons Aged 12 to 20, by Parental Alcohol Use: Annual Averages, 2002-2006.

Household Structure

Analyses of the link between alcohol use disorders among underage persons and alcohol use by their parents for one-parent and two-parent households are limited by small sample sizes, especially for fathers in one-parent households. Looking just at two-parent households, underage persons whose mothers had consumed alcohol in the past year were more likely to meet the criteria for alcohol dependence or abuse (7.6 percent) than those whose mothers did not drink in the past year (4.8 percent) (Table 3.12). This pattern held for fathers as well, with 7.9 percent of underage persons whose fathers had drunk alcohol in the past year meeting the criteria for an alcohol use disorder compared with 5.4 percent of those whose fathers did not drink in the past year. In addition, 12 to 20 year olds in two-parent households had a higher rate of past year alcohol use disorder if their father was a binge drinker (9.9 percent) than if their father was a past month drinker but was not a binge drinker (6.9 percent). There was no significant difference in alcohol use disorders between underage persons in two-parent households whose mothers were binge drinkers and those whose mothers were past month drinkers but were not binge drinkers.

3.4. Summary

Combined data from 2002 to 2006 indicated that among persons aged 12 to 20, rates of current (past month), binge, and heavy alcohol use were higher for those who were older than for those who were younger and for males than for females. Among all persons aged 12 to 20, non- Hispanic whites had higher rates of current and heavy alcohol use than any other racial/ethnic group. Whites aged 12 to 14 had a lower rate of binge drinking than Hispanics and American Indians or Alaska Natives, but among those aged 15 to 17 or those aged 18 to 20, whites had higher rates of current, binge, and heavy drinking compared with Hispanics. Underage persons whose family income was less than \$20,000 or \$75,000 or higher had higher rates of current, binge, and heavy drinking compared with those whose family income was \$20,000 to \$74,999. Underage persons who lived in urbanized nonmetropolitan counties had higher rates of current, binge, and heavy drinking than those who lived in counties in large metropolitan areas, counties in small metropolitan areas, or rural areas. The pattern of underage alcohol use by racial/ethnic group differed between county types, with a higher rate for current drinking among non-Hispanic whites (33.2 percent) than among Hispanics (25.3 percent) in metropolitan areas. In rural areas, however, the rate for current drinking was higher among Hispanics (32.4 percent) than among whites (28.9 percent).

Among youths aged 12 to 14, a higher percentage of females (2.2 percent) than males (1.6 percent) were classified with an alcohol use disorder. This pattern was reversed for those aged 18 to 20, with a higher percentage of males (19.6 percent) than females (13.4 percent) who were classified with an alcohol use disorder. Among all persons aged 12 to 20, more than one in seven American Indians or Alaska Natives (14.9 percent) and one in eight Native Hawaiians or Other Pacific Islanders (12.7 percent) met the criteria for an alcohol use disorder. As was the case with alcohol use, persons aged 12 to 20 who lived in urbanized nonmetropolitan counties had higher rates of alcohol use disorders than those who lived in counties in large metropolitan areas, small metropolitan areas, or rural areas. Also, the prevalence of alcohol dependence or abuse in the past year among those who lived in counties in metropolitan areas was higher for non-Hispanic whites (10.9 percent) than for Hispanics (8.4 percent). However, there were no statistically significant differences in the prevalence of alcohol use disorders between underage whites and Hispanics who lived in urbanized metropolitan counties or rural counties. Within counties in metropolitan or rural areas, blacks were less likely to be classified with alcohol dependence or abuse in the past year than either whites or Hispanics.

Among underage persons, rates of current alcohol use, binge use, and heavy use, as well as rates of alcohol use disorders, were higher among persons who lived with a parent who had consumed alcohol in the past year compared with those who lived with a parent who had not consumed alcohol in the past year. Furthermore, rates of underage binge drinking were higher among those who lived with a mother or father who was a binge drinker than among those whose mother or father had used alcohol in the past month but had not binged. Underage persons who lived with a father who was a binge drinker also had higher rates of alcohol use disorders in the past year compared with those whose father was a current drinker but was not a binge drinker, whereas there was no difference in alcohol use disorders between those whose mothers were binge drinkers and those whose mothers were current drinkers but were not binge drinkers.

4. Characteristics of Recent Drinking Episodes

This chapter presents information on the social context and location of underage drinking, the sources of alcohol for underage drinkers, and the co-occurrence of underage drinking and illicit drug use. These estimates are based on new items from the 2006 National Survey on Drug Use and Health (NSDUH) and include only data from current (past month) drinkers aged 12 to 20. Findings are presented by age group and gender.

4.1. Social Context of Alcohol Use

Among persons aged 12 to 20 who had used alcohol in the past month, most (80.9 percent) were with two or more people the last time they drank alcohol, 14.3 percent were with one other person the last time they drank, and 4.9 percent were alone (see Table 4.1 in Appendix C). Underage persons who drank with two or more other people on the last occasion in the past month had more drinks on the last occasion on average (4.9 drinks) than those who drank with one other person (3.1 drinks) or those who drank alone (2.9 drinks) (Table 4.2).

4.1.1. Age

In 2006, the majority of underage current drinkers in each age group (i.e., those aged 12 to 14, 15 to 17, and 18 to 20) consumed alcohol with two or more other people the last time they drank (Table 4.1 and Figure 4.1). Among current drinkers, youths aged 12 to 14 were more likely to have been alone (9.0 percent) or with one other person (21.9 percent) the last time they drank compared with youths aged 15 to 17 (5.2 percent alone and 14.6 percent with one other person) or 18 to 20 year olds (4.2 percent alone and 13.2 percent with one other person).

Current drinkers aged 12 to 14 who drank with two or more other people the last time they drank averaged more drinks on the last occasion (3.1 drinks) than those who drank with one other person (2.0 drinks) (Table 4.2 and Figure 4.2). Among current drinkers aged either 15 to 17 or 18 to 20, those who drank with two or more people on the last occasion consumed more drinks on average than those who drank either with one other person or by themselves.

4.1.2. Gender

Among underage drinkers, the majority of both males and females were with two or more other people on their last drinking occasion (Table 4.1). However, female drinkers were more likely to have been with two or people the last time they drank (83.6 percent) than were male drinkers (78.4 percent). Conversely, male drinkers were more likely to have been alone the last time they drank (6.3 percent) than were female drinkers (3.3 percent).

For both males and females, underage persons who drank with two or more other people on the last occasion consumed more drinks on average than those who drank alone or with one other person (Table 4.2 and Figure 4.3). Males and females who drank alone on the last occasion reported a similar number of drinks on their last drinking occasion (3.1 drinks for males, 2.6

drinks for females), but males consumed more drinks than females when the last occasion was with one other person (3.5 drinks for males, 2.5 drinks for females) or with two or more people (5.8 drinks for males, 3.9 drinks for females).

4.2. Location of Alcohol Use

Overall, a majority of underage drinkers in 2006 reported that when they last used alcohol they were either in someone else's home (53.4 percent) or their own home (30.3 percent) (Table 4.1 and Figure 4.4). The next most popular drinking locations for this age group were at a restaurant, bar, or club (9.4 percent); in a car or vehicle (5.5 percent); or at a park, on a beach, or in a parking lot (4.8 percent).

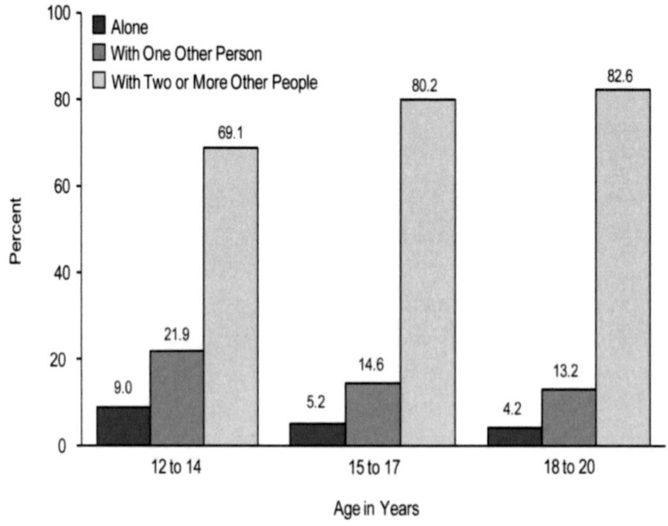

Figure 4.1. Social Context of Last Alcohol Use in the Past Month among Current Drinkers Aged 12 to 20, by Age: 2006.

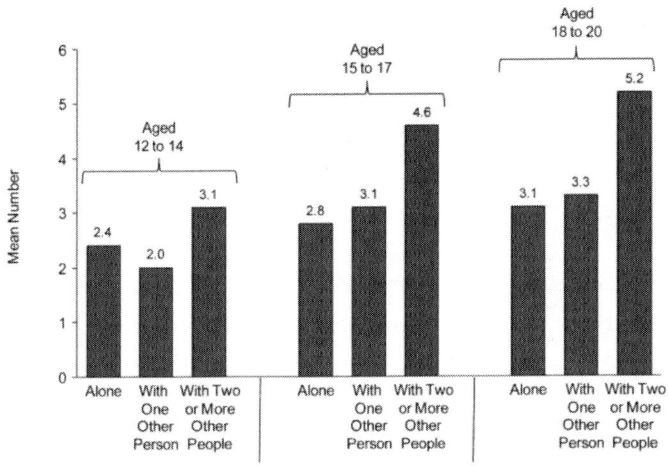

Figure 4.2. Drinks Consumed on Last Occasion of Alcohol Use in the Past Month among Current Drinkers Aged 12 to 20, by Social Context and Age: 2006.

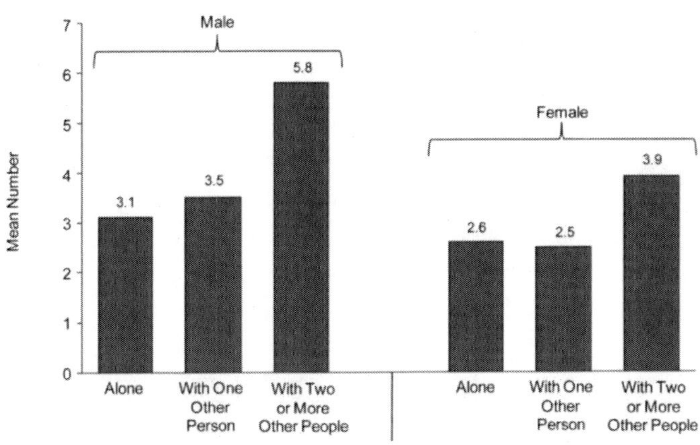

Figure 4.3. Drinks Consumed on Last Occasion of Alcohol Use in the Past Month among Current Drinkers Aged 12 to 20, by Social Context and Gender: 2006.

Underage drinkers whose last drinking occasion was at someone else's home consumed an average of 4.9 drinks, while those whose last drinking occasion was at their own home consumed an average of 4.0 drinks (Table 4.2 and Figure 4.5). Among the next most popular drinking locations, underage current drinkers whose last alcohol use was at a restaurant or bar averaged 4.6

drinks, and those whose last alcohol use was at school, in a car or vehicle, or at a park, on a beach, or in a parking lot averaged 5.1 drinks. Current drinkers aged 12 to 20 who last drank at a concert or sports game (1.6 percent of all underage drinkers) consumed an average of 6.0 drinks on their last drinking occasion.

4.2.1. Age

More than 80 percent of underage drinkers in each age group (i.e., those aged 12 to 14, 15 to 17, or 18 to 20) drank at their own or someone else's home when they last used alcohol. However, there were differences in drinking locations between these age groups. Current drinkers aged 12 to 14 were more likely to have been at their own home the last time they drank (38.8 percent) and less likely to have been at someone else's home (45.0 percent) compared with those aged 15 to 17 (26.0 and 60.9 percent, respectively) or those aged 18 to 20 (31.4 and 50.7 percent, respectively) (Table 4.1 and Figure 4.6). In addition, drinkers aged 18 to 20 were more likely than younger age groups to have been in a restaurant, bar, or club on their last drinking occasion (12.9 percent for those aged 18 to 20 vs. 4.6 percent for those aged 12 to 14 and 3.7 percent for those aged 15 to 17), and they were less likely than younger age groups to have been at a park, on the beach, or in a parking lot on their last drinking occasion (2.9 percent for those aged 18 to 20 vs. 8.3 percent for those aged 12 to 14 and 7.7 percent for those aged 15 to 17).

Current drinkers aged 12 to 14 who last drank at home consumed an average of 2.2 drinks on their last drinking occasion, whereas those who last drank at someone else's home consumed an average of 3.4 drinks on their last occasion (Table 4.2). This pattern was similar for youths aged 15 to 17 (average of 3.6 drinks if they last drank in their own home, 4.7 drinks if they last drank in someone else's home) and 18 to 20 year olds (average of 4.4 drinks if they last drank in their own home, 5.2 drinks if they last drank in someone else's home).

4.2.2. Gender

Among underage current drinkers, males were more likely than females to have been in their own home on their last drinking occasion (32.2 percent for males, 28.1 for females), whereas females were more likely than males to have been in a restaurant, bar, or club on their last drinking occasion (12.0 percent for females, 7.2 percent for males) (Table 4.1).

Underage male drinkers who last drank alcohol at their own home consumed more drinks on average on their last drinking occasion (4.6 drinks) than underage female drinkers who last drank at their own home (3.3 drinks) (Table 4.2). The pattern was similar for underage drinkers who last drank at someone else's home, with males averaging 5.8 drinks on this last drinking occasion and females averaging 4.0 drinks.

4.3. Sources of Alcohol among Underage Drinkers

This section provides information on the source of last alcohol use in the past month among current drinkers aged 12 to 20 in 2006. The sources of last alcohol use are divided into two categories: (a) underage drinker paid (he or she purchased it or gave someone else money to purchase it) and (b) underage drinker did not pay (he or she received it for free from someone or took it from his or her own or someone else’s home).

Among all underage current drinkers, 31.0 percent paid for the alcohol the last time they drank, including 9.3 percent who purchased the alcohol themselves and 21.6 percent who gave money to someone else to purchase it (Table 4.3). The remaining 69.0 percent of underage drinkers did not pay for the alcohol on their last drinking occasion. More than one in four underage drinkers (25.8 percent) indicated that on their last drinking occasion they were given alcohol for free by an unrelated person aged 21 or older. Nearly one in five underage drinkers were given alcohol for free by a member of their family or took the alcohol from their own home on their last drinking occasion, including 6.4 percent who were given alcohol by their parent or guardian, 8.3 percent who were given alcohol by another family member aged 21 or older, and 3.9 percent who took it from their own home.

Persons aged 12 to 20 who paid for alcohol themselves consumed more drinks on their last drinking occasion (5.9 drinks) than did those who did not pay for the alcohol themselves (3.9 drinks) (Table 4.4).

4.3.1. Age

The most common sources of alcohol among underage current drinkers varied substantially by age group. For youths aged 12 to 14, the most common sources were receiving it for free from someone under the age of 21 (17.5 percent), receiving it from a parent or guardian (17.1 percent), or taking it from their own home (15.0 percent) (Table 4.3 and Figure 4.7). For youths aged 15 to 17, the most common sources were receiving it for free from an unrelated person aged 21 or older (20.1 percent), receiving it from someone under the age of 21 (19.9 percent), and giving somebody else money to purchase the alcohol (17.9 percent). For persons aged 18 to 20, the majority of current drinkers either received alcohol for free from an unrelated person aged 21 or older (30.0 percent) or gave somebody else money to purchase the alcohol (25.3 percent).

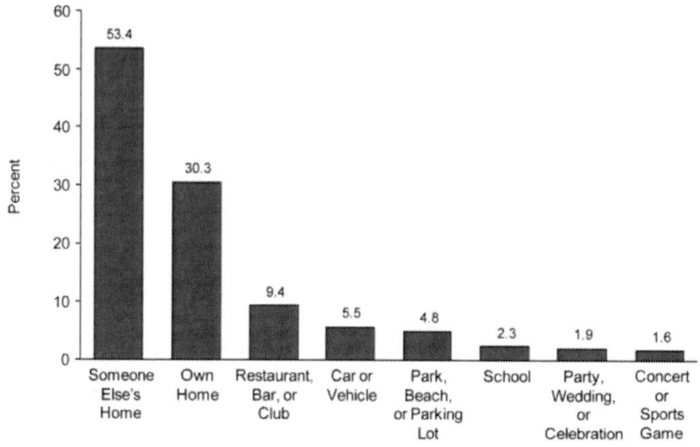

Figure 4.4. Location of Last Alcohol Use in the Past Month among Current Drinkers Aged 12 to 20: 2006.

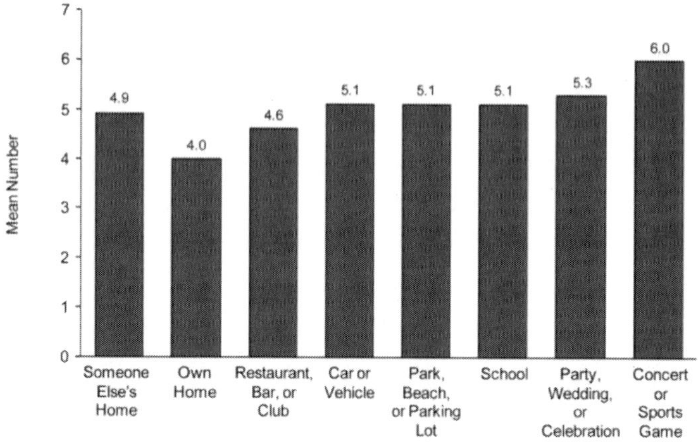

Figure 4.5. Drinks Consumed on Last Alcohol Use in the Past Month among Current Drinkers Aged 12 to 20, by Location of Last Alcohol Use: 2006.

Those in older age groups were more likely to have paid for alcohol themselves on their last drinking occasion, with 37.6 percent of 18 to 20 year olds paying for it themselves compared with 23.5 percent of 15 to 17 year olds and 6.6 percent of 12 to 14 year olds.

Within each of these age groups, persons who paid for alcohol themselves on the last occasion had more drinks on average than those who did not pay for alcohol themselves (Table 4.4 and Figure 4.8). For example, youths aged 12 to 14 had 4.8 drinks when they paid for their own drinks, but they had 2.7 drinks when they did not pay for them.

4.3.2. Gender

Among underage current drinkers, males were more likely to have paid for alcohol themselves on their last drinking occasion (36.7 percent) than were females (24.5 percent) (Table 4.3). That is, female drinkers aged 12 to 20 were more likely to have others give them alcohol for free than were male drinkers in this age group. Among underage drinkers, similar percentages of females and males reported getting alcohol from their parent or guardian, another family member aged 21 or older, or from their own home. However, underage females were more likely than underage males to have received alcohol without paying from someone not related aged 21 or older (29.8 percent for females, 22.2 percent for males) or from someone under the age of 21 (16.0 percent for females, 12.5 percent for males).

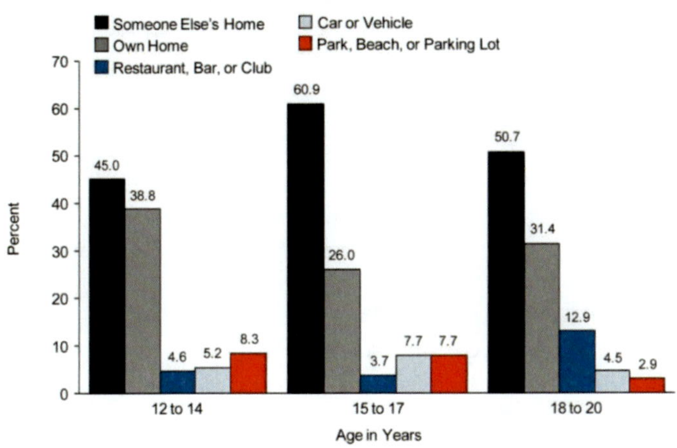

Figure 4.6. Location of Last Alcohol Use in the Past Month among Current Drinkers Aged 12 to 20, by Age: 2006.

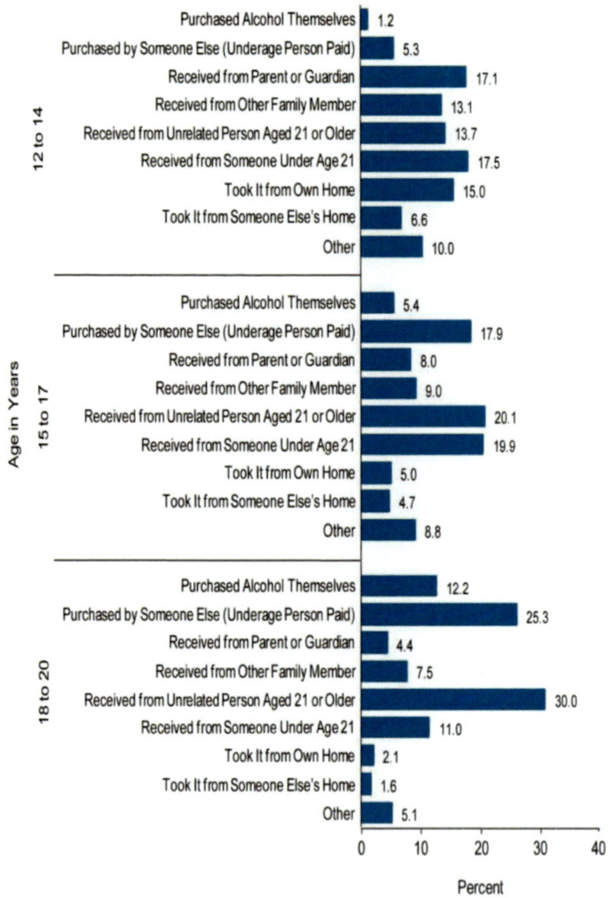

Figure 4.7. Source of Alcohol Used in the Past Month among Current Drinkers Aged 12 to 20, by Age: 2006.

Among both underage males and females, persons who paid for alcohol themselves on the last occasion had more drinks on average (6.8 drinks for males, 4.5 drinks for females) than those who did not pay for alcohol themselves (4.4 drinks for males, 3.4 drinks for females) (Table 4.4).

4.4. Use of Illicit Drugs with Alcohol

In 2006, more than one third (35.8 percent) of persons aged 12 to 20 who used alcohol in the past month also had used an illicit drug in the past month (Table 4.5). Among underage drinkers, marijuana was the drug most often used in the past month (30.0 percent), followed by pain relievers (8.8 percent). Furthermore, 16.0 percent of underage drinkers had used an illicit drug within 2 hours of using alcohol on their last occasion in the past month (Table 4.5). The drug most often used within 2 hours of their last alcohol use in the past month was marijuana (15.0 percent), followed by pain relievers (1.2 percent).

4.4.1. Age

Approximately one in four youths aged 12 to 14 who had used alcohol in the past month had also used an illicit drug in the past month (25.2 percent), as had more than one in three current drinkers aged 15 to 17 (37.0 percent) and those aged 18 to 20 (36.4 percent) (Table 4.5). Current drinkers aged 12 to 14 were less likely to have used marijuana in the past month (15.5 percent) compared with those aged 15 to 17 (31.0 percent) or those aged 18 to 20 (31.2 percent); however, 12- to 14-year-old drinkers used illicit drugs other than marijuana at a similar rate (15.2 percent) as those aged 15 to 17 (15.3 percent).

Among current drinkers, 5.4 percent of 12 to 14 year olds had used an illicit drug within 2 hours of alcohol use on their last drinking occasion, as did 15.7 percent of 15 to 17 year olds and 17.4 percent of 18 to 20 year olds (Table 4.5 and Figure 4.9). For all three age groups, marijuana was used more often with alcohol than any other illicit drug. Drinkers aged 12 to 14 were less likely to have used illicit drugs other than marijuana within 2 hours of their last alcohol (1.1 percent) than those aged 18 to 20 (2.9 percent).

4.4.2. Gender

Among underage drinkers, males were more likely than females to have used an illicit drug in the past month (37.3 percent for males, 34.0 percent for females) or to have used an illicit drug within 2 hours of their last alcohol use in the past month (18.3 percent for males, 13.4 percent for females) (Table 4.5). Among underage drinkers, males were more likely than females to have used marijuana within 2 hours of their last alcohol use in the past month (17.2 percent for males, 12.6 percent for females), but males and females had similar rates of use of illicit drugs other than marijuana within 2 hours of drinking in the past month.

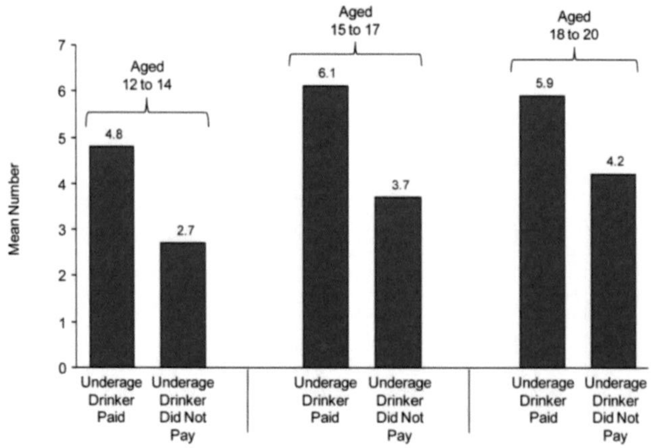

Figure 4.8. Drinks Consumed on Last Occasion of Alcohol Use in the Past Month among Current Drinkers Aged 12 to 20, by Source of Last Alcohol Used and Age: 2006.

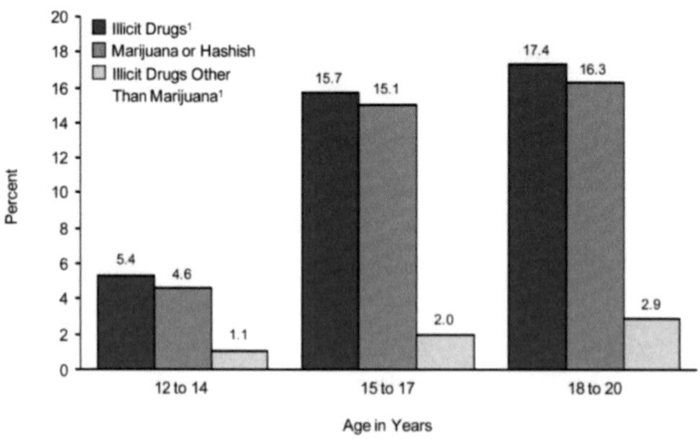

[1]Illicit Drugs include marijuana/hashish, cocaine (including crack), heroin, hallucinogens, inhalants, or prescription-type psychotherapeutics used nonmedically. Illicit Drugs Other Than Marijuana include cocaine (including crack), heroin, hallucinogens, inhalants, or prescription-type psychotherapeutics used nonmedically. These summary estimates do not include data from the methamphetamine use items added in 2005 and 2006.

Figure 4.9. Illicit Drug Use within 2 Hours of Alcohol Use in the Past Month among Current Drinkers Aged 12 to 20, by Age: 2006.

4.5. Summary

In 2006, most (80.9 percent) of the persons aged 12 to 20 who had consumed alcohol in the past month were with two or more people the last time they drank alcohol, 14.3 percent were with one other person the last time they drank, and 4.9 percent were alone. Among underage drinkers, females were more likely to have been with two or people the last time they drank (83.6 percent) than were males (78.4 percent), whereas males were more likely to have been alone the last time they drank (6.3 percent) than were females (3.3 percent). Males and females who drank alone on the last occasion reported a similar number of drinks on their last drinking occasion (3.1 drinks for males, 2.6 drinks for females), but males consumed more drinks than females did when their last drinking occasion was with one other person (3.5 drinks for males, 2.5 drinks for females) or with two or more people (5.8 drinks for males, 3.9 drinks for females). A majority of underage drinkers reported that when they last used alcohol they were either in someone else's home (53.4 percent) or their own home (30.3 percent). Drinkers aged 12 to 14 were more likely to have been at their own home the last time they drank and less likely to have been at someone else's home compared with drinkers in older age groups, and drinkers aged 18 to 20 were more likely than those in younger age groups to have been in a restaurant, bar, or club on their last drinking occasion.

Among all underage current drinkers, 9.3 percent purchased the alcohol themselves, and 21.6 percent gave money to someone else to purchase it. Underage persons who paid for alcohol themselves consumed more drinks on their last drinking occasion (average of 5.9 drinks) than did those who did not pay for the alcohol themselves (average of 3.9 drinks). More than one in four underage drinkers (25.8 percent) indicated that on their last drinking occasion they were given alcohol for free by an unrelated person aged 21 or older. Among underage drinkers, males were more likely to have paid for alcohol themselves on their last drinking occasion (36.7 percent) than were females (24.5 percent).

In 2006, more than one third (35.8 percent) of persons aged 12 to 20 who used alcohol in the past month also had used an illicit drug in the past month, and 16.0 percent of underage drinkers used an illicit drug with alcohol or within 2 hours of alcohol use on their last occasion of alcohol use in the past month. Marijuana was the illicit drug most used by underage drinkers, with nearly one third (30.0 percent) having used marijuana in the past month, and 15.0 percent having used marijuana with alcohol or within 2 hours of their last alcohol use. Males were more likely than females to have used an illicit drug within 2 hours of their last alcohol use in the past month (18.3 percent for males, 13.4 percent for females).

REFERENCES

American Psychiatric Association. (1994). *Diagnostic and statistical manual of mental disorders* (DSM-IV) (4th ed.). Washington, DC: American Psychiatric Association.

Aquilino, W. S. (1994). Interview mode effects in surveys of drug and alcohol use: A field experiment. *Public Opinion Quarterly, 58*, 2 10-240.

Biglan, M., Gilpin, E. A., Rohrbach, L. A., & Pierce, J. P. (2004). Is there a simple correction factor for comparing adolescent tobacco-use estimates from school- and home-based surveys? *Nicotine & Tobacco Research, 6*, 427-437.

Bradburn, N. M., & Sudman, S. (1983). *Improving interview method and questionnaire design*. Washington, DC: Jossey-Bass.

Butler, M. A., & Beale, C. L. (1994, September). *Rural–urban continuum codes for metro and non-metro counties, 1993* (Staff Report No. AGES 9425). Washington, DC: U.S. Department of Agriculture, Economic Research Service. [Current codes *http://ers.usda. gov/Briefing/ Rurality/ ruralurbcon]*

Chen, P., Dai, L., Gordek, H., Shi, W., Singh, A., & Westlake, M. (2005, January). Person-level sampling weight calibration for the 2003 NSDUH. In *2003 National Survey on Drug Use and Health: Methodological resource book* (Section 3, prepared for the Substance Abuse and Mental Health Services Administration, Office of Applied Studies, under Contract No. 283-98-9008, Deliverable No. 28, RTI/07190.574.100). Research Triangle Park, NC: RTI International. [Available as a PDF at http://oas.samhsa.gov/nhsda/methods.cfm]

Deville, J. C., & Särndal, C. E. (1992). Calibration estimators in survey sampling. *Journal of the American Statistical Association, 87*, 376-382.

Fendrich, M., Johnson, T. P., Sudman, S., Wislar, J. S., & Spiehler, V. (1999). Validity of drug use reporting in a high-risk community sample: A comparison of cocaine and heroin survey reports with hair tests. *American Journal of Epidemiology, 149*, 955-962.

Folsom, R. E., & Singh, A. C. (2000). The generalized exponential model for sampling weight calibration for extreme values, nonresponse, and poststratification. In *Proceedings of the 2000 Joint Statistical Meetings, American Statistical Association, Survey Research Methods Section, Indianapolis, IN* (pp. 598-603). Alexandria, VA: American Statistical Association. http://www.amstat. org/ sections/SRMS/proceedings/]

Grant, B. F., & Dawson, D. A. (1997). Age at onset of alcohol use and its association with DSMIV alcohol abuse and dependence: Results from the National Longitudinal Alcohol Epidemiologic Survey. *Journal of Substance Abuse, 9*, 103-110.

Hingson, R., & Kenkel, D. (2004). Social, health, and economic consequences of underage drinking. In R. J. Bonnie & M. E. O'Connell (Eds.), *Reducing underage drinking: A collective responsibility* (pp. 351-382). Washington, DC: National Academies Press. http://www.nap. edu/books/0309089352/ html]

Hser, Y. I., & Anglin, M. D. (Eds.). (1993). Prevalence estimation techniques for drug-using populations [Special issue]. *Journal of Drug Issues, 23*(2), 163-360.

Johnston, L. D., O'Malley, P. M., Bachman, J. G. , & Schulenberg, J. E. (2007a). *Monitoring the Future national survey results on drug use, 1975-2006: Secondary school students* (NIH Publication No. 07-6205, Vol. I). Bethesda, MD: National Institute on Drug Abuse. [Available as a PDF at http://monitoringthefuture.org/pubs.html#monographs]

Johnston, L. D., O'Malley, P. M., Bachman, J. G. , & Schulenberg, J. E. (2007b). *Monitoring the Future national survey results on drug use, 1975-2006: College students and adults ages 19-45* (NIH Publication No. 07-6206, Vol. II). Bethesda, MD: National Institute on Drug Abuse. [Available as a PDF at http://monitoringthefuture.org/ pubs.html# monographs]

Manly, B. F. J. (1986). *Multivariate statistical methods: A primer*. London, England: Chapman and Hall.

Morton, K. B., Chromy, J. R., Hunter, S. R., & Martin, P. C. (2007, January; revised February 2008). Sample design report [2006]. In *2006 National Survey on Drug Use and Health: Methodological resource book* (Section 2, prepared for the Substance Abuse and Mental Health Services Administration, Office of Applied Studies, under Contract No. 283-2004-00022, Phase II, Deliverable No. 8, RTI/0209009.230.004). Research Triangle Park, NC: RTI International. *http://oas.samhsa.gov/ nsduh/ methods.cfm]*

National Highway Traffic Safety Administration. (2002). *Youth fatal crash and alcohol facts 2000* (DOT HS 809 406). Washington, DC: Author.

National Institute on Alcohol Abuse and Alcoholism. (2004, Winter). NIAAA council approves definition of binge drinking. *NIAAA Newsletter, 3*, 3. [Available as NIH Publication No. 04-5346 at *http://pubs.niaaa.nih.gov/publications/Newsletter/winter2004/Newsletter_Number3.pdf]*

National Institute on Alcohol Abuse and Alcoholism. (2006, January). *Alcohol Alert No. 67: Underage drinking: Why do adolescents drink, what are the risks, and how can underage drinking be prevented?* Retrieved January 28, 2008, from http://pubs.niaaa.nih.gov/publications/AA67/AA67.htm

Office of Applied Studies. (2007a). *Results from the 2006 National Survey on Drug Use and Health: National findings* (DHHS Publication No. SMA 07-4293, NSDUH Series H-32). Rockville, MD: Substance Abuse and Mental Health Services Administration. [Available at http://oas.samhsa.gov/ p0000016.htm]

Office of Applied Studies. (2007b). Table 7.36A. Alcohol dependence or abuse in the past year among persons aged 21 or older, by age first used alcohol and age group: Numbers in thousands, 2005 and 2006. In *Results from the 2006 National Survey on Drug Use and Health: Detailed tables*. Rockville, MD: Substance Abuse and Mental Health Services Administration. *http://oas.samhsa.gov/WebOnly. htm# NHSDAtabs]*

Office of Management and Budget. (2003, June 6). *OMB Bulletin No. 03-04: Revised definitions of metropolitan statistical areas, new definitions of micropolitan statistical areas and combined statistical areas, and guidance on uses of the statistical definitions of these areas.* Retrieved March 21, 2008, from http://www.whitehouse.gov/omb/bulletins/b03-04.html

Office of Management and Budget. (1997). Revisions to the standards for the classification of federal data on race and ethnicity. *Federal Register, 62*(210), 58781-58790. [Available at http://www.whitehouse.gov/omb/fedreg/1997standards.html].

RTI International. (2004). *SUDAAN® language manual, Release 9.0.* Research Triangle Park, NC: Author.

RTI International. (2008). *2006 National Survey on Drug Use and Health: Methodological resource book* (RTI 0209009, prepared for the Substance Abuse and Mental Health Services Administration, Office of Applied Studies, under Contract No. 283-2004-00022, Deliverable No. 39). Research Triangle Park, NC: Author. [Available as PDFs at http://oas.samhsa.gov/nsduh/methods.cfm]

Rubin, D. B. (1986). Statistical matching using file concatenation with adjusted weights and multiple imputations. *Journal of Business and Economic Statistics, 4*(1), 87-94.

Singh, A., Grau, E., & Folsom, R., Jr. (2001). Predictive mean neighborhood imputation with application to the person-pair data of the National Household Survey on Drug Abuse. In *Proceedings of the 2001 Joint Statistical Meetings, American Statistical Association, Survey Research Methods Section, Atlanta, GA* [CD-ROM] . Alexandria, VA: American Statistical Association. http://www. amstat.org/sections/ SRMS/ proceedings/]

Singh, A., Grau, E., & Folsom, R., Jr. (2002). Predictive mean neighborhood imputation for NHSDA substance use data. In J. Gfroerer, J. Eyerman, & J. Chromy (Eds.), *Redesigning an ongoing national household survey: Methodological issues* (DHHS Publication No. SMA 03- 3768, pp. 111-133). Rockville, MD: Substance Abuse and Mental Health Services Administration, Office of Applied Studies. *http://oas.samhsa.gov/ nhsda/methods.cfm]*

SRNT Subcommittee on Biochemical Verification. (2002). Biochemical verification of tobacco use and cessation. *Nicotine & Tobacco Research, 4*(2), 149-159.

Stueve, A., & O'Donnell, L. N. (2005). Early alcohol initiation and subsequent sexual and alcohol risk behaviors among urban youths. *American Journal of Public Health, 95*, 887-893.

Substance Abuse and Mental Health Data Archive. (2008). *Online analysis of data from the 2006 Treatment Episode Data Set.* Retrieved on April 1, 2008, from http://www.icpsr.umich.edu/SAMHDA/

Swahn, M. H., Bossarte, R. M., & Sullivent, E. E. 3rd. (2008). Age of alcohol use initiation, suicidal behavior, and peer and dating violence victimization and perpetration among high-risk, seventh-grade adolescents. *Pediatrics, 121*, 297-305.

Turner, C. F., Lessler, J. T., & Gfroerer, J. C. (Eds.). (1992). *Survey measurement of drug use: Methodological studies* (DHHS Publication No. ADM 92-1929). Rockville, MD: National Institute on Drug Abuse.

U.S. Department of Health and Human Services. (2006, January). *A comprehensive plan for preventing and reducing underage drinking* (DHHS Publication No. SMA 01-35 17). Rockville, MD: U.S. Department of Health and Human Services, Substance Abuse and Mental Health Services Administration.

U.S. Department of Health and Human Services. (2007). *The Surgeon General's call to action to prevent and reduce underage drinking.* Rockville, MD: Office of the Surgeon General. [Available at http://www.surgeongeneral.gov/topics/underagedrinking/]

Wright, D., Sathe, N., & Spagnola, K. (2007). *State estimates of substance use from the 2004- 2005 National Surveys on Drug Use and Health* (DHHS Publication No. SMA 07-423 5, NSDUH Series H-31). Rockville, MD: Substance Abuse and Mental Health Services Administration, Office of Applied Studies. [Available at http://oas.samhsa.gov/states.htm]

APPENDIX A: DESCRIPTION OF THE SURVEYS

A.1. Sample Design

The designs for the 2002 to 2006 National Surveys on Drug Use and Health (NSDUH)[3] are part of coordinated sample designs providing estimates for all 50 States plus the District of Columbia. Survey years 2002 to 2004 come from a coordinated 5-year design for the 1999 through 2004 surveys, while the 2005 and 2006 designs are from a coordinated 5-year design for the 2005 through 2009 NSDUHs. The respondent universe is the civilian, noninstitutionalized population aged 12 years old or older residing within the 50 States and the District of Columbia. The survey includes persons living in noninstitutionalized group quarters (e.g., shelters, rooming/boarding houses, college dormitories, migratory workers' camps, halfway houses), and civilians living on military bases. Persons excluded from NSDUH include persons with no fixed household address (e.g., homeless and/or transient persons not in shelters), active-duty military personnel, and residents of institutional group quarters, such as correctional facilities, nursing homes, mental institutions, and long-term hospitals.

For the 50-State design, 8 States were designated as large sample States (California, Florida, Illinois, Michigan, New York, Ohio, Pennsylvania, and Texas) with samples large enough to support direct State estimates. In 2006, sample sizes in these States ranged from 3,512 to 3,671. For the remaining 42 States and the District of Columbia, smaller, but adequate, samples were selected to support State estimates using small area estimation (SAE).[4] Sample sizes in these States ranged from 862 to 1,000 in 2006.

In 2005 and 2006, States were first stratified into a total of 900 State sampling (SS) regions (48 regions in each large sample State and 12 regions in each small sample State). These regions were contiguous geographic areas designed to yield the same number of interviews on average.[5] Unlike the 2002 through 2004 NSDUHs in which the first-stage sampling units were clusters of census blocks called "area segments," the first stage of selection for the 2005 through 2009 NSDUHs was census tracts.[6] This stage was included to contain sample segments within a single census tract to the extent possible.[7]

For each SS region, 48 census tracts were selected with probability proportional to size. Within sampled census tracts, adjacent census blocks were combined to form the second-stage sampling units or area segments. One area segment was selected within each sampled census tract with probability proportional to population size to support the 5-year sample and any supplemental studies that the Substance Abuse and Mental Health Services Administration (SAMHSA) may choose to field.[8] Of these segments, 24 were designated for the coordinated 5- year sample and 24 were designated as "reserve" segments. Eight sample segments per SS region were fielded during the 2006 survey year.

These sampled segments were allocated equally into four separate samples, one for each 3-month period (calendar quarter) during the year, so that the survey was essentially continuous in the field. In each of these area segments, a listing of all addresses was constructed and used as the frame for selecting a sample of addresses. Selected addresses were determined to be eligible sample units or to be ineligible. In the eligible sample units (which can be either households or units within group quarters), sample persons were randomly selected using an automated screening procedure programmed in a handheld computer carried by the interviewers. Persons aged 12 to 17 years and those aged 18 to 25 years were oversampled at this stage. Because of the large sample sizes in each year, there was no need to oversample racial/ethnic groups, as was done on surveys prior to 1999. Consistent with previous surveys in this series, the final respondent samples in each survey year were representative of the U.S. general population (since 1991, the civilian, noninstitutionalized population) aged 12 or older. In addition, State samples were representative of their respective State populations. More detailed information on the disposition of the national screening and interview samples can be found in Appendix B.

NSDUH covers residents of households (living in houses/townhouses, apartments, condominiums, etc.), persons in noninstitutional group quarters (e.g., shelters, rooming/boarding houses, college dormitories, migratory workers' camps, halfway houses), and civilians living on military bases. Although the survey covers residents of these types of units (they are given a nonzero probability of selection), the sample sizes of most specific groups are too small to provide separate estimates.

More information on the sample design can be found in the 2006 NSDUH sample design report by Morton et al. (2007) on the Office of Applied Studies (OAS) website (available at http://oas.samhsa.gov/nsduh/methods.cfm).

A.2. Data Collection Methodology

The data collection method used in NSDUH involves in-person interviews with sample persons, incorporating procedures designed to maximize respondents' cooperation and willingness to report honestly about their illicit drug use behavior. Confidentiality is stressed in all written and oral communications with potential respondents. Respondents' names are not collected with the data, and computer-assisted interviewing (CAI) methods, including audio computer-assisted self-interviewing (ACASI), are used to provide a private and confidential setting to complete the interview.

Introductory letters are sent to sampled addresses, followed by an interviewer visit. A 5- minute screening procedure using a handheld computer involves listing all household members along with their basic demographic data. The computer uses the demographic data in a preprogrammed selection algorithm to select zero, one, or two sample person(s), depending on the composition of the household. This selection process is designed to provide the necessary sample sizes for the specified population age groupings and to select a subsample of pairs of individual respondents within the same households.

Interviewers immediately attempt to conduct the NSDUH interview with each selected person in the household. The interviewer requests the selected respondent to identify a private area in the home to conduct the interview away from other household members. The interview averages about an hour and includes a combination of CAPI (computer-assisted personal interviewing, in which the interviewer reads the questions) and ACASI (which is self-administered by the respondent).

The NSDUH interview consists of a core and supplemental sections. A core set of questions critical for basic trend measurement of prevalence estimates remains in the survey every year and comprises the first part of the interview. Supplemental questions, or modules, that can be revised, dropped, or added from year to year make up the remainder of the interview. The core consists of initial demographic items (which are interviewer-administered) and self-administered questions pertaining to the use of tobacco, alcohol, marijuana, cocaine, crack cocaine, heroin, hallucinogens, inhalants, pain relievers, tranquilizers, stimulants, and sedatives. Supplemental topics in the remaining self-administered sections include (but are not limited to) injection drug use, perceived risks of substance use, substance dependence or abuse, arrests, treatment for substance use problems, pregnancy and health care issues, and mental health issues. Supplemental demographic questions (which are interviewer-administered and follow the ACASI questions) address such topics as immigration, current school enrollment, employment and workplace issues, health insurance coverage, and income. It should be noted that some of the supplemental portions of the interview have remained in the survey, relatively unchanged, from year to year (e.g., current health insurance coverage, employment).

Thus, the interview begins in CAPI mode with the field interviewer (FI) reading the questions from the computer screen and entering the respondent's replies into the computer. The interview then transitions to the ACASI mode for the sensitive questions. In this mode, the respondent can read the questions silently on the computer screen and/or listen to the questions read through headphones and enter his or her responses directly into the computer. At the conclusion of the ACASI section, the interview returns to the CAPI mode with the interviewer completing the questionnaire. Each respondent who completes a full interview is given a $30.00 cash payment as a token of appreciation for his or her time.

No personal identifying information is captured in the CAI record for the respondent. Interviewers transmit the completed interview data to RTI in Research Triangle Park, North Carolina, via home telephone lines.

A.3. Data Processing

Computers at RTI direct the information to a raw data file that consists of one record for each completed interview. Even though editing and consistency checks are done by the CAI program during the interview, additional, more complex edits and consistency checks are completed at RTI. Cases are retained only if respondents provided data on lifetime use of cigarettes and at least nine other substances in the core section of the questionnaire. An important aspect of subsequent editing routines involves assignment of codes when respondents legitimately were skipped out of questions that definitely did not apply to them (e.g., if respondents never used a drug of interest). For key alcohol and other drug use measures, the editing procedures identify inconsistencies between related variables. Inconsistencies in variables pertaining to the most recent period that respondents used alcohol or other drugs are edited by assigning an "indefinite" period of use (e.g., use at some point in the lifetime, which could mean use in the past 30 days or past 12 months). Inconsistencies in other key substance use variables are edited by assigning missing data codes. These inconsistencies then are resolved through statistical imputation procedures, as discussed in Section A.3.1.

In addition, an important principle that was followed in editing NSDUH data was that data from core substance use modules (i.e., tobacco through sedatives, and including the core alcohol module) generally were not used to edit data in noncore modules, such as the consumption of alcohol module that was the source of estimates in some chapters of this report. In particular, noncore self-administered data (including the consumption of alcohol module in 2006) were *never* used to edit related variables in the core self-administered modules, such as alcohol. Consequently, variables in noncore sections of the interview could be inconsistent with variables in core sections. For example, respondents could report in the core alcohol module that they did not engage in binge alcohol use in the past 30 days (i.e., consumed five or more drinks in a single occasion on 0 days in the past 30 days), but they also could report in the noncore consumption of alcohol module that they had five or more drinks the last time they drank alcohol in the past 30 days. No further editing was done to make these core and noncore reports about binge alcohol use consistent with one another.

In an exception to the principle that items from noncore modules not be used to edit core variables, new methamphetamine items added to the special drugs noncore module in 2005 and 2006 were considered in the estimates of methamphetamine use in the past year among past year alcohol users in the top section of Table 4.5 in Appendix C. These methamphetamine items were added to better account for how methamphetamine is supplied and obtained. Unlike other stimulants that are available, most methamphetamine in the United States is supplied through illicit manufacturing and trafficking, rather than through conventional prescription drug distribution process. Therefore, one concern is that methamphetamine use may have been underestimated in NSDUH due to its inclusion within a set of questions about prescription-type drugs. Specifically, survey respondents who used methamphetamine might not have reported its use when questions about it were asked in the context of other questions about prescription pharmaceuticals. Section B.4.6 in Appendix B of the 2006 NSDUH national findings report (Office of Applied Studies [OAS], 2007a) provides a discussion of the new items and the process used to generate the prevalence estimates based on them.

A.3.1. Statistical Imputation

For some key variables that still had missing or ambiguous values after editing, statistical imputation was used to replace these values with appropriate response codes. For example, the response is ambiguous if the editing procedures assigned a respondent's most recent use of alcohol or other drugs to "use at some point in the lifetime," with no definite period within the lifetime. In this case, the imputation procedures assign a definite value for when the respondent last used the substance (e.g., in the past 30 days, more than 30 days ago but within the past 12 months, more than 12 months ago). Similarly, if a response is completely missing, the imputation procedures replace missing values with nonmissing ones.

In most cases, missing or ambiguous values are imputed in NSDUH using a methodology called predictive mean neighborhoods (PMN), which was developed specifically for the 1999 survey and used in all subsequent survey years. The PMN method offers a rigorous and flexible method that was implemented to improve the quality of estimates and allow more variables to be imputed. Some of the key reasons for implementing this method include the following: (1) the ability to use covariates to determine donors is far greater than that offered in the hot deck, (2) the relative importance of covariates can be determined by standard estimating equation techniques, (3) the correlations across response variables can be accounted for by making the imputation multivariate, and (4) sampling weights can be easily incorporated in the models. The PMN method has some similarity with the predictive mean matching method of Rubin (1986) except that, for the donor records, Rubin used the observed variable value (not the predictive mean) to compute the distance function. Also, the well-known method of nearest neighbor imputation is similar to PMN, except that the distance function is in terms of the original predictor variables and often requires somewhat arbitrary scaling of discrete variables. PMN is a combination of a model-assisted imputation methodology and a random nearest neighbor hot- deck procedure. The hot-deck procedure is set up in such a way that imputed values are made consistent with preexisting nonmis sing values for other variables. Whenever feasible, the imputation of variables using PMN is multivariate, in which imputation is accomplished on several response variables at once. Variables requiring imputation using PMN are the core demographic variables, core alcohol and other drug use variables (recency of use, frequency of use, and age at first use), income, health insurance, and noncore demographic variables for work status, immigrant status, and the household roster.

In the modeling stage of PMN, the model chosen depends on the nature of the response variable *Y*. In the 2006 NSDUH, the models included binomial logistic regression, multinomial logistic regression, Poisson regression, and ordinary linear regression, where the models incorporated the sampling design weights.

In general, hot-deck imputation replaces an item nonresponse (missing or ambiguous value) with a recorded response that is donated from a "similar" respondent who has nonmissing data. For random nearest neighbor hot-deck imputation, the missing or ambiguous value is replaced by a responding value from a donor randomly selected from a set of potential donors. Potential donors are defined to be "close" to the unit with the missing or ambiguous value according to a predefined function called a distance metric. In the hot-deck stage of PMN, the set of candidate donors (the "neighborhood") consists of respondents with complete data who have a predicted mean close to that of the item nonrespondent. The predicted means are computed both for respondents with and without missing data, which differs from Rubin's method where predicted means are not computed for the donor respondent (Rubin, 1986). In particular, the neighborhood consists of either the set of the closest 30 respondents or the set of respondents with a predicted mean (or means) within 5 percent of the predicted mean(s) of the item nonrespondent, whichever set is smaller. If no respondents are available who have a predicted mean (or means) within 5 percent of the item nonrespondent, the respondent with the predicted mean(s) closest to that of the item nonrespondent is selected as the donor.

In the univariate case (where only one variable is imputed using PMN), the neighborhood of potential donors is determined by calculating the relative distance between the predicted mean for an item nonrespondent and the predicted mean for each potential donor, then choosing those means defined by the distance metric. The pool of donors is restricted further to satisfy logical constraints whenever necessary (e.g., age at first crack use must not be less than age at first cocaine use).

Whenever possible, missing or ambiguous values for more than one response variable are considered at a time. In this (multivariate) case, the distance metric is a Mahalanobis distance (Manly, 1986) rather than a relative Euclidean distance. Whether the imputation is univariate or multivariate, only missing or ambiguous values are replaced, and donors are restricted to be logically consistent with the response variables that are not missing. Furthermore, donors are restricted to satisfy "likeness constraints" whenever possible. That is, donors are required to have the same values for variables highly correlated with the response. If no donors are available who meet these conditions, these likeness constraints can be loosened. For example, donors for the age at first use variable are required to be of the same age as recipients, if at all possible. Further details on the PMN methodology are provided in RTI International (2008) and by Singh, Grau, and Folsom (2001, 2002).

Although statistical imputation could not proceed separately within each State due to insufficient pools of donors, information about each respondent's State of residence was incorporated in the modeling and hot-deck steps. For most drugs, respondents were separated into three "State usage" categories as follows: respondents from States with high usage of a given drug were placed in one category, respondents from States with medium usage into another, and the remainder into a third category. This categorical "State rank" variable was used as one set of covariates in the imputation models. In addition, eligible donors for each item nonrespondent were restricted to be of the same State usage category (i.e., the same "State rank") as the nonrespondent.

A.3.2. Development of Analysis Weights

The general approach to developing and calibrating analysis weights involved developing design-based weights, d_k, as the product of the inverse of the selection probabilities at each selection stage. The 2005 and 2006 NSDUHs used a four-stage sample selection scheme in which an extra selection stage of census tracts was added before the selection of a segment. Thus, the design-based weights, d_k, for the 2005 and 2006 NSDUHs incorporated the extra layer of sampling selection to reflect the change in sample design relative to the 2002 to 2004 NSDUHs. Adjustment factors, $a_k(\lambda)$, then were applied to the design-based weights to adjust for nonresponse, to poststratify to known population control totals, and to control for extreme weights when necessary. In view of the importance of State-level estimates with the 50-State design, it was necessary to control for a much larger number of known population totals. Several other modifications to the general weight adjustment strategy that had been used in past surveys also were implemented for the first time beginning with the 1999 CAI sample.

Weight adjustments were based on a generalization of Deville and Särndal's (1992) logit model. This generalized exponential model (GEM)

(Folsom & Singh, 2000) incorporates unit- specific bounds (l_k, u_k), $k \in s$, for the adjustment factor $a_k(\lambda)$ as follows:

$$a_k(\lambda) = \frac{\ell_k(u_k - c_k) + u_k(c_k - \ell_k)\exp(A_k x_k' \lambda)}{(u_k - c_k) + (c_k - \ell_k)\exp(A_k x_k' \lambda)},$$

where c_k are pre specified centering constants, such that $l_k < c_k < u_k$ and $A_k = (u_k - l_k) / (u_k - c_k)(c_k - l_k)$. The variables l_k, c_k, and u_k are user-specified bounds, and λ is the column vector of p model parameters corresponding to the p covariates x. The λ-parameters are estimated by solving

$$\sum_s x_k d_k a_k(\lambda) - \tilde{T}_x = 0,$$

where $\tilde{T}_x$ denotes control totals that could be either nonrandom, as is generally the case with poststratification, or random, as is generally the case for nonresponse adjustment.

The final weights $w_k = d_k a_k(\lambda)$ minimize the distance function $\Delta(w, d)$ defined as

$$\Delta(w,d) = \sum_{k \in s} \frac{d_k}{A_k} \left\{ (a_k - \ell_k)\log\frac{a_k - \ell_k}{c_k - \ell_k} + (u_k - a_k)\log\frac{u_k - a_k}{u_k - c_k} \right\}.$$

This general approach was used at several stages of the weight adjustment process, including (1) adjustment of household weights for nonresponse at the screener level, (2) poststratification of household weights to meet population controls for various demographic groups by State, (3) adjustment of household weights for extremes, (4) poststratification of selected person weights, (5) adjustment of responding person weights for nonresponse at the questionnaire level, (6) poststratification of responding person weights, and (7) adjustment of responding person weights for extremes.

Every effort was made to include as many relevant State-specific covariates (typically defined by demographic domains within States) as possible in the multivariate models used to calibrate the weights (nonresponse adjustment and poststratification steps). Because further subdivision of State samples by demographic covariates often produced small cell sample sizes, it was not possible to retain all State-specific covariates (even after meaningful collapsing of covariate categories) and still estimate the necessary model parameters with reasonable precision. Therefore, a hierarchical structure was used in grouping States with covariates defined at the national level, at the census division level within the Nation, at the State group within the census division, and, whenever possible, at the State level. In every case, the controls for the total population within a State and the five age groups (12 to 17, 18 to 25, 26 to 34, 35 to 49, 50 or older) within a State were maintained except that, in the last step of poststratification of person weights, six age groups (12 to 17, 18 to 25, 26 to 34, 35 to 49, 50 to 64, 65 or older) were used. Census control totals by age, race, gender, and Hispanicity were required for the civilian, noninstitutionalized population of each State. Beginning with the 2002 NSDUH, the Population Estimates Branch of the U.S. Census Bureau has produced the necessary population estimates in response to a special request based on the 2000 census.

Consistent with the surveys from 1999 onward, control of extreme weights through separate bounds for adjustment factors was incorporated into the GEM calibration processes for both nonresponse and poststratification. This is unlike the traditional method of winsorization in which extreme weights are truncated at prespecified levels and the trimmed portions of weights are distributed to the nontruncated cases. In GEM, it is possible to set bounds around the prespecified levels for extreme weights, and then the calibration process provides an objective way of deciding the extent of adjustment (or truncation) within the specified bounds. A step was added to poststratify the household-level weights to obtain census-consistent estimates based on the household rosters from all screened households; these household roster-based estimates then provided the control totals needed to calibrate the respondent pair weights for subsequent planned analyses. An additional step poststratified the selected person sample to conform to the adjusted roster estimates. This additional step takes advantage of the inherent two-phase nature of the NSDUH design. The final step poststratified the respondent person sample to external census data (defined within the State whenever possible, as discussed above). For more detailed information, see the *2006 NSDUH Methodological Resource Book* (RTI International, 2008).

In addition to the person-level analysis weights discussed above, person pair–level analysis weights also were calculated. In each year of NSDUH, the person pair–level analysis weights and person-level analysis weights shared the same weight components at the screening dwelling unit (SDU) level. In addition to these common weight components, the person pair– level analysis weights had several specific weight components: (1) inverse of person-pair selection probability, (2) poststratification of selected person-pair weights, (3) adjustment of responding person-pair weights for nonresponse, (4) poststratification of responding person-pair weights, and (5) adjustment of responding person-pair weights for extremes. The person-pair analysis weights were the product of all of the weight components. For more detailed information, see the *2006 NSDUH Methodological Resource Book* (RTI International, 2008).

APPENDIX B: STATISTICAL METHODS AND MEASUREMENT

B.1. Target Population

An important limitation of estimates of drug use prevalence from the National Survey on Drug Use and Health (NSDUH) is that they are only designed to describe the target population of the survey—the civilian, noninstitutionalized population aged 12 or older. Although this population includes almost 98 percent of the total U.S. population aged 12 or older, it excludes some important and unique subpopulations who may have very different alcohol and drug use patterns. Within the population aged 12 or older, this chapter focuses on persons between the ages of 12 and 20, that is, those who are below the legal drinking age.

B.2. Sampling Error and Statistical Significance

This chapter includes tables for national and State estimates, produced using a multiprocedure package called SUDAAN® Software for Statistical Analysis of Correlated Data. SUDAAN was designed for the statistical analysis of data collected using stratified, multistage cluster sampling designs, as well as other observational and experimental studies involving repeated measures or studies subject to cluster correlation effects (RTI International, 2004). The final, nonresponse-adjusted, and poststratified analysis weights were used in SUDAAN to compute unbiased design-based drug use estimates.

The sampling error (i.e., the standard error or SE) of an estimate is the error caused by the selection of a sample instead of conducting a census of the population. The sampling error may be reduced by selecting a large sample and/or by using efficient sample design and estimation strategies, such as stratification, optimal allocation, and ratio estimation.

With the use of probability sampling methods in NSDUH, it is possible to develop estimates of sampling error from the survey data. These estimates have been calculated using SUDAAN for all estimates presented in this chapter using a Taylor series linearization approach that takes into account the effects of NSDUH's complex design features. The sampling errors are used to identify unreliable estimates and to test for the statistical significance of differences between estimates.

B.2.1. Variance Estimation for Totals

Estimates of means or proportions, $\hat{p}_d$, such as drug use prevalence estimates for a domain *d*, can be expressed as a ratio estimate:

$$\hat{p}_d = \frac{\hat{Y}_d}{\hat{N}_d},$$

where $\hat{Y}_d$ is a linear statistic estimating number of substance users in the domain, and $\hat{N}_d$ is a linear statistic estimating the total number of persons in domain *d* (both users and nonusers). The SUDAAN software used to develop estimates and their SEs produces direct estimates $\hat{Y}_d$ and $\hat{N}_d$ and their SEs. The SUDAAN application also uses a Taylor series approximation method to estimate the SEs of the ratio estimate $\hat{p}_d$.

When the domain size, $\hat{N}_d$, is free of sampling error, an appropriate estimate of the SE for the total number of substance users is

$$\text{SE}(\hat{Y}_d) = \hat{N}_d \text{SE}(\hat{p}_d).$$

This approach is theoretically correct when the domain size estimates, $\hat{N}_d$, are among those forced to match their respective U.S. Census Bureau population projections through the weight calibration process (Chen et al., 2005). In these cases, $\hat{N}_d$ is not subject to sampling error. For a more detailed explanation of the weight calibration process, see Section A.3.2 in Appendix A.

For estimated domain totals, $\hat{Y}_d$, where is not fixed (i.e., where domain size estimates are not forced to match the U.S. Census Bureau population projections), this formulation may still provide a good approximation if it can be assumed that the sampling variation in $\hat{N}_d$ is negligible relative to the sampling variation in $\hat{p}_d$. This is a reasonable assumption for most cases in this study.

For a subset of the estimates produced from the 2002 to 2006 data, the above approach yielded an underestimate of the variance of a total because $\hat{N}_d$ was subject to considerable variation. In these cases, the SEs for the total estimates calculated directly within SUDAAN are reported. Using the SEs from the total estimates directly from SUDAAN does not affect the SE estimates for the corresponding proportions presented in the same sets of tables.

B.2.2. Suppression Criteria for Unreliable Estimates

As has been done in other NSDUH reports, direct survey estimates produced for this study that are considered to be unreliable due to unacceptably large sampling errors are not shown in this chapter and are noted by asterisks (*) in the tables containing such estimates. The criteria used for suppressing all direct survey estimates were based on the relative standard error (RSE) (defined as the ratio of the SE over the estimate), nominal (actual) sample size, and effective sample size for each estimate.

Proportion estimates $(\hat{p})$ within the range $[0 < \hat{p} < 1]$., rates, and the corresponding estimated number of users were suppressed if

$$\text{RSE}[-\ln(\hat{p})] > .175 \text{ when } \hat{p} \le .5$$

or

$$\text{RSE}[-\ln(1 - \hat{p})] > .175 \text{ when } \hat{p} > .5.$$

Using a first-order Taylor series approximation to estimate $\text{RSE}[-\ln(\hat{p})]$ and RSE[-ln(1 – $p^\wedge$)], the following equation was derived and used for computational purposes:

$$\frac{SE(\hat{p})/\hat{p}}{-\ln(\hat{p})} > .175 \text{ when } \hat{p} \leq .5$$

or

$$\frac{SE(\hat{p})/(1-\hat{p})}{-\ln(1-\hat{p})} > .175 \text{ when } \hat{p} > .5.$$

The separate formulas for $p\hat{}$ $\leq .5$ and $p\hat{}$ $>.5$ produce a symmetric suppression rule; that is, if $p\hat{}$ is suppressed, $1-p\hat{}$ will be suppressed as well. This ad hoc rule requires an effective sample size in excess of 50. When $.05 < p\hat{} < .95$, the symmetric property of the rule produces a local maximum effective sample size of 68 at $p\hat{} = .5$. Thus, estimates with these values of $p\hat{}$ along with effective sample sizes falling below 68 are suppressed. See Figure B. 1 for a representation of the required minimum effective sample sizes as a function of the proportion estimated.

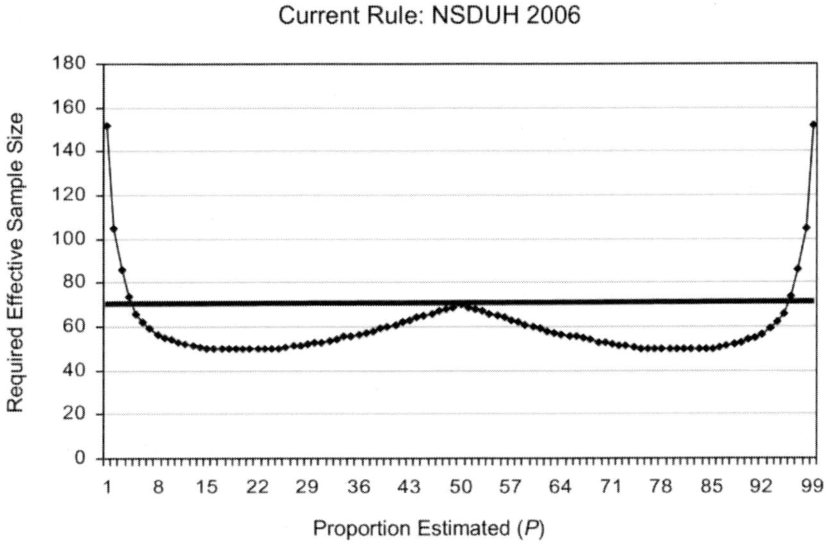

Figure B.1 Required Effective Sample as a Function of the Proportion Estimated Current Rule: NSDUH 2006.

A minimum nominal sample size suppression criterion (n = 100) that protects against unreliable estimates caused by small design effects and small nominal sample sizes was employed. Prevalence estimates also were suppressed if they were close to 0 or 100 percent (i.e., if $\hat{p} < .00005$ or if $\hat{p} \geq .99995$).

Estimates of other totals along with means and rates that are not bounded between 0 and 1 (e.g., mean age at first use and incidence rates) were suppressed if the RSEs of the estimates were larger than .5. Additionally, estimates of the mean age at first use were suppressed if the sample size was smaller than 10 respondents. Also, the estimated incidence rate and number of initiates were suppressed if they rounded to 0.

The suppression criteria for various NSDUH estimates are summarized in Table B. 1 at the end of this appendix.

B.2.3. Statistical Significance of Differences

This section describes the methods used to compare prevalence estimates in this report. Customarily, the observed difference between estimates is evaluated in terms of its statistical significance. Statistical significance is based on the p value of the test statistic and refers to the probability that a difference as large as that observed would occur due to random variability in the estimates if there were no difference in the prevalence estimates for the population groups being compared. The significance of observed differences in this chapter is reported at the .05 level. When comparing prevalence estimates, the null hypothesis (no difference between prevalence estimates) was tested against the alternative hypothesis (there is a difference in prevalence estimates) using the standard difference in proportions test expressed as

$$Z = \frac{\hat{p}_1 - \hat{p}_2}{\sqrt{\text{var}(\hat{p}_1) + \text{var}(\hat{p}_2) - 2\text{cov}(\hat{p}_1, \hat{p}_2)}},$$

where $\hat{p}_1$ = first prevalence estimate, $\hat{p}_2$ = second prevalence estimate, var ($\hat{p}_1$) = variance of first prevalence estimate, var ($\hat{p}_2$) = variance of second prevalence estimate, and cov ($\hat{p}_1$, $\hat{p}_2$) . covariance between $\hat{p}_1$ and $\hat{p}_2$. In cases where significance tests between years were performed, the prevalence estimate from the earlier year (2002, 2003, 2004, or 2005) becomes the first prevalence estimate, and the prevalence estimate from the later year (2006) becomes the second prevalence estimate.

Under the null hypothesis, Z is asymptotically distributed as a normal random variable. Therefore, calculated values of Z can be referred to the unit normal distribution to determine the corresponding probability level (i.e., p value). Because the covariance term between the two estimates is not necessarily zero, SUDAAN was used to compute estimates of Z along with the associated p values using the analysis weights and accounting for the sample design as described in Appendix A. A similar procedure and formula for Z were used for estimated totals; however, it should be noted that because it was necessary to calculate the SE outside of SUDAAN for domains forced by the weighting process to match their respective U.S. Census Bureau population estimates, the corresponding test statistics also were computed outside of SUDAAN.

When comparing population subgroups across three or more levels of a categorical variable, log-linear chi-square tests of independence of the subgroups and the prevalence variables were conducted first to control the error level for multiple comparisons. If the chi- square test indicated overall significant differences, the significance of each particular pairwise comparison of interest was tested using SUDAAN analytic procedures to properly account for the sample design. Using the published estimates and SEs to perform independent t tests for the difference of proportions usually will provide the same results as tests performed in SUDAAN. However, where the significance level is borderline, results may differ for two reasons: (1) the covariance term is included in SUDAAN tests, whereas it is not included in independent t tests; and (2) the reduced number of significant digits shown in the published estimates may cause rounding errors in the independent t tests.

B.3. Other Information on Data Accuracy

The accuracy of survey estimates can be affected by nonresponse, coding errors, computer processing errors, errors in the sampling frame, reporting errors, and other errors not due to sampling. They are sometimes referred to as "nonsampling errors." These types of errors and their impact are reduced through data editing, statistical adjustments for nonresponse, close monitoring and periodic retraining of interviewers, and improvement in various quality control procedures.

Although these types of errors often can be much larger than sampling errors, measurement of most of these errors is difficult. However, some indication of the effects of some types of these errors can be obtained through proxy measures, such as response rates and from other research studies.

B.3.1. Screening and Interview Response Rate Patterns

Beginning in 2002 and continuing through 2006, respondents received a $30 incentive in an effort to maximize response rates. Of the 151,288 eligible households sampled for the 2006 NSDUH, 137,057 were screened successfully, for a weighted screening response rate of 90.6 percent. In these screened households, a total of 85,034 sample persons were selected, and completed interviews were obtained from 67,802 of these sample persons, for a weighted interview response rate of 74.2 percent. The overall weighted response rate, defined as the product of the weighted screening response rate and weighted interview response rate, was 67.2 percent in 2006. The interview response rate for persons aged 12 to 20 was 84.9 percent.

The weighted screening rates for the 2002 to 2005 NSDUHs ranged from 90.7 to 91.3 percent, the interviewer response rates ranged from 76.2 to 78.6 percent, and the overall response rates ranged from 71.3 percent in 2002 to 69.2 percent in 2005. For the sample aged 12 to 20, the interview response rates ranged from 84.9 to 89.2 percent.

Nonresponse bias can be expressed as the product of the nonresponse rate $(1 - R)$ and the difference between the characteristic of interest between respondents and nonrespondents in the population $(P_r - P_{nr})$. By maximizing NSDUH response rates, it is hoped that the bias due to the difference between the estimates from respondents and nonrespondents is minimized. Alcohol and drug use surveys are particularly vulnerable to nonresponse due to the difficult nature of accessing heavy alcohol and drug users.

B.3.2. Inconsistent Responses and Item Nonresponse

Among survey participants, item response rates were above 99 percent for most drug use items. However, inconsistent responses for some items were common. Estimates of substance use from NSDUH are based on responses to multiple questions by respondents, so that the maximum amount of information is used in determining whether a respondent is classified as a drug user. Inconsistencies in responses are resolved through a logical editing process that involves some judgment on the part of survey analysts. Additionally, missing or inconsistent responses are imputed using statistical methodology. Editing and imputation of missing responses are potential sources of error.

B.3.3. Validity of Self-Reported Substance Use

Most drug use prevalence estimates, including those produced for NSDUH, are based on self-reports of use. Although studies have generally supported the validity of self-report data, it is well documented that these data often are biased (underreported or overreported) by several factors, including the mode of administration, the population under investigation, and the type of drug (Bradburn & Sudman, 1983; Hser & Anglin, 1993). Higher levels of bias also are observed among younger respondents and those with higher levels of drug use (Biglan, Gilpin, Rohrbach, & Pierce, 2004). Methodological procedures, such as biological specimens (e.g., urine, hair, saliva), proxy reports (e.g., family member, peer), and repeated measures (e.g., recanting), have been used to validate self-report data (Fendrich, Johnson, Sudman, Wislar, & Spiehler, 1999). However, these procedures often are impractical or too costly for community-based epidemiological studies (SRNT Subcommittee on Biochemical Verification, 2002). NSDUH utilizes widely accepted methodological practices for ensuring validity, such as encouraging privacy through audio computer-assisted self-interviewing (ACASI). Comparisons using these methods within NSDUH have been shown to reduce reporting bias (Aquilino, 1994; Turner, Lessler, & Gfroerer, 1992).

B.4. Measurement Issues and Additional Findings for Alcohol Items Added in 2006

As noted in Section 1.4 of Chapter 1, NSDUH in 2006 incorporated a new consumption of alcohol module that collected additional information about respondents' last use of alcohol for those who indicated that they had consumed alcohol at least once in the past month.

Table B.1. Summary of NSDUH Suppression Rules.

Estimate	Suppress if:
Prevalence Rate, $p\hat{}$, with Nominal Sample Size, n, and Design Effect, *deff*	1. The estimated prevalence rate, $p\hat{}$, is $< .00005$ or $\geq .99995$, or 2. $\frac{SE(\hat{p}) / \hat{p}}{-\ln(\hat{p})} > .175$ when $\hat{p} \leq .5$, or $\frac{SE(\hat{p}) / (1-\hat{p})}{-\ln(1-\hat{p})} > .175$ when $\hat{p} \leq .5$, or 3. Effective $n < 68$, where Effective $n - \frac{n}{deff}$ or 4. $n < 100$. Note: The rounding portion of this suppression rule for prevalence rates will produce some estimates that round at one decimal place to 0.0 or 100.0 percent but are not suppressed from the tables.
Estimated Number (Numerator of $p\hat{}$)	The estimated prevalence rate, $p\hat{}$, is suppressed. Note: In some instances when $p\hat{}$ is not suppressed, the estimated number may appear as a 0 in the tables. This means that the estimate is greater than 0 but less than 500 (estimated numbers are shown in thousands).
Mean Age at First Use, $\bar{x}$, with Nominal Sample Size, n	1. $RSE(\bar{x}) > .5$, or 2. $n < 10$.

SE = standard error; RSE = relative standard error; deff = design effect.

Source: SAMHSA, Office of Applied Studies, National Survey on Drug Use and Health, 2006.

Table B.2AB. Number of Drinks Consumed on Last Occasion of Alcohol Use in the Past Month among Past Month Alcohol Users Aged 12 to 20, by Gender and Age Group: Numbers in Thousands, Percentage Distribution and Mean, 2006.

	TOTAL	AGE GROUP			GENDER	
		12 to 14	15 to 17	18 to 20	Male	Female
Number of Drinks Consumed on Last Occasion of Alcohol Use	**Numbers in Thousands, by Number of Drinks Consumed**					
1 Drink	2,166	318	754	1,094	1,056	1,111
2 Drinks	1,821	177	565	1,078	839	982
3 or 4 Drinks	2,403	116	721	1,566	1,087	1,316
5 to 8 Drinks	2,633	74	799	1,760	1,461	1,172
9 or More Drinks	1,330	43	345	942	1,046	284
Number of Drinks Consumed on Last Occasion of Alcohol Use	**Percentage Distribution, by Number of Drinks Consumed**					
1 Drink	20.9	43.7	23.7	17.0	19.2	22.8
2 Drinks	17.6	24.4	17.8	16.7	15.3	20.2
3 or 4 Drinks	23.2	15.9	22.6	24.3	19.8	27.1
5 to 8 Drinks	25.4	10.1	25.1	27.3	26.6	24.1
9 or More Drinks	12.8	5.9	10.8	14.6	19.1	5.8
	Number of Drinks Consumed					
Mean Number of Drinks Consumed	4.5	2.8	4.3	4.8	5.3	3.7

*Low precision; no estimate reported.

NOTE: Respondents with unknown responses to number of drinks consumed on last occasion of alcohol use were excluded.

Source: SAMHSA, Office of Applied Studies, National Survey on Drug Use and Health, 2006.

Table B.3A. Binge Alcohol Use in the Lifetime and Past Month and Binge Alcohol Use Initiates among Persons Aged 12 to 20, by Binge Drinking Definition, Age Group, and Gender: Numbers in Thousands, 2006.

	Binge Alcohol Use Defined as Five or More Drinks on One Occasion			Binge Alcohol Use Defined as Four or More Drinks on One Occasion–Females Only[1]	Binge Alcohol Use Defined as Five Drinks for Males and Four Drinks for Females[1]
	TOTAL	Male	Female		
Age Group		Engaged in Binge Alcohol Use in Lifetime			
12 to 20 Years	11,488	6,310	5,178	5,723	12,034
12 to 14 Years	689	339	350	380	719
15 to 17 Years	3,832	2,003	1,829	2,007	4,010
18 to 20 Years	6,967	3,968	2,999	3,336	7,305
Age Group		Engaged in Binge Alcohol Use in Past Month			
12 to 20 Years	7,421	4,293	3,128	3,427	7,719
12 to 14 Years	409	196	213	222	418
15 to 17 Years	2,298	1,239	1,059	1,148	2,387
18 to 20 Years	4,713	2,858	1,855	2,057	4,915
Age Group		Initiated Binge Alcohol Use in Past 12 Months[2,3]			
12 to 20 Years	3,798	2,087	1,712	†	†
12 to 14 Years	423	191	231	†	†
15 to 17 Years	1,761	921	840	†	†
18 to 20 Years	1,615	975	640	†	†

*Low precision; no estimate reported.

† Estimate is available but has not been reported because of an invalid anomaly in the data collection.

1 The Four or More Drinks definition corresponds to that used by the National Institute on Alcohol Abuse and Alcoholism (NIAAA, 2004).

2 Respondents with unknown responses were excluded.

3 Binge Alcohol Use Initiates are defined as persons who binged on alcohol for the first time in the 12 months prior to the date of the interview.

Source: SAMHSA, Office of Applied Studies, National Survey on Drug Use and Health, 2006.

Table B.3B. Binge Alcohol Use in the Lifetime and Past Month and Binge Alcohol Use Initiates among Persons Aged 12 to 20, by Binge Drinking Definition, Age Group, and Gender: Percentages, 2006.

	Binge Alcohol Use Defined as Five or More Drinks on One Occasion			Binge Alcohol Use Defined as Four or More Drinks on One Occasion–Females Only[1]	Binge Alcohol Use Defined as Five Drinks for Males and Four Drinks for Females[1]
	TOTAL	Male	Female		
Age Group		**Engaged in Binge Alcohol Use in Lifetime**			
12 to 20 Years	30.1	32.0	28.0	31.0	31.5
12 to 14 Years	5.6	5.3	5.9	6.4	5.8
15 to 17 Years	29.3	30.4	28.3	31.0	30.7
18 to 20 Years	54.5	59.0	49.5	55.0	57.1
Age Group		**Engaged in Binge Alcohol Use in Past Month**			
12 to 20 Years	19.4	21.8	16.9	18.5	20.2
12 to 14 Years	3.3	3.1	3.6	3.7	3.4
15 to 17 Years	17.6	18.8	16.4	17.8	18.3
18 to 20 Years	36.8	42.5	30.6	33.9	38.4
Age Group		**Initiated Binge Alcohol Use in Past 12 Months[2,3]**			
12 to 20 Years	10.2	10.9	9.5	†	†
12 to 14 Years	3.5	3.0	3.9	†	†
15 to 17 Years	13.9	14.4	13.3	†	†
18 to 20 Years	13.1	15.2	10.9	†	†

*Low precision; no estimate reported.

† Estimate is available but has not been reported because of an invalid anomaly in the data collection. See Section B.4. 1 in this appendix.

1 The Four or More Drinks definition corresponds to that used by the National Institute on Alcohol Abuse and Alcoholism (NIAAA, 2004).

2 Respondents with unknown responses were excluded.

3 Binge Alcohol Use Initiates are defined as persons who binged on alcohol for the first time in the 12 months prior to the date of the interview.

Source: SAMHSA, Office of Applied Studies, National Survey on Drug Use and Health, 2006.

Other items in the consumption of alcohol module included the source of alcohol, location, and social context of the last drinking episode among past month alcohol users aged 12 to 20; the number of drinks consumed on the last drinking occasion; and the use of illicit drugs in combination with alcohol or within 2 hours of consuming alcohol on the last drinking occasion. Findings for many of these items are covered in the tables in Appendix C and discussed in Chapter 4. This section provides further information on some of the items in the new module, including a discussion of data collection issues with the new four-drink binge drinking measure for females and additional findings for this and selected other variables.

B.4.1. Data Issues Involving the Measurement of Binge Alcohol Use for Females

In 2006, new items were added within the consumption of alcohol module to investigate whether the current binge drinking definition based on drinking five or more drinks on the same occasion should be changed to a lower threshold of four or more drinks on the same occasion for females. The four or more drinks definition corresponds to that used by the National Institute on Alcohol Abuse and Alcoholism (NIAAA, 2004). Although all persons aged 12 or older were asked the new items regarding lifetime binge use and age of initiation of binge use based on the five or more drinks definition, the question pertaining to binge use based on four or more drinks and related follow-up questions were asked only of females. The intent was to route all female respondents who were lifetime drinkers into the questions regarding their history of having four or more drinks on the same occasion.

During the editing process, it was discovered that females who had some history of consuming five or more drinks on the same occasion were skipped out of the questions regarding their history of having four or more drinks. The sole exception to this was that females who had a history of having five or more drinks on the same occasion and who also indicated that they had four or more drinks when they last used alcohol were properly routed into the questions about their history of having five or more drinks on the same occasion. As a result of this error, 1,235 females aged 12 to 20 who were lifetime alcohol users (8.0 percent of all females in this group) were not asked the questions regarding their history of having four or more drinks on the same occasion.

In most cases, females who were incorrectly skipped out of the four or more drinks questions could be assigned a four or more drinks status for both past month and lifetime use either from previous responses to questions about the number of drinks on the last occasion or questions about binge use based on five or more drinks earlier in the same module. In cases where there was unknown data, the information from the core computer-assisted interviewing (CAI) module about binge use status, an imputed revised measure, was used to determine whether the female should be recoded to be a binge drinker based on the four or more drinks definition. Data on initiation of binge alcohol use based on the four or more drinks definition were not available for those females incorrectly skipped from these questions. Because of the large number of females who were improperly skipped, estimates of the age of initiation of binge drinking based on four or more drinks definition are not presented in this report.

B.4.2. Results from Selected Alcohol Use Items Added in 2006

The results based on many of the new items in the consumption of alcohol module are presented in Chapter 4. This section presents supplementary tables on the number of drinks consumed when persons aged 12 to 20 last consumed alcohol, as well as comparisons of binge drinking rates using the criterion of five more drinks on the same occasion for males and females and the criterion of four or more drinks on the same occasion for females.

Table B.2AB presents the number of drinks consumed the last time past month drinkers aged 12 to 20 drank alcohol, both for the full sample and by gender and age group. The majority of underage drinkers in each age and gender group reported drinking four or fewer drinks the last time they used alcohol. Current drinkers aged 12 to 14 were more likely to have had only one drink on their last drinking occasion (43.7 percent) compared with those aged 15 to 17 (23.7 percent) or those aged 18 to 20 (17.0 percent). The 18 to 20 year olds had the highest percentage of persons who reported drinking nine or more drinks at the last occasion (14.6 percent) compared with the other age groups (5.9 percent for those aged 12 to 14, 10.8 percent for those aged 15 to 17). Females were more likely than males to have had one drink (22.8 percent for females, 19.2 percent for males), two drinks (20.2 percent for females, 15.3 percent for males), or three or four drinks (27.1 percent for females, 19.8 percent for males) when they last drank alcohol. In contrast, underage males were more likely than underage females to have had five to eight drinks (26.6 percent for males, 24.1 percent for females) or nine or more drinks (19.1 percent for males, 5.8 percent for females) when they last drank alcohol.

Information on the mean number of drinks for these groups is also included in Table B.2AB. Overall, current drinkers aged 12 to 20 averaged 4.5 drinks when they last used alcohol. The mean number of drinks reported increased with age. Persons aged 12 to 14 had the lowest mean number of drinks (2.8 drinks), those aged 15 to 17 reported a higher amount at 4.3 drinks on average, and the 18 to 20 age group reported the highest average number at 4.8 drinks on the last occasion. Among current drinkers, underage males consumed more drinks on their last drinking occasion (mean of 5.3 drinks) than underage females (mean of 3.7 drinks).

Tables B.3A and B.3B present information from 2006 on binge alcohol use as defined by drinking five or more drinks on one occasion for both males and females, and an alternative definition based on five or more drinks for males but four or more drinks for females. Using the definition of five or more drinks on one occasion for both males and females, the rate of lifetime binge drinking was higher for underage males (32.0 percent) than for underage females (28.0 percent). This difference was principally found for those aged 18 to 20, where males had a higher rate of lifetime binge use (59.0 percent) compared with females (49.5 percent). A similar pattern was found for past month binge use using the five or more drinks criterion, with males having a higher rate than females (21.8 to 16.9 percent, respectively). Among both 15 to 17 year olds and 18 to 20 year olds, males had higher rates of past month binge drinking compared with females when binge drinking was defined as five or more drinks for both males and females.

Although a statistical comparison cannot be drawn between the binge drinking rates based on the two different definitions, it can be seen that using the less stringent definition for lifetime binge use increased the rate of lifetime binge alcohol use for females from 28.0 to 31.0 percent, and it increased the rate of past month binge alcohol use for females from 16.9 to 18.5 percent. This higher rate of binge drinking for females using the four or more drinks criterion also can be seen in the overall rate of binge drinking including both males and females; lifetime binge drinking increased from 30.1 to 31.5 percent, and past month binge drinking increased from 19.4 to 20.2 percent. The increase in the prevalence of binge drinking among females using the four or more drinks criterion was primarily found for females aged 18 to 20.

APPENDIX C: PREVALENCE TABLES

Table 2.1A. Alcohol Use in the Lifetime, Past Year, and Past Month; Binge and Heavy Alcohol Use in the Past Month; and Alcohol Dependence or Abuse in the Past Year among Persons Aged 12 to 20, by Gender: Numbers in Thousands, 2002-2006.

Gender/Alcohol Measure	2002	2003	2004	2005	2006
TOTAL					
Lifetime Use	20,911	20,936	20,709	20,671	20,574
Past Year Use	17,492	17,554	17,568	17,729	17,598
Past Month Use	10,713	10,876	10,838	10,819	10,823
Binge Alcohol Use[1]	7,175	7,190	7,397	7,197	7,239
Heavy Alcohol Use[1]	2,301	2,297	2,375	2,296	2,359
Past Year Dependence or Abuse[2]	3,570	3,468	3,616	3,592	3,475
MALE					
Lifetime Use	10,719	10,537	10,624	10,500	10,647
Past Year Use	8,847	8,735	8,946	8,927	9,064
Past Month Use	5,619	5,720	5,723	5,658	5,752
Binge Alcohol Use[1]	4,140	4,162	4,271	4,175	4,192
Heavy Alcohol Use[1]	1,544	1,506	1,582	1,492	1,561
Past Year Dependence or Abuse[2]	2,079	1,905	2,092	1,958	1,893
FEMALE					
Lifetime Use	10,192	10,399[a]	10,085	10,171	9,927

Table 2.1A. (Continued)

Gender/Alcohol Measure	2002	2003	2004	2005	2006
Past Year Use	8,645	8,819	8,622	8,802	8,534
Past Month Use	5,094	5,156	5,115	5,160	5,072
Binge Alcohol Use[1]	3,035	3,027	3,127	3,022	3,047
Heavy Alcohol Use[1]	756	791	793	803	798
Past Year Dependence or Abuse[2]	1,491	1,563	1,524	1,634	1,582

*Low precision; no estimate reported.

[a]Difference between estimate and 2006 estimate is statistically significant at the 0.05 level.

[b]Difference between estimate and 2006 estimate is statistically significant at the 0.01 level.

[1]Binge Alcohol Use is defined as drinking five or more drinks on the same occasion (i.e., at the same time or within a couple of hours of each other) on at least 1 day in the past 30 days. Heavy Alcohol Use is defined as drinking five or more drinks on the same occasion on each of 5 or more days in the past 30 days; all heavy alcohol users are also binge alcohol users.

[2]Dependence or abuse is based on definitions found in the 4th edition of the *Diagnostic and Statistical Manual of Mental Disorders* (DSM-IV).

Source: SAMHSA, Office of Applied Studies, National Survey on Drug Use and Health, 2002, 2003, 2004, 2005, and 2006.

Table 2.1B. Alcohol Use in the Lifetime, Past Year, and Past Month; Binge and Heavy Alcohol Use in the Past Month; and Alcohol Dependence or Abuse in the Past Year among Persons Aged 12 to 20, by Gender: Percentages, 2002-2006.

Gender/Alcohol Measure	2002	2003	2004	2005	2006
TOTAL					
Lifetime Use	56.2[b]	55.8[b]	54.9	53.9	53.9
Past Year Use	47.0	46.8	46.6	46.3	46.1
Past Month Use	28.8	29.0	28.7	28.2	28.3
Binge Alcohol Use[1]	19.3	19.2	19.6	18.8	19.0
Heavy Alcohol Use[1]	6.2	6.1	6.3	6.0	6.2
Past Year Dependence or Abuse[2]	9.6	9.2	9.6	9.4	9.1
MALE					
Lifetime Use	56.5[b]	55.0	54.9	53.7	54.0
Past Year Use	46.6	45.6	46.3	45.6	46.0
Past Month Use	29.6	29.9	29.6	28.9	29.2
Binge Alcohol Use[1]	21.8	21.7	22.1	21.3	21.3
Heavy Alcohol Use[1]	8.1	7.9	8.2	7.6	7.9
Past Year Dependence or Abuse[2]	10.9[b]	9.9	10.8[a]	10.0	9.6
FEMALE					
Lifetime Use	56.0[b]	56.6[b]	54.8	54.2	53.7
Past Year Use	47.5	48.0[a]	46.9	46.9	46.2
Past Month Use	28.0	28.1	27.8	27.5	27.4
Binge Alcohol Use[1]	16.7	16.5	17.0	16.1	16.5
Heavy Alcohol Use[1]	4.2	4.3	4.3	4.3	4.3
Past Year Dependence or Abuse[2]	8.2	8.5	8.3	8.7	8.6

*Low precision; no estimate reported.

[a] Difference between estimate and 2006 estimate is statistically significant at the 0.05 level.

[b] Difference between estimate and 2006 estimate is statistically significant at the 0.01 level.

[1] Binge Alcohol Use is defined as drinking five or more drinks on the same occasion (i.e., at the same time or within a couple of hours of each other) on at least 1 day in the past 30 days. Heavy Alcohol Use is defined as drinking five or more drinks on the same occasion on each of 5 or more days in the past 30 days; all heavy alcohol users are also binge alcohol users.

[2] Dependence or abuse is based on definitions found in the 4th edition of the *Diagnostic and Statistical Manual of Mental Disorders* (DSM-IV).

Source: SAMHSA, Office of Applied Studies, National Survey on Drug Use and Health, 2002, 2003, 2004, 2005, and 2006.

Table 2.2A. Alcohol Use in the Lifetime, Past Year, and Past Month; Binge and Heavy Alcohol Use in the Past Month; and Alcohol Dependence or Abuse in the Past Year among Persons Aged 12 to 20, by Age Group: Numbers in Thousands, 2002-2006.

Age Group/Alcohol Measure	2002	2003	2004	2005	2006
AGE 12 TO 14					
Lifetime Use	3,149[b]	3,001[b]	3,008[b]	2,739	2,723
Past Year Use	2,231[b]	2,154	2,193[a]	2,074	2,002
Past Month Use	940[a]	924[a]	902	805	815
Binge Alcohol Use[1]	455	423	415	386	381
Heavy Alcohol Use[1]	81	64	64	61	49
Past Year Dependence or Abuse[2]	247	267[a]	252	213	211
AGE 15 TO 17					
Lifetime Use	7,598	7,713	7,587	7,567	7,532
Past Year Use	6,333	6,409	6,344	6,380	6,359
Past Month Use	3,424	3,501	3,534	3,387	3,406
Binge Alcohol Use[1]	2,186	2,235	2,379	2,127	2,232
Heavy Alcohol Use[1]	549	588	607	550	554
Past Year Dependence or Abuse[2]	1,206	1,204	1,265	1,194	1,149
AGE 18 TO 20					
Lifetime Use	10,164	10,223	10,113	10,365	10,319
Past Year Use	8,928	8,991	9,031	9,275	9,236
Past Month Use	6,348	6,451	6,402	6,628	6,602
Binge Alcohol Use[1]	4,534	4,531	4,604	4,684	4,625
Heavy Alcohol Use[1]	1,671	1,645	1,704	1,685	1,756
Past Year Dependence or Abuse[2]	2,117	1,997	2,099	2,185	2,115

*Low precision; no estimate reported.

[a] Difference between estimate and 2006 estimate is statistically significant at the 0.05 level.

[b] Difference between estimate and 2006 estimate is statistically significant at the 0.01 level.

[1] Binge Alcohol Use is defined as drinking five or more drinks on the same occasion (i.e., at the same time or within a couple of hours of each other) on at least 1 day in the past 30 days. Heavy Alcohol Use is defined as drinking five or more drinks on the same occasion on each of 5 or more days in the past 30 days; all heavy alcohol users are also binge alcohol users.

[2] Dependence or abuse is based on definitions found in the 4th edition of the *Diagnostic and Statistical Manual of Mental Disorders* (DSM-IV).

Source: SAMHSA, Office of Applied Studies, National Survey on Drug Use and Health, 2002, 2003, 2004, 2005, and 2006.

Table 2.2B. Alcohol Use in the Lifetime, Past Year, and Past Month; Binge and Heavy Alcohol Use in the Past Month; and Alcohol Dependence or Abuse in the Past Year among Persons Aged 12 to 20, by Age Group: Percentages, 2002-2006.

Age Group/Alcohol Measure	2002	2003	2004	2005	2006
AGE 12 TO 14					
Lifetime Use	24.9[b]	23.9[a]	23.6[a]	21.8	22.1
Past Year Use	17.6[a]	17.1	17.2	16.5	16.2
Past Month Use	7.4	7.3	7.1	6.4	6.6
Binge Alcohol Use[1]	3.6	3.4	3.3	3.1	3.1
Heavy Alcohol Use[1]	0.6	0.5	0.5	0.5	0.4
Past Year Dependence or Abuse[2]	2.0	2.1	2.0	1.7	1.7
AGE 15 TO 17					
Lifetime Use	62.7[b]	62.1[b]	60.8[b]	59.2	57.7
Past Year Use	52.3[b]	51.6[b]	50.9[a]	49.9	48.7
Past Month Use	28.3[b]	28.2[b]	28.3[b]	26.5	26.1
Binge Alcohol Use[1]	18.1	18.0	19.1[b]	16.6	17.1
Heavy Alcohol Use[1]	4.5	4.7	4.9	4.3	4.2
Past Year Dependence or Abuse[2]	10.0[a]	9.7	10.1[b]	9.3	8.8
AGE 18 TO 20					
Lifetime Use	81.7	81.6	80.8	79.9	80.7
Past Year Use	71.7	71.8	72.1	71.5	72.2
Past Month Use	51.0	51.5	51.1	51.1	51.6
Binge Alcohol Use[1]	36.4	36.2	36.8	36.1	36.2
Heavy Alcohol Use[1]	13.4	13.1	13.6	13.0	13.7
Past Year Dependence or Abuse[2]	17.0	16.0	16.8	16.9	16.5

*Low precision; no estimate reported.

[a] Difference between estimate and 2006 estimate is statistically significant at the 0.05 level.

[b] Difference between estimate and 2006 estimate is statistically significant at the 0.01 level.

[1] Binge Alcohol Use is defined as drinking five or more drinks on the same occasion (i.e., at the same time or within a couple of hours of each other) on at least 1 day in the past 30 days. Heavy Alcohol Use is defined as drinking five or more drinks on the same occasion on each of 5 or more days in the past 30 days; all heavy alcohol users are also binge alcohol users.

[2] Dependence or abuse is based on definitions found in the 4th edition of the *Diagnostic and Statistical Manual of Mental Disorders* (DSM-IV).

Source: SAMHSA, Office of Applied Studies, National Survey on Drug Use and Health, 2002, 2003, 2004, 2005, and 2006.

Table 3.1A. Alcohol Use in the Lifetime, Past Year, and Past Month; Binge and Heavy Alcohol Use in the Past Month; and Alcohol Dependence or Abuse in the Past Year among Persons Aged 12 to 20, by Demographic Characteristics: Numbers in Thousands, Annual Averages Based on 2002-2006.

Demographic Characteristic	Lifetime Use	Past Year Use	Past Month Use	Binge Use in Past Month[1]	Heavy Use in Past Month[1]	Dependence or Abuse in Past Year[2]
TOTAL GENDER	20,760	17,588	10,814	7,240	2,325	3,544
Male	10,605	8,904	5,694	4,188	1,537	1,985
Female	10,155	8,684	5,119	3,052	788	1,559
AGE						
12	441	263	94	38	3	20
13	954	682	257	109	16	67
14	1,530	1,185	526	266	45	151
15	2,178	1,765	858	499	100	280
16	2,577	2,174	1,171	749	181	420
17	2,845	2,427	1,422	984	288	504
18	3,478	3,082	2,062	1,461	507	671
19	3,313	2,930	2,119	1,527	572	719
20	3,445	3,081	2,305	1,607	612	712
GENDER/RACE/HISPANIC ORIGIN						
Male, White, Not Hispanic	6,851	5,938	3,967	3,013	1,214	1,381
Female, White, Not Hispanic	6,673	5,899	3,640	2,269	654	1,157
Male, Black, Not Hispanic	1,326	1,005	561	310	71	159
Female, Black, Not Hispanic	1,259	974	485	207	25	95
Male, Hispanic	1,849	1,494	911	684	201	334
Female, Hispanic	1,635	1,323	732	434	82	222

[*] Low precision; no estimate reported.

[1] Binge Alcohol Use is defined as drinking five or more drinks on the same occasion (i.e., at the same time or within a couple of hours of each other) on at least 1 day in the past 30 days. Heavy Alcohol Use is defined as drinking five or more drinks on the same occasion on each of 5 or more days in the past 30 days; all heavy alcohol users are also binge alcohol users.

[2] Dependence or abuse is based on definitions found in the 4th edition of the *Diagnostic and Statistical Manual of Mental Disorders* (DSM-IV).

Source: SAMHSA, Office of Applied Studies, National Survey on Drug Use and Health, 2002, 2003, 2004, 2005, and 2006.

Table 3.1B. Alcohol Use in the Lifetime, Past Year, and Past Month; Binge and Heavy Alcohol Use in the Past Month; and Alcohol Dependence or Abuse in the Past Year among Persons Aged 12 to 20, by Demographic Characteristics: Percentages, Annual Averages Based on 2002-2006.

Demographic Characteristic	Lifetime Use	Past Year Use	Past Month Use	Binge Use in Past Month[1]	Heavy Use in Past Month[1]	Dependence or Abuse in Past Year[2]
TOTAL	54.9	46.5	28.6	19.2	6.2	9.4
GENDER						
Male	54.8	46.0	29.4	21.6	7.9	10.3
Female	55.1	47.1	27.8	16.5	4.3	8.5
AGE						
12	11.0	6.5	2.3	0.9	0.1	0.5
13	22.4	16.0	6.0	2.6	0.4	1.6
14	35.6	27.6	12.3	6.2	1.0	3.5
15	50.8	41.2	20.0	11.6	2.3	6.5
16	61.4	51.8	27.9	17.8	4.3	10.0
17	69.7	59.4	34.8	24.1	7.1	12.3
18	76.5	67.8	45.4	32.2	11.2	14.8
19	81.3	71.9	52.0	37.5	14.0	17.7
20	85.5	76.4	57.2	39.9	15.2	17.7
GENDER/RACE/HISPANIC ORIGIN						
Male, White, Not Hispanic	57.5	49.8	33.3	25.3	10.2	11.6
Female, White, Not Hispanic	58.5	51.7	31.9	19.9	5.7	10.1
Male, Black, Not Hispanic	46.8	35.5	19.8	11.0	2.5	5.6
Female, Black, Not Hispanic	46.2	35.8	17.8	7.6	0.9	3.5
Male, Hispanic	55.4	44.7	27.3	20.5	6.0	10.0
Female, Hispanic	53.5	43.3	23.9	14.2	2.7	7.3

*Low precision; no estimate reported.

[1]Binge Alcohol Use is defined as drinking five or more drinks on the same occasion (i.e., at the same time or within a couple of hours of each other) on at least 1 day in the past 30 days. Heavy Alcohol Use is defined as drinking five or more drinks on the same occasion on each of 5 or more days in the past 30 days; all heavy alcohol users are also binge alcohol users.

[2] Dependence or abuse is based on definitions found in the 4th edition of the *Diagnostic and Statistical Manual of Mental Disorders* (DSM-IV).

Source: SAMHSA, Office of Applied Studies, National Survey on Drug Use and Health, 2002, 2003, 2004, 2005, and 2006.

Table 3.2A. Alcohol Use in the Lifetime, Past Year, and Past Month; Binge and Heavy Alcohol Use in the Past Month; and Alcohol Dependence or Abuse in the Past Year among Persons Aged 12 to 20, by Racial/Ethnic Subgroups: Numbers in Thousands, Annual Averages Based on 2002-2006.

Racial/Ethnic Subgroup	Lifetime Use	Past Year Use	Past Month Use	Binge Use in Past Month[1]	Heavy Use in Past Month[1]	Dependence or Abuse in Past Year[2]
TOTAL[3]	20,760	17,588	10,814	7,240	2,325	3,544
NOT HISPANIC OR LATINO[3]	17,276	14,771	9,171	6,122	2,043	2,988
White	13,523	11,837	7,607	5,282	1,868	2,538
Black or African American	2,585	1,979	1,046	517	96	255
American Indian or Alaska Native	139	112	67	51	11	37
Native Hawaiian or Other Pacific Islander	75	60	34	26	6	18
Asian	654	529	268	143	28	77
Chinese	131	106	48	22	6	12
Filipino	137	106	56	33	5	17
Japanese	34	30	17	9	2	2
Indian	89	79	44	24	3	11
Korean	83	70	40	22	4	16
Vietnamese	77	59	25	9	1	6
HISPANIC OR LATINO[3]	3,484	2,817	1,643	1,118	283	556
Mexican	2,420	1,938	1,113	780	201	396
Puerto Rican	391	321	176	114	28	48
Central or South American	374	301	182	123	23	60
Cuban	107	94	62	33	10	16

*Low precision; no estimate reported.

[1] Binge Alcohol Use is defined as drinking five or more drinks on the same occasion (i.e., at the same time or within a couple of hours of each other) on at least 1 day in the past 30 days. Heavy Alcohol Use is defined as drinking five or more drinks on the same occasion on each of 5 or more days in the past 30 days; all heavy alcohol users are also binge alcohol users.

[2] Dependence or abuse is based on definitions found in the 4th edition of the *Diagnostic and Statistical Manual of Mental Disorders* (DSM-IV).

[3] Totals include data from respondents reporting racial/ethnic subgroups not shown, as well as respondents reporting more than one subgroup.

Source: SAMHSA, Office of Applied Studies, National Survey on Drug Use and Health, 2002, 2003, 2004, 2005, and 2006.

Table 3.2B. Alcohol Use in the Lifetime, Past Year, and Past Month; Binge and Heavy Alcohol Use in the Past Month; and Alcohol Dependence or Abuse in the Past Year among Persons Aged 12 to 20, by Racial/Ethnic Subgroups: Percentages, Annual Averages Based on 2002-2006.

Racial/Ethnic Subgroup	Lifetime Use	Past Year Use	Past Month Use	Binge Use in Past Month[1]	Heavy Use in Past Month[1]	Dependence or Abuse in Past Year[2]
TOTAL[3]	54.9	46.5	28.6	19.2	6.2	9.4
NOT HISPANIC OR LATINO[3]	55.0	47.0	29.2	19.5	6.5	9.5
White	58.0	50.8	32.6	22.6	8.0	10.9
Black or African American	46.5	35.6	18.8	9.3	1.7	4.6
American Indian or Alaska Native	56.7	45.5	27.2	20.8	4.5	14.9
Native Hawaiian or Other Pacific Islander	53.4	42.6	24.3	18.8	4.0	12.7
Asian	41.7	33.7	17.1	9.1	1.8	4.9
Chinese	41.9	33.9	15.2	7.2	1.9	3.9
Filipino	49.0	37.9	20.0	12.0	1.9	6.1
Japanese	47.7	42.6	24.0	12.9	2.7	3.0
Indian	26.7	23.6	13.1	7.1	1.0	3.4
Korean	48.3	40.6	23.4	12.9	2.2	9.3
Vietnamese	46.6	36.1	14.9	5.2	0.9	3.9
HISPANIC OR LATINO[3]	54.4	44.0	25.7	17.5	4.4	8.7
Mexican	54.1	43.3	24.9	17.4	4.5	8.9
Puerto Rican	55.5	45.6	25.0	16.2	4.1	6.8
Central or South American	53.3	42.9	26.0	17.6	3.4	8.5
Cuban	55.9	48.8	32.0	17.4	5.3	8.1

*Low precision; no estimate reported.

[1] Binge Alcohol Use is defined as drinking five or more drinks on the same occasion (i.e., at the same time or within a couple of hours of each other) on at least 1 day in the past 30 days. Heavy Alcohol Use is defined as drinking five or more drinks on the same occasion on each of 5 or more days in the past 30 days; all heavy alcohol users are also binge alcohol users.

[2] Dependence or abuse is based on definitions found in the 4th edition of the *Diagnostic and Statistical Manual of Mental Disorders* (DSM-IV).

[3] Totals include data from respondents reporting racial/ethnic subgroups not shown, as well as respondents reporting more than one subgroup.

Source: SAMHSA, Office of Applied Studies, National Survey on Drug Use and Health, 2002, 2003, 2004, 2005, and 2006.

Table 3.3A. Alcohol Use in the Lifetime, Past Year, and Past Month; Binge and Heavy Alcohol Use in the Past Month; and Alcohol Dependence or Abuse in the Past Year among Persons Aged 12 to 14, by Demographic Characteristics: Numbers in Thousands, Annual Averages Based on 2002-2006.

Demographic Characteristic	Lifetime Use	Past Year Use	Past Month Use	Binge Use in Past Month[1]	Heavy Use in Past Month[1]	Dependence or Abuse in Past Year[2]
TOTAL	2,924	2,131	877	412	64	238
GENDER						
Male	1,506	1,025	403	200	32	103
Female	1,418	1,106	474	212	32	135
HISPANIC ORIGIN AND RACE						
Not Hispanic or Latino	2,377	1,732	705	318	47	190
White	1,829	1,379	571	255	40	157
Black or African American	399	245	91	40	3	20
American Indian or Alaska Native	24	19	9	7	1	4
Native Hawaiian or Other Pacific Islander	6	6	3	2	0	1
Asian	62	41	15	7	1	3
Two or More Races	57	42	16	7	2	5
Hispanic or Latino	548	398	172	94	17	48
GENDER/RACE/HISPANIC ORIGIN						
Male, White, Not Hispanic	943	663	260	121	17	64
Female, White, Not Hispanic	886	716	311	133	23	93
Male, Black, Not Hispanic	198	113	42	19	2	9
Female, Black, Not Hispanic	201	132	49	22	1	12
Male, Hispanic	286	195	83	50	11	25
Female, Hispanic	262	204	89	44	6	23

*Low precision; no estimate reported.

[1] Binge Alcohol Use is defined as drinking five or more drinks on the same occasion (i.e., at the same time or within a couple of hours of each other) on at least 1 day in the past 30 days. Heavy Alcohol Use is defined as drinking five or more drinks on the same occasion on each of 5 or more days in the past 30 days; all heavy alcohol users are also binge alcohol users.

[2] Dependence or abuse is based on definitions found in the 4th edition of the *Diagnostic and Statistical Manual of Mental Disorders* (DSM-IV).

Source: SAMHSA, Office of Applied Studies, National Survey on Drug Use and Health, 2002, 2003, 2004, 2005, and 2006.

Table 3.3B. Alcohol Use in the Lifetime, Past Year, and Past Month; Binge and Heavy Alcohol Use in the Past Month; and Alcohol Dependence or Abuse in the Past Year among Persons Aged 12 to 14, by Demographic Characteristics: Percentages, Annual Averages Based on 2002- 2006.

Demographic Characteristic	Lifetime Use	Past Year Use	Past Month Use	Binge Use in Past Month[1]	Heavy Use in Past Month[1]	Dependence or Abuse in Past Year[2]
TOTAL	23.3	16.9	7.0	3.3	0.5	1.9
GENDER						
Male	23.4	15.9	6.3	3.1	0.5	1.6
Female	23.1	18.0	7.7	3.5	0.5	2.2
HISPANIC ORIGIN AND RACE						
Not Hispanic or Latino	22.9	16.7	6.8	3.1	0.5	1.8
White	24.1	18.2	7.5	3.4	0.5	2.1
Black or African American	20.6	12.7	4.7	2.1	0.2	1.0
American Indian or Alaska Native	27.7	22.0	10.3	8.1	1.0	4.2
Native Hawaiian or Other Pacific Islander	15.1	14.4	6.4	4.6	0.1	1.8
Asian	12.8	8.5	3.2	1.5	0.1	0.7
Two or More Races	25.2	18.3	7.2	3.1	0.8	2.3
Hispanic or Latino	24.8	18.1	7.8	4.3	0.8	2.2
GENDER/RACE/HISPANIC ORIGIN						
Male, White, Not Hispanic	24.3	17.1	6.7	3.1	0.4	1.6
Female, White, Not Hispanic	23.8	19.2	8.3	3.6	0.6	2.5
Male, Black, Not Hispanic	20.1	11.5	4.2	1.9	0.2	0.9
Female, Black, Not Hispanic	21.2	14.0	5.2	2.3	0.1	1.2
Male, Hispanic	24.9	17.0	7.2	4.4	1.0	2.2
Female, Hispanic	24.7	19.2	8.4	4.1	0.6	2.2

*Low precision; no estimate reported.

[1] Binge Alcohol Use is defined as drinking five or more drinks on the same occasion (i.e., at the same time or within a couple of hours of each other) on at least 1 day in the past 30 days. Heavy Alcohol Use is defined as drinking five or more drinks on the same occasion on each of 5 or more days in the past 30 days; all heavy alcohol users are also binge alcohol users.

[2] Dependence or abuse is based on definitions found in the 4th edition of the *Diagnostic and Statistical Manual of Mental Disorders* (DSM-IV).

Source: SAMHSA, Office of Applied Studies, National Survey on Drug Use and Health, 2002, 2003, 2004, 2005, and 2006.

Table 3.4A. Alcohol Use in the Lifetime, Past Year, and Past Month; Binge and Heavy Alcohol Use in the Past Month; and Alcohol Dependence or Abuse in the Past Year among Persons Aged 15 to 17, by Demographic Characteristics: Numbers in Thousands, Annual Averages Based on 2002-2006.

Demographic Characteristic	Lifetime Use	Past Year Use	Past Month Use	Binge Use in Past Month[1]	Heavy Use in Past Month[1]	Dependence or Abuse in Past Year[2]
TOTAL	7,599	6,365	3,451	2,232	569	1,204
GENDER						
Male	3,819	3,142	1,751	1,217	354	604
Female	3,780	3,223	1,700	1,014	216	600
HISPANIC ORIGIN AND RACE						
Not Hispanic or Latino	6,334	5,340	2,922	1,885	495	1,009
White	4,999	4,339	2,468	1,650	458	873
Black or African American	932	679	310	147	20	71
American Indian or Alaska Native	52	40	21	16	4	15
Native Hawaiian or Other Pacific Islander	26	20	8	4	1	3
Asian	213	168	66	33	4	21
Two or More Races	112	93	49	34	8	25
Hispanic or Latino	1,265	1,025	529	347	75	195
GENDER/RACE/HISPANIC ORIGIN						
Male, White, Not Hispanic	2,516	2,149	1,260	905	281	434
Female, White, Not Hispanic	2,483	2,190	1,209	745	176	439
Male, Black, Not Hispanic	472	337	160	84	14	42
Female, Black, Not Hispanic	460	342	150	63	5	30
Male, Hispanic	627	503	263	184	48	97
Female, Hispanic	638	522	265	163	27	97

*Low precision; no estimate reported.

[1] Binge Alcohol Use is defined as drinking five or more drinks on the same occasion (i.e., at the same time or within a couple of hours of each other) on at least 1 day in the past 30 days. Heavy Alcohol Use is defined as drinking five or more drinks on the same occasion on each of 5 or more days in the past 30 days; all heavy alcohol users are also binge alcohol users.

[2] Dependence or abuse is based on definitions found in the 4th edition of the *Diagnostic and Statistical Manual of Mental Disorders* (DSM-IV).

Source: SAMHSA, Office of Applied Studies, National Survey on Drug Use and Health, 2002, 2003, 2004, 2005, and 2006.

Table 3.4B. Alcohol Use in the Lifetime, Past Year, and Past Month; Binge and Heavy Alcohol Use in the Past Month; and Alcohol Dependence or Abuse in the Past Year among Persons Aged 15 to 17, by Demographic Characteristics: Percentages, Annual Averages Based on 2002-2006.

Demographic Characteristic	Lifetime Use	Past Year Use	Past Month Use	Binge Use in Past Month[1]	Heavy Use in Past Month[1]	Dependence or Abuse in Past Year[2]
TOTAL	60.5	50.6	27.5	17.8	4.5	9.6
GENDER						
Male	59.6	49.0	27.3	19.0	5.5	9.4
Female	61.4	52.3	27.6	16.5	3.5	9.7
HISPANIC ORIGIN AND RACE						
Not Hispanic or Latino	60.1	50.7	27.7	17.9	4.7	9.6
White	63.7	55.3	31.4	21.0	5.8	11.1
Black or African American	50.3	36.6	16.7	7.9	1.1	3.8
American Indian or Alaska Native	65.2	50.3	26.3	20.0	4.7	19.0
Native Hawaiian or Other Pacific Islander	58.5	46.7	17.4	9.1	3.0	7.3
Asian	40.3	31.7	12.4	6.3	0.8	3.9
Two or More Races	62.0	51.6	27.0	18.8	4.7	13.8
Hispanic or Latino	62.3	50.5	26.0	17.1	3.7	9.6
GENDER/RACE/HISPANIC ORIGIN						
Male, White, Not Hispanic	62.4	53.3	31.2	22.4	7.0	10.8
Female, White, Not Hispanic	65.0	57.4	31.7	19.5	4.6	11.5
Male, Black, Not Hispanic	50.2	35.9	17.0	8.9	1.5	4.4
Female, Black, Not Hispanic	50.3	37.4	16.5	6.9	0.6	3.2
Male, Hispanic	61.6	49.5	25.9	18.1	4.7	9.6
Female, Hispanic	63.0	51.6	26.2	16.1	2.7	9.6

*Low precision; no estimate reported.

[1] Binge Alcohol Use is defined as drinking five or more drinks on the same occasion (i.e., at the same time or within a couple of hours of each other) on at least 1 day in the past 30 days. Heavy Alcohol Use is defined as drinking five or more drinks on the same occasion on each of 5 or more days in the past 30 days; all heavy alcohol users are also binge alcohol users.

[2] Dependence or abuse is based on definitions found in the 4th edition of the *Diagnostic and Statistical Manual of Mental Disorders* (DSM-IV).

Source: SAMHSA, Office of Applied Studies, National Survey on Drug Use and Health, 2002, 2003, 2004, 2005, and 2006.

Table 3.5A. Alcohol Use in the Lifetime, Past Year, and Past Month; Binge and Heavy Alcohol Use in the Past Month; and Alcohol Dependence or Abuse in the Past Year among Persons Aged 18 to 20, by Demographic Characteristics: Numbers in Thousands, Annual Averages Based on 2002-2006.

Demographic Characteristic	Lifetime Use	Past Year Use	Past Month Use	Binge Use in Past Month[1]	Heavy Use in Past Month[1]	Dependence or Abuse in Past Year[2]
TOTAL	10,237	9,092	6,486	4,596	1,692	2,103
GENDER						
Male	5,280	4,736	3,541	2,770	1,152	1,278
Female	4,957	4,356	2,945	1,825	540	824
HISPANIC ORIGIN AND RACE						
Not Hispanic or Latino	8,566	7,698	5,544	3,919	1,501	1,789
White	6,696	6,119	4,567	3,377	1,370	1,508
Black or African American	1,254	1,054	645	330	73	163
American Indian or Alaska Native	63	52	37	28	6	18
Native Hawaiian or Other Pacific Islander	44	34	24	21	4	14
Asian	379	320	187	102	24	53
Two or More Races	131	119	85	62	24	34
Hispanic or Latino	1,671	1,394	942	677	191	313
GENDER/RACE/HISPANIC ORIGIN						
Male, White, Not Hispanic	3,392	3,126	2,447	1,986	915	883
Female, White, Not Hispanic	3,304	2,993	2,121	1,390	455	625
Male, Black, Not Hispanic	656	555	359	208	54	109
Female, Black, Not Hispanic	598	499	285	122	18	54
Male, Hispanic	937	797	565	450	142	212
Female, Hispanic	734	597	377	227	49	101

*Low precision; no estimate reported.

[1] Binge Alcohol Use is defined as drinking five or more drinks on the same occasion (i.e., at the same time or within a couple of hours of each other) on at least 1 day in the past 30 days. Heavy Alcohol Use is defined as drinking five or more drinks on the same occasion on each of 5 or more days in the past 30 days; all heavy alcohol users are also binge alcohol users.

[2] Dependence or abuse is based on definitions found in the 4th edition of the *Diagnostic and Statistical Manual of Mental Disorders* (DSM-IV).

Source: SAMHSA, Office of Applied Studies, National Survey on Drug Use and Health, 2002, 2003, 2004, 2005, and 2006.

Table 3.5B. Alcohol Use in the Lifetime, Past Year, and Past Month; Binge and Heavy Alcohol Use in the Past Month; and Alcohol Dependence or Abuse in the Past Year among Persons Aged 18 to 20, by Demographic Characteristics: Percentages, Annual Averages Based on 2002- 2006.

Demographic Characteristic	Lifetime Use	Past Year Use	Past Month Use	Binge Use in Past Month[1]	Heavy Use in Past Month[1]	Dependence or Abuse in Past Year[2]
TOTAL	80.9	71.9	51.3	36.3	13.4	16.6
GENDER						
Male	81.2	72.8	54.4	42.6	17.7	19.6
Female	80.7	70.9	47.9	29.7	8.8	13.4
HISPANIC ORIGIN AND RACE						
Not Hispanic or Latino	81.7	73.4	52.9	37.4	14.3	17.1
White	85.1	77.7	58.0	42.9	17.4	19.2
Black or African American	70.7	59.5	36.4	18.6	4.1	9.2
American Indian or Alaska Native	79.1	65.9	46.3	35.4	7.9	22.1
Native Hawaiian or Other Pacific Islander	75.9	58.8	41.9	35.9	7.4	24.5
Asian	68.5	57.8	33.7	18.4	4.3	9.6
Two or More Races	86.0	78.2	55.6	40.5	15.9	22.4
Hispanic or Latino	77.3	64.5	43.5	31.3	8.8	14.5
GENDER/RACE/HISPANIC ORIGIN						
Male, White, Not Hispanic	84.5	77.9	61.0	49.5	22.8	22.0
Female, White, Not Hispanic	85.6	77.6	55.0	36.0	11.8	16.2
Male, Black, Not Hispanic	71.9	60.9	39.4	22.8	5.9	12.0
Female, Black, Not Hispanic	69.4	58.0	33.1	14.1	2.1	6.3
Male, Hispanic	79.6	67.7	48.0	38.2	12.1	18.0
Female, Hispanic	74.5	60.6	38.2	23.0	5.0	10.2

*Low precision; no estimate reported.

[1]Binge Alcohol Use is defined as drinking five or more drinks on the same occasion (i.e., at the same time or within a couple of hours of each other) on at least 1 day in the past 30 days. Heavy Alcohol Use is defined as drinking five or more drinks on the same occasion on each of 5 or more days in the past 30 days; all heavy alcohol users are also binge alcohol users.

[2] Dependence or abuse is based on definitions found in the 4th edition of the *Diagnostic and Statistical Manual of Mental Disorders* (DSM-IV).

Source: SAMHSA, Office of Applied Studies, National Survey on Drug Use and Health, 2002, 2003, 2004, 2005, and 2006.

Table 3.6A. Alcohol Use in the Lifetime, Past Year, and Past Month; Binge and Heavy Alcohol Use in the Past Month; and Alcohol Dependence or Abuse in the Past Year among Persons Aged 12 to 20, by Family Income and Geographic Characteristics: Numbers in Thousands, Annual Averages Based on 2002-2006.

Family Income/ Geographic Characteristic	Lifetime Use	Past Year Use	Past Month Use	Binge Use in Past Month[1]	Heavy Use in Past Month[1]	Dependence or Abuse in Past Year[2]
TOTAL	20,760	17,588	10,814	7,240	2,325	3,544
FAMILY INCOME						
Less Than $20,000	5,365	4,504	3,002	2,102	767	1,030
$20,000 - $49,999	6,817	5,619	3,274	2,136	602	1,056
$50,000 - $74,999	3,408	2,911	1,726	1,132	326	555
$75,000 or More	5,171	4,555	2,812	1,870	631	903
GEOGRAPHIC REGION						
Northeast	3,890	3,401	2,156	1,445	481	645
Midwest	4,881	4,225	2,664	1,875	635	917
South	7,246	6,014	3,584	2,330	743	1,135
West	4,743	3,949	2,410	1,589	467	847
COUNTY TYPE						
Metropolitan	17,120	14,527	8,942	5,914	1,888	2,872
Large Metropolitan	10,680	9,066	5,465	3,518	1,048	1,686
Small Metropolitan	6,440	5,461	3,477	2,396	840	1,187
250K - 1 Mil. Pop.	4,171	3,522	2,213	1,513	519	749
< 250K Pop.	2,268	1,939	1,264	883	321	437
Nonmetropolitan	3,640	3,061	1,872	1,326	437	672
Urbanized (Urban Pop. > 20K)	1,552	1,323	830	589	218	309
Rural (Urban Pop. < 20K)	2,089	1,739	1,042	737	219	363
Urban Pop. 2,500-19,999	1,730	1,449	874	613	180	296
Urban Pop. < 2,500	359	289	168	123	39	67

*Low precision; no estimate reported.

[1] Binge Alcohol Use is defined as drinking five or more drinks on the same occasion (i.e., at the same time or within a couple of hours of each other) on at least 1 day in the past 30 days. Heavy Alcohol Use is defined as drinking five or more drinks on the same occasion on each of 5 or more days in the past 30 days; all heavy alcohol users are also binge alcohol users.

[2] Dependence or abuse is based on definitions found in the 4th edition of the *Diagnostic and Statistical Manual of Mental Disorders* (DSM-IV).

Source: SAMHSA, Office of Applied Studies, National Survey on Drug Use and Health, 2002, 2003, 2004, 2005, and 2006.

Table 3.6B. Alcohol Use in the Lifetime, Past Year, and Past Month; Binge and Heavy Alcohol Use in the Past Month; and Alcohol Dependence or Abuse in the Past Year among Persons Aged 12 to 20, by Family Income and Geographic Characteristics: Percentages, Annual Averages Based on 2002-2006.

Family Income/ Geographic Characteristic	Lifetime Use	Past Year Use	Past Month Use	Binge Use in Past Month[1]	Heavy Use in Past Month[1]	Dependence or Abuse in Past Year[2]
TOTAL	54.9	46.5	28.6	19.2	6.2	9.4
FAMILY INCOME						
Less Than $20,000	60.6	50.9	33.9	23.7	8.7	11.6
$20,000 - $49,999	54.2	44.7	26.0	17.0	4.8	8.4
$50,000 - $74,999	52.2	44.6	26.4	17.3	5.0	8.5
$75,000 or More	52.6	46.3	28.6	19.0	6.4	9.2
GEOGRAPHIC REGION						
Northeast	57.5	50.3	31.9	21.4	7.1	9.5
Midwest	56.8	49.2	31.0	21.8	7.4	10.7
South	53.7	44.6	26.6	17.3	5.5	8.4
West	53.0	44.2	26.9	17.8	5.2	9.5
COUNTY TYPE						
Metropolitan	54.5	46.2	28.5	18.8	6.0	9.1
Large Metropolitan	53.7	45.6	27.5	17.7	5.3	8.5
Small Metropolitan	55.8	47.3	30.1	20.8	7.3	10.3
250K - 1 Mil. Pop.	54.6	46.1	29.0	19.8	6.8	9.8
< 250K Pop.	58.1	49.6	32.4	22.6	8.2	11.2
Nonmetropolitan	57.2	48.1	29.4	20.8	6.9	10.6
Urbanized (Urban Pop. > 20K)	58.4	49.8	31.3	22.2	8.2	11.7
Rural (Urban Pop. < 20K)	56.2	46.8	28.1	19.8	5.9	9.8
Urban Pop. 2,500-19,999	56.3	47.2	28.5	20.0	5.9	9.6
Urban Pop. < 2,500	55.8	45.0	26.1	19.2	6.0	10.5

*Low precision; no estimate reported.

[1] Binge Alcohol Use is defined as drinking five or more drinks on the same occasion (i.e., at the same time or within a couple of hours of each other) on at least 1 day in the past 30 days. Heavy Alcohol Use is defined as drinking five or more drinks on the same occasion on each of 5 or more days in the past 30 days; all heavy alcohol users are also binge alcohol users.

[2] Dependence or abuse is based on definitions found in the 4th edition of the *Diagnostic and Statistical Manual of Mental Disorders* (DSM-IV).

Source: SAMHSA, Office of Applied Studies, National Survey on Drug Use and Health, 2002, 2003, 2004, 2005, and 2006.

Table 3.7A. Alcohol Use in the Lifetime, Past Year, and Past Month; Binge and Heavy Alcohol Use in the Past Month; and Alcohol Dependence or Abuse in the Past Year among Persons Aged 12 to 20 Residing in Metropolitan Counties, by Demographic Characteristics: Numbers in Thousands, Annual Averages Based on 2002-2006.

Demographic Characteristic	Lifetime Use	Past Year Use	Past Month Use	Binge Use in Past Month[1]	Heavy Use in Past Month[1]	Dependence or Abuse in Past Year[2]
TOTAL	17,120	14,527	8,942	5,914	1,888	2,872
AGE						
12 to 14	2,375	1,728	700	320	47	183
15 to 17	6,251	5,244	2,824	1,802	461	967
18 to 20	8,494	7,555	5,417	3,792	1,381	1,722
GENDER						
Male	8,729	7,329	4,673	3,396	1,240	1,611
Female	8,391	7,198	4,269	2,517	648	1,261
HISPANIC ORIGIN AND RACE						
Not Hispanic or Latino	13,909	11,933	7,438	4,900	1,643	2,370
White	10,637	9,380	6,081	4,191	1,495	1,995
Black or African American	2,266	1,731	911	441	83	216
American Indian or Alaska Native	65	52	31	23	5	16
Native Hawaiian or Other Pacific Islander	65	52	30	23	5	15
Asian	625	505	257	136	27	74
Two or More Races	251	213	128	87	29	54
Hispanic or Latino	3,211	2,594	1,503	1,014	245	502

*Low precision; no estimate reported.

Note: Metropolitan Counties include both large metropolitan areas (≥ 1 million population) and small metropolitan areas (<1 million population). For more detailed definitions of county types, see Section 1.5 in Chapter 1.

[1] Binge Alcohol Use is defined as drinking five or more drinks on the same occasion (i.e., at the same time or within a couple of hours of each other) on at least 1 day in the past 30 days. Heavy Alcohol Use is defined as drinking five or more drinks on the same occasion on each of 5 or more days in the past 30 days; all heavy alcohol users are also binge alcohol users.

[2] Dependence or abuse is based on definitions found in the 4th edition of the *Diagnostic and Statistical Manual of Mental Disorders* (DSM-IV).

Source: SAMHSA, Office of Applied Studies, National Survey on Drug Use and Health, 2002, 2003, 2004, 2005, and 2006.

Table 3.7B. Alcohol Use in the Lifetime, Past Year, and Past Month; Binge and Heavy Alcohol Use in the Past Month; and Alcohol Dependence or Abuse in the Past Year among Persons Aged 12 to 20 Residing in Metropolitan Counties, by Demographic Characteristics: Percentages, Annual Averages Based on 2002-2006.

Demographic Characteristic	Lifetime Use	Past Year Use	Past Month Use	Binge Use in Past Month[1]	Heavy Use in Past Month[1]	Dependence or Abuse in Past Year[2]
TOTAL	54.5	46.2	28.5	18.8	6.0	9.1
AGE						
12 to 14	22.7	16.5	6.7	3.1	0.4	1.7
15 to 17	60.0	50.3	27.1	17.3	4.4	9.3
18 to 20	80.8	71.9	51.5	36.1	13.1	16.4
GENDER						
Male	54.3	45.6	29.1	21.1	7.7	10.0
Female	54.7	46.9	27.8	16.4	4.2	8.2
HISPANIC ORIGIN AND RACE						
Not Hispanic or Latino	54.6	46.8	29.2	19.2	6.4	9.3
White	58.0	51.2	33.2	22.9	8.2	10.9
Black or African American	46.1	35.2	18.5	9.0	1.7	4.4
American Indian or Alaska Native	54.9	44.0	26.5	19.1	4.1	13.3
Native Hawaiian or Other Pacific Islander	52.2	41.5	23.8	18.3	3.7	12.1
Asian	41.3	33.3	17.0	9.0	1.8	4.9
Two or More Races	53.5	45.4	27.4	18.5	6.3	11.6
Hispanic or Latino	54.0	43.6	25.3	17.0	4.1	8.4

*Low precision; no estimate reported.

Note: Metropolitan Counties include both large metropolitan areas (≥ 1 million population) and small metropolitan areas (<1 million population). For more detailed definitions of county types, see Section 1.5 in Chapter 1.

[1] Binge Alcohol Use is defined as drinking five or more drinks on the same occasion (i.e., at the same time or within a couple of hours of each other) on at least 1 day in the past 30 days. Heavy Alcohol Use is defined as drinking five or more drinks on the same occasion on each of 5 or more days in the past 30 days; all heavy alcohol users are also binge alcohol users.

[2] Dependence or abuse is based on definitions found in the 4th edition of the *Diagnostic and Statistical Manual of Mental Disorders* (DSM-IV).

Source: SAMHSA, Office of Applied Studies, National Survey on Drug Use and Health, 2002, 2003, 2004, 2005, and 2006.

Table 3.8A. Alcohol Use in the Lifetime, Past Year, and Past Month; Binge and Heavy Alcohol Use in the Past Month; and Alcohol Dependence or Abuse in the Past Year among Persons Aged 12 to 20 Residing in Urbanized Nonmetropolitan Counties, by Demographic Characteristics: Numbers in Thousands, Annual Averages Based on 2002-2006.

Demographic Characteristic	Lifetime Use	Past Year Use	Past Month Use	Binge Use in Past Month[1]	Heavy Use in Past Month[1]	Dependence or Abuse in Past Year[2]
TOTAL	1,552	1,323	830	589	218	309
AGE						
12 to 14	217	159	69	32	6	22
15 to 17	537	445	240	165	44	94
18 to 20	798	719	521	392	168	193
GENDER						
Male	799	677	449	350	147	170
Female	753	646	381	239	71	139
HISPANIC ORIGIN AND RACE						
Not Hispanic or Latino	1,427	1,221	768	544	200	285
White	1,211	1,049	673	481	186	247
Black or African American	142	111	62	39	7	21
American Indian or Alaska Native	21	16	9	8	2	7
Native Hawaiian or Other Pacific Islander	*	*	*	*	*	*
Asian	15	13	8	5	*	3
Two or More Races	31	26	13	9	3	5
Hispanic or Latino	125	101	62	45	19	24

*Low precision; no estimate reported.

Note: Urbanized Nonmetropolitan Counties include counties containing populations of 20,000 or more in urbanized areas. For more detailed definitions of county types, see Section 1.5 in Chapter 1.

[1] Binge Alcohol Use is defined as drinking five or more drinks on the same occasion (i.e., at the same time or within a couple of hours of each other) on at least 1 day in the past 30 days. Heavy Alcohol Use is defined as drinking five or more drinks on the same occasion on each of 5 or more days in the past 30 days; all heavy alcohol users are also binge alcohol users.

[2] Dependence or abuse is based on definitions found in the 4th edition of the *Diagnostic and Statistical Manual of Mental Disorders* (DSM-IV).

Source: SAMHSA, Office of Applied Studies, National Survey on Drug Use and Health, 2002, 2003, 2004, 2005, and 2006.

Table 3.8B. Alcohol Use in the Lifetime, Past Year, and Past Month; Binge and Heavy Alcohol Use in the Past Month; and Alcohol Dependence or Abuse in the Past Year among Persons Aged 12 to 20 Residing in Urbanized Nonmetropolitan Counties, by Demographic Characteristics: Percentages, Annual Averages Based on 2002-2006.

Demographic Characteristic	Lifetime Use	Past Year Use	Past Month Use	Binge Use in Past Month[1]	Heavy Use in Past Month[1]	Dependence or Abuse in Past Year[2]
TOTAL	58.4	49.8	31.3	22.2	8.2	11.7
AGE						
12 to 14	25.5	18.7	8.1	3.7	0.7	2.5
15 to 17	62.9	52.1	28.1	19.3	5.2	11.1
18 to 20	83.8	75.5	54.8	41.2	17.7	20.3
GENDER						
Male	58.7	49.7	33.0	25.7	10.8	12.5
Female	58.2	49.9	29.4	18.5	5.5	10.7
HISPANIC ORIGIN AND RACE						
Not Hispanic or Latino	58.4	50.0	31.5	22.3	8.2	11.7
White	59.4	51.4	33.0	23.6	9.1	12.1
Black or African American	52.3	41.1	23.0	14.2	2.4	7.8
American Indian or Alaska Native	58.2	46.0	24.8	21.3	5.2	19.6
Native Hawaiian or Other Pacific Islander	*	*	*	*	*	*
Asian	49.2	41.6	25.5	15.6	*	9.7
Two or More Races	57.0	47.5	23.9	17.3	5.3	9.4
Hispanic or Latino	58.7	47.7	29.1	21.1	8.7	11.3

*Low precision; no estimate reported.

Note: Urbanized Nonmetropolitan Counties include counties containing populations of 20,000 or more in urbanized areas. For more detailed definitions of county types, see Section 1.5 in Chapter 1.

[1] Binge Alcohol Use is defined as drinking five or more drinks on the same occasion (i.e., at the same time or within a couple of hours of each other) on at least 1 day in the past 30 days. Heavy Alcohol Use is defined as drinking five or more drinks on the same occasion on each of 5 or more days in the past 30 days; all heavy alcohol users are also binge alcohol users.

[2] Dependence or abuse is based on definitions found in the 4th edition of the *Diagnostic and Statistical Manual of Mental Disorders* (DSM-IV).

Source: SAMHSA, Office of Applied Studies, National Survey on Drug Use and Health, 2002, 2003, 2004, 2005, and 2006.

Table 3.9A. Alcohol Use in the Lifetime, Past Year, and Past Month; Binge and Heavy Alcohol Use in the Past Month; and Alcohol Dependence or Abuse in the Past Year among Persons Aged 12 to 20 Residing in Rural Counties, by Demographic Characteristics: Numbers in Thousands, Annual Averages Based on 2002-2006.

Demographic Characteristic	Lifetime Use	Past Year Use	Past Month Use	Binge Use in Past Month[1]	Heavy Use in Past Month[1]	Dependence or Abuse in Past Year[2]
TOTAL	2,089	1,739	1,042	737	219	363
AGE						
12 to 14	332	243	108	60	11	33
15 to 17	812	676	386	265	65	143
18 to 20	945	819	548	411	143	187
GENDER						
Male	1,077	898	573	442	150	204
Female	1,011	840	469	295	69	159
HISPANIC ORIGIN AND RACE						
Not Hispanic or Latino	1,941	1,616	964	678	200	333
White	1,676	1,407	853	610	186	295
Black or African American	177	137	73	38	7	18
American Indian or Alaska Native	54	44	27	21	4	14
Native Hawaiian or Other Pacific Islander	*	*	*	*	*	*
Asian	*	*	*	*	*	*
Two or More Races	19	15	8	6	2	5
Hispanic or Latino	148	123	78	59	19	30

*Low precision; no estimate reported.

Note: Rural Counties include nonmetropolitan counties containing populations of fewer than 20,000 in urbanized areas. For more detailed definitions of county types, see Section 1.5 in Chapter 1.

[1] Binge Alcohol Use is defined as drinking five or more drinks on the same occasion (i.e., at the same time or within a couple of hours of each other) on at least 1 day in the past 30 days. Heavy Alcohol Use is defined as drinking five or more drinks on the same occasion on each of 5 or more days in the past 30 days; all heavy alcohol users are also binge alcohol users.

[2] Dependence or abuse is based on definitions found in the 4th edition of the *Diagnostic and Statistical Manual of Mental Disorders* (DSM-IV).

Source: SAMHSA, Office of Applied Studies, National Survey on Drug Use and Health, 2002, 2003, 2004, 2005, and 2006.

Table 3.9B. Alcohol Use in the Lifetime, Past Year, and Past Month; Binge and Heavy Alcohol Use in the Past Month; and Alcohol Dependence or Abuse in the Past Year among Persons Aged 12 to 20 Residing in Rural Counties, by Demographic Characteristics: Percentages, Annual Averages Based on 2002-2006.

Demographic Characteristic	Lifetime Use	Past Year Use	Past Month Use	Binge Use in Past Month[1]	Heavy Use in Past Month[1]	Dependence or Abuse in Past Year[2]
TOTAL	56.2	46.8	28.1	19.8	5.9	9.8
AGE						
12 to 14	26.8	19.7	8.7	4.9	0.9	2.7
15 to 17	62.9	52.4	30.0	20.6	5.0	11.1
18 to 20	79.6	68.9	46.1	34.6	12.0	15.7
GENDER						
Male	56.3	47.0	30.0	23.1	7.8	10.7
Female	56.1	46.6	26.0	16.4	3.8	8.8
HISPANIC ORIGIN AND RACE						
Not Hispanic or Latino	55.9	46.5	27.8	19.5	5.8	9.6
White	56.8	47.7	28.9	20.7	6.3	10.0
Black or African American	48.0	37.0	19.6	10.4	1.8	4.9
American Indian or Alaska Native	58.4	47.2	29.0	22.9	4.7	15.1
Native Hawaiian or Other Pacific Islander	*	*	*	*	*	*
Asian	*	*	*	*	*	*
Two or More Races	49.0	40.8	22.3	16.8	5.9	12.3
Hispanic or Latino	61.7	51.2	32.4	24.7	7.9	12.5

*Low precision; no estimate reported.

Note: Rural Counties include nonmetropolitan counties containing populations of fewer than 20,000 in urbanized areas. For more detailed definitions of county types, see Section 1.5 in Chapter 1.

[1] Binge Alcohol Use is defined as drinking five or more drinks on the same occasion (i.e., at the same time or within a couple of hours of each other) on at least 1 day in the past 30 days. Heavy Alcohol Use is defined as drinking five or more drinks on the same occasion on each of 5 or more days in the past 30 days; all heavy alcohol users are also binge alcohol users.

[2] Dependence or abuse is based on definitions found in the 4th edition of the *Diagnostic and Statistical Manual of Mental Disorders* (DSM-IV).

Source: SAMHSA, Office of Applied Studies, National Survey on Drug Use and Health, 2002, 2003, 2004, 2005, and 2006.

Table 3.10A. Alcohol Use in the Lifetime, Past Year, and Past Month; Binge and Heavy Alcohol Use in the Past Month; and Alcohol Dependence or Abuse in the Past Year among Persons Aged 12 to 20, by State: Numbers in Thousands, Annual Averages Based on 2002-2006.

State	Lifetime Use	Past Year Use	Past Month Use	Binge Use in Past Month[1]	Heavy Use in Past Month[1]	Dependence or Abuse in Past Year[2]
Total United States	20,760	17,588	10,814	7,240	2,325	3,544
Alabama	315	254	154	102	32	48
Alaska	51	43	26	18	5	9
Arizona	401	328	208	142	45	71
Arkansas	200	161	97	71	25	38
California	2,484	2,054	1,222	782	205	414
Colorado	344	302	191	123	34	65
Connecticut	243	215	141	94	28	41
Delaware	59	50	31	20	6	9
District of Columbia	32	26	18	11	4	5
Florida	1,140	975	573	361	124	188
Georgia	582	469	271	173	48	84
Hawaii	81	66	40	28	8	15
Idaho	94	79	49	35	14	23
Illinois	899	776	485	335	109	166
Indiana	448	374	220	156	56	77
Iowa	222	199	128	95	38	50
Kansas	215	184	121	89	28	44
Kentucky	291	240	145	100	25	39
Louisiana	360	306	185	116	36	58
Maine	94	81	51	35	11	16
Maryland	377	323	194	114	41	57
Massachusetts	447	396	259	186	67	77
Michigan	746	645	403	276	90	128
Minnesota	366	323	207	147	48	71
Mississippi	208	162	96	64	22	29
Missouri	440	374	239	165	56	82
Montana	77	68	47	35	12	21

Table 3.10A. (Continued)

State	Lifetime Use	Past Year Use	Past Month Use	Binge Use in Past Month[1]	Heavy Use in Past Month[1]	Dependence or Abuse in Past Year[2]
Nebraska	131	115	78	54	18	31
Nevada	156	128	76	49	15	26
New Hampshire	100	90	59	42	19	21
New Jersey	599	526	323	195	53	92
New Mexico	162	134	83	57	18	34
New York	1,366	1,196	763	504	168	225
North Carolina	539	443	262	176	49	81
North Dakota	59	53	37	28	12	16
Ohio	835	718	440	310	104	141
Oklahoma	255	213	124	87	27	47
Oregon	250	210	127	85	30	43
Pennsylvania	904	777	477	331	114	146
Rhode Island	85	76	52	36	14	17
South Carolina	272	212	126	84	28	40
South Dakota	67	60	39	29	9	17
Tennessee	368	304	167	106	37	57
Texas	1,644	1,361	816	522	166	249
Utah	137	111	71	52	17	30
Vermont	51	45	31	22	8	10
Virginia	480	409	260	177	58	86
Washington	463	391	248	166	58	85
West Virginia	125	105	63	47	15	23
Wisconsin	453	404	268	191	67	94
Wyoming	43	36	23	17	6	10

*Low precision; no estimate reported.

[1] Binge Alcohol Use is defined as drinking five or more drinks on the same occasion (i.e., at the same time or within a couple of hours of each other) on at least 1 day in the past 30 days. Heavy Alcohol Use is defined as drinking five or more drinks on the same occasion on each of 5 or more days in the past 30 days; all heavy alcohol users are also binge alcohol users.

[2] Dependence or abuse is based on definitions found in the 4th edition of the *Diagnostic and Statistical Manual of Mental Disorders* (DSM-IV).

Source: SAMHSA, Office of Applied Studies, National Survey on Drug Use and Health, 2002, 2003, 2004, 2005, and 2006.

Table 3.10B. Alcohol Use in the Lifetime, Past Year, and Past Month; Binge and Heavy Alcohol Use in the Past Month; and Alcohol Dependence or Abuse in the Past Year among Persons Aged 12 to 20, by State: Percentages, Annual Averages Based on 2002-2006.

State	Lifetime Use	Past Year Use	Past Month Use	Binge Use in Past Month[1]	Heavy Use in Past Month[1]	Dependence or Abuse in Past Year[2]
Total United States	54.9	46.5	28.6	19.2	6.2	9.4
Alabama	52.5	42.4	25.7	17.0	5.4	7.9
Alaska	53.0	44.0	26.8	18.2	5.4	9.8
Arizona	54.9	44.8	28.5	19.4	6.1	9.7
Arkansas	55.6	44.6	27.0	19.8	7.1	10.4
California	51.5	42.5	25.3	16.2	4.2	8.6
Colorado	59.7	52.4	33.1	21.4	5.8	11.2
Connecticut	57.3	50.6	33.1	22.0	6.6	9.7
Delaware	57.2	47.9	29.5	19.2	5.7	8.2
District of Columbia	53.6	44.7	30.2	19.0	6.3	8.1
Florida	55.1	47.1	27.7	17.4	6.0	9.1
Georgia	50.5	40.7	23.5	15.0	4.1	7.3
Hawaii	53.7	43.9	26.7	18.9	5.2	9.9
Idaho	47.8	40.2	24.9	18.0	7.2	11.7
Illinois	54.9	47.4	29.7	20.5	6.6	10.2
Indiana	53.8	44.9	26.4	18.7	6.7	9.2
Iowa	58.0	51.8	33.4	24.8	9.9	13.2
Kansas	58.4	50.1	32.9	24.2	7.7	11.9
Kentucky	57.9	47.9	29.0	19.9	4.9	7.9
Louisiana	59.0	50.2	30.4	19.0	5.9	9.4
Maine	57.0	48.8	30.7	21.4	6.5	9.7
Maryland	53.8	46.1	27.6	16.3	5.9	8.1
Massachusetts	58.5	51.8	33.9	24.3	8.7	10.1
Michigan	55.6	48.1	30.0	20.5	6.7	9.6
Minnesota	56.1	49.5	31.7	22.6	7.3	10.9
Mississippi	51.9	40.4	24.1	15.9	5.6	7.1
Missouri	59.1	50.2	32.1	22.2	7.5	11.0
Montana	64.0	56.7	38.5	29.3	10.2	17.8

Table 3.10B. (Continued)

State	Lifetime Use	Past Year Use	Past Month Use	Binge Use in Past Month[1]	Heavy Use in Past Month[1]	Dependence or Abuse in Past Year[2]
Nebraska	57.4	50.3	34.0	23.6	8.1	13.5
Nevada	56.0	45.8	27.1	17.4	5.5	9.3
New Hampshire	59.0	53.2	34.9	24.6	11.5	12.6
New Jersey	57.3	50.3	30.9	18.7	5.0	8.7
New Mexico	61.3	50.8	31.3	21.4	6.8	13.0
New York	57.3	50.2	32.0	21.2	7.1	9.4
North Carolina	51.5	42.3	25.1	16.8	4.6	7.7
North Dakota	66.2	59.1	41.2	31.7	12.9	17.7
Ohio	56.6	48.7	29.8	21.0	7.0	9.5
Oklahoma	55.3	46.3	26.9	18.9	5.9	10.2
Oregon	56.3	47.4	28.6	19.2	6.8	9.7
Pennsylvania	56.9	48.8	30.0	20.8	7.1	9.2
Rhode Island	61.0	54.8	37.8	26.2	9.9	12.2
South Carolina	52.0	40.6	24.2	16.0	5.3	7.7
South Dakota	63.6	56.8	37.2	27.9	8.9	15.9
Tennessee	50.1	41.3	22.7	14.4	5.0	7.7
Texas	54.0	44.7	26.8	17.2	5.5	8.2
Utah	37.1	30.0	19.3	14.1	4.6	8.0
Vermont	61.8	54.9	37.2	26.5	9.2	12.4
Virginia	52.8	45.0	28.6	19.5	6.4	9.4
Washington	56.4	47.6	30.3	20.3	7.1	10.4
West Virginia	57.1	48.0	29.0	21.6	6.7	10.6
Wisconsin	61.9	55.2	36.6	26.1	9.2	12.9
Wyoming	62.6	53.2	33.8	24.4	8.2	14.8

*Low precision; no estimate reported.

[1] Binge Alcohol Use is defined as drinking five or more drinks on the same occasion (i.e., at the same time or within a couple of hours of each other) on at least 1 day in the past 30 days. Heavy Alcohol Use is defined as drinking five or more drinks on the same occasion on each of 5 or more days in the past 30 days; all heavy alcohol users are also binge alcohol users.

[2] Dependence or abuse is based on definitions found in the 4th edition of the *Diagnostic and Statistical Manual of Mental Disorders* (DSM-IV).

Source: SAMHSA, Office of Applied Studies, National Survey on Drug Use and Health, 2002, 2003, 2004, 2005, and 2006.

Table 3.11A. Alcohol Use in the Lifetime, Past Year, and Past Month; Binge and Heavy Alcohol Use in the Past Month; and Alcohol Dependence or Abuse in the Past Year among Persons Aged 12 to 20, by Parental Alcohol Use: Numbers in Thousands, Annual Averages Based on 2002- 2006.

Parental Alcohol Use[1]	Lifetime Use	Past Year Use	Past Month Use	Binge Use in Past Month[2]	Heavy Use in Past Month[2]	Dependence or Abuse in Past Year[3]
Mother's Alcohol Use						
No Use in Past Year	4,067	3,025	1,465	966	260	537
Used in Past Year	11,593	9,956	5,916	3,820	1,128	1,712
Used in Past Month But No Binge Use[2]	5,759	5,083	3,043	1,908	557	841
Binge Use at Least Once in Past Month[2]	2,778	2,395	1,536	1,039	368	440
Father's Alcohol Use						
No Use in Past Year	2,607	1,979	999	665	147	341
Used in Past Year	9,594	8,132	4,798	3,083	944	1,493
Used in Past Month But No Binge Use[2]	3,799	3,321	1,865	1,203	313	551
Binge Use at Least Once in Past Month[2]	4,274	3,693	2,319	1,482	570	773

*Low precision; no estimate reported.

Note: Estimates were created from mother-child and father-child pair data. For further details, see Section A.2 in Appendix A.

[1] Parent was female in 60 percent of the cases.

[2] Binge Alcohol Use is defined as drinking five or more drinks on the same occasion (i.e., at the same time or within a couple of hours of each other) on at least 1 day in the past 30 days. Heavy Alcohol Use is defined as drinking five or more drinks on the same occasion on each of 5 or more days in the past 30 days; all heavy alcohol users are also binge alcohol users.

[3] Dependence or abuse is based on definitions found in the 4th edition of the *Diagnostic and Statistical Manual of Mental Disorders* (DSM-IV).

Source: SAMHSA, Office of Applied Studies, National Survey on Drug Use and Health, 2002, 2003, 2004, 2005, and 2006.

Table 3.11B. Alcohol Use in the Lifetime, Past Year, and Past Month; Binge and Heavy Alcohol Use in the Past Month; and Alcohol Dependence or Abuse in the Past Year among Persons Aged 12 to 20, by Parental Alcohol Use: Percentages, Annual Averages Based on 2002-2006.

Parental Alcohol Use[1]	Lifetime Use	Past Year Use	Past Month Use	Binge Use in Past Month[2]	Heavy Use in Past Month[2]	Dependence or Abuse in Past Year[3]
Mother's Alcohol Use						
No Use in Past Year	39.1	29.1	14.1	9.3	2.5	5.2
Used in Past Year	53.5	46.0	27.3	17.6	5.2	7.9
Used in Past Month But No Binge Use[2]	52.7	46.5	27.9	17.5	5.1	7.7
Binge Use at Least Once in Past Month[2]	57.0	49.1	31.5	21.3	7.5	9.0
Father's Alcohol Use						
No Use in Past Year	39.9	30.3	15.3	10.2	2.2	5.2
Used in Past Year	51.5	43.6	25.7	16.5	5.1	8.0
Used in Past Month But No Binge Use[2]	48.6	42.5	23.9	15.4	4.0	7.1
Binge Use at Least Once in Past Month[2]	56.1	48.5	30.5	19.5	7.5	10.2

*Low precision; no estimate reported.

Note: Estimates were created from mother-child and father-child pair data. For further details, see Section A.2 in Appendix A.

[1] Parent was female in 60 percent of the cases.

[2] Binge Alcohol Use is defined as drinking five or more drinks on the same occasion (i.e., at the same time or within a couple of hours of each other) on at least 1 day in the past 30 days. Heavy Alcohol Use is defined as drinking five or more drinks on the same occasion on each of 5 or more days in the past 30 days; all heavy alcohol users are also binge alcohol users.

[3] Dependence or abuse is based on definitions found in the 4th edition of the *Diagnostic and Statistical Manual of Mental Disorders* (DSM-IV).

Source: SAMHSA, Office of Applied Studies, National Survey on Drug Use and Health, 2002, 2003, 2004, 2005, and 2006.

Table 3.12A. Alcohol Use in the Lifetime, Past Year, and Past Month; Binge and Heavy Alcohol Use in the Past Month; and Alcohol Dependence or Abuse in the Past Year among Persons Aged 12 to 20, by Parental Alcohol Use and Household Structure: Numbers in Thousands, Annual Averages Based on 2002-2006.

Parental Alcohol Use/ Household Structure[1]	Lifetime Use	Past Year Use	Past Month Use	Binge Use in Past Month[2]	Heavy Use in Past Month[2]	Dependence or Abuse in Past Year[3]
MOTHER'S ALCOHOL USE						
One-Parent Household						
No Use in Past Year	1,066	752	295	184	19	151
Used in Past Year	2,482	2,097	1,239	761	242	427
Used in Past Month But No Binge Use[2]	1,004	883	572	322	80	147
Binge Use at Least Once in Past Month[2]	798	678	422	272	101	145
Two-Parent Household[4]						
No Use in Past Year	3,001	2,273	1,170	782	241	386
Used in Past Year	9,111	7,859	4,676	3,059	886	1,285
Used in Past Month But No Binge Use[2]	4,755	4,200	2,471	1,586	477	694
Binge Use at Least Once in Past Month[2]	1,981	1,716	1,113	767	267	295
FATHER'S ALCOHOL USE						
One-Parent Household[4]						
No Use in Past Year	*	*	*	18	3	*
Used in Past Year	580	514	278	190	53	108
Used in Past Month But No Binge Use[2]	*	*	*	50	*	*
Binge Use at Least Once in Past Month[2]	*	*	154	112	22	63
Two-Parent Household[4]						
No Use in Past Year	2,494	1,887	967	647	144	334
Used in Past Year	9,014	7,619	4,519	2,894	891	1,385

Table 3.12A. (Continued)

Parental Alcohol Use/ Household Structure[1]	Lifetime Use	Past Year Use	Past Month Use	Binge Use in Past Month[2]	Heavy Use in Past Month[2]	Dependence or Abuse in Past Year[3]
Used in Past Month But No Binge Use[2]	3,613	3,158	1,793	1,153	284	518
Binge Use at Least Once in Past Month[2]	3,985	3,437	2,165	1,370	548	711

*Low precision; no estimate reported.

Note: Estimates were created from mother-child and father-child pair data. For further details, see Section A.2 in Appendix A.

[1] Parent was female in 60 percent of the cases.

[2] Binge Alcohol Use is defined as drinking five or more drinks on the same occasion (i.e., at the same time or within a couple of hours of each other) on at least 1 day in the past 30 days. Heavy Alcohol Use is defined as drinking five or more drinks on the same occasion on each of 5 or more days in the past 30 days; all heavy alcohol users are also binge alcohol users.

[3] Dependence or abuse is based on definitions found in the 4th edition of the *Diagnostic and Statistical Manual of Mental Disorders* (DSM-IV).

[4] Includes parent-child pairs reporting more than two parents in the household, which may occur because the definition of parent includes all biological, adoptive, step-, and foster relationships.

Source: SAMHSA, Office of Applied Studies, National Survey on Drug Use and Health, 2002, 2003, 2004, 2005, and 2006.

Table 3.12B. Alcohol Use in the Lifetime, Past Year, and Past Month; Binge and Heavy Alcohol Use in the Past Month; and Alcohol Dependence or Abuse in the Past Year among Persons Aged 12 to 20, by Parental Alcohol Use and Household Structure: Percentages, Annual Averages Based on 2002-2006.

Parental Alcohol Use/ Household Structure[1]	Lifetime Use	Past Year Use	Past Month Use	Binge Use in Past Month[2]	Heavy Use in Past Month[2]	Dependence or Abuse in Past Year[3]
MOTHER'S ALCOHOL USE						
One-Parent Household						
No Use in Past Year	45.3	31.9	12.5	7.8	0.8	6.4
Used in Past Year	51.7	43.7	25.8	15.9	5.0	8.9
Used in Past Month But No Binge Use[2]	53.1	46.7	30.3	17.0	4.2	7.8
Binge Use at Least Once in Past Month[2]	52.6	44.7	27.8	17.9	6.6	9.6
Two-Parent Household[4]						
No Use in Past Year	37.4	28.3	14.6	9.7	3.0	4.8
Used in Past Year	54.0	46.6	27.7	18.1	5.3	7.6
Used in Past Month But No Binge Use[2]	52.7	46.5	27.4	17.6	5.3	7.7
Binge Use at Least Once in Past Month[2]	59.0	51.1	33.2	22.9	8.0	8.8
FATHER'S ALCOHOL USE						
One-Parent Household[4]						
No Use in Past Year	*	*	*	5.6	0.9	*

Table 3.12B. (Continued)

Parental Alcohol Use/ Household Structure[1]	Lifetime Use	Past Year Use	Past Month Use	Binge Use in Past Month[2]	Heavy Use in Past Month[2]	Dependence or Abuse in Past Year[3]
Used in Past Year	57.5	50.9	27.5	18.8	5.2	10.7
Used in Past Month But No Binge Use[2]	*	*	*	15.0	*	*
Binge Use at Least Once in Past Month[2]	*	*	33.0	23.8	4.7	13.4
Two-Parent Household[4]						
No Use in Past Year	40.2	30.4	15.6	10.4	2.3	5.4
Used in Past Year	51.1	43.2	25.6	16.4	5.1	7.9
Used in Past Month But No Binge Use[2]	48.3	42.2	24.0	15.4	3.8	6.9
Binge Use at Least Once in Past Month[2]	55.8	48.1	30.3	19.2	7.7	9.9

*Low precision; no estimate reported.

Note: Estimates were created from mother-child and father-child pair data. For further details, see Section A.2 in Appendix A.

[1] Parent was female in 60 percent of the cases.

[2] Binge Alcohol Use is defined as drinking five or more drinks on the same occasion (i.e., at the same time or within a couple of hours of each other) on at least 1 day in the past 30 days. Heavy Alcohol Use is defined as drinking five or more drinks on the same occasion on each of 5 or more days in the past 30 days; all heavy alcohol users are also binge alcohol users.

[3] Dependence or abuse is based on definitions found in the 4th edition of the *Diagnostic and Statistical Manual of Mental Disorders* (DSM-IV).

[4] Includes parent-child pairs reporting more than two parents in the household, which may occur because the definition of parent includes all biological, adoptive, step-, and foster relationships.

Source: SAMHSA, Office of Applied Studies, National Survey on Drug Use and Health, 2002, 2003, 2004, 2005, and 2006.

Table 4.1A Social Context and Location of Last Alcohol Use in the Past Month among Past Month Alcohol Users Aged 12 to 20, by Age Group and Gender: Numbers in Thousands, 2006.

Social Context and Location of Last Alcohol Use	TOTAL	AGE GROUP			GENDER	
		12-14	15-17	18-20	Male	Female
SOCIAL CONTEXT OF LAST ALCOHOL USE[1]						
Alone	514	68	171	275	351	164
With One Other Person	1,506	167	481	858	859	647
With Two or More Other People	8,540	525	2,645	5,371	4,398	4,143
LOCATION OF LAST ALCOHOL USE[1,2]						
In a Car or Other Vehicle	580	39	251	290	295	285
At Home	3,174	290	846	2,038	1,790	1,383
At Someone Else's Home	5,606	335	1,985	3,287	2,910	2,696
At a Park, on a Beach, or in a Parking Lot	500	62	250	188	255	245
At a Restaurant, Bar, or Club	990	35	120	836	400	590
At a Concert or Sports Game	172	8	69	96	89	83
At School	240	21	60	158	117	123
At Some Other Place[3]	686	53	238	395	381	304
Party, Wedding, or Celebration	199	18	70	112	87	112
Outside; location not specified	98	12	46	40	66	32
Hotel, Motel, or Resort	80	4	21	55	30	50
Camping, Hunting, or Fishing	40	3	20	18	18	23
Cabin, Cottage, Vaca-tion Home, etc.	35	3	13	18	28	6
Dorm Room	19	*	2	18	9	11

*Low precision; no estimate reported.

[1] Respondents with unknown responses were excluded.

[2] Respondents could indicate multiple locations for the last time they used alcohol; thus, these response categories are not mutually exclusive.

[3] Some Other Place includes only valid responses from the other-specify questions, including these six most commonly reported locations.

Source: SAMHSA, Office of Applied Studies, National Survey on Drug Use and Health, 2006.

Table 4.1B. Social Context and Location of Last Alcohol Use in the Past Month among Past Month Alcohol Users Aged 12 to 20, by Age Group and Gender: Percentages, 2006.

Social Context and Location of Last Alcohol Use	TOTAL	AGE GROUP			GENDER	
		12-14	15-17	18-20	Male	Female
SOCIAL CONTEXT OF LAST ALCOHOL USE[1]						
Alone	4.9	9.0	5.2	4.2	6.3	3.3
With One Other Person	14.3	21.9	14.6	13.2	15.3	13.1
With Two or More Other People	80.9	69.1	80.2	82.6	78.4	83.6
LOCATION OF LAST ALCOHOL USE[1,2]						
In a Car or Other Vehicle	5.5	5.2	7.7	4.5	5.3	5.8
At Home	30.3	38.8	26.0	31.4	32.2	28.1
At Someone Else's Home	53.4	45.0	60.9	50.7	52.3	54.7
At a Park, on a Beach, or in a Parking Lot	4.8	8.3	7.7	2.9	4.6	5.0
At a Restaurant, Bar, or Club	9.4	4.6	3.7	12.9	7.2	12.0
At a Concert or Sports Game	1.6	1.0	2.1	1.5	1.6	1.7
At School	2.3	2.8	1.9	2.4	2.1	2.5
At Some Other Place[3]	6.6	7.2	7.5	6.2	7.0	6.3
Party, Wedding, or Celebration	1.9	2.4	2.2	1.7	1.6	2.3
Outside; location not specified	0.9	1.6	1.4	0.6	1.2	0.7
Hotel, Motel, or Resort	0.8	0.6	0.7	0.9	0.5	1.0
Camping, Hunting, or Fishing	0.4	0.4	0.6	0.3	0.3	0.5
Cabin, Cottage, Vacation Home, etc.	0.3	0.4	0.4	0.3	0.5	0.1
Dorm Room	0.2	*	0.1	0.3	0.2	0.2

*Low precision; no estimate reported.

Source: SAMHSA, Office of Applied Studies, National Survey on Drug Use and Health, 2006.

[1]Respondents with unknown responses were excluded.

[2]Respondents could indicate multiple locations for the last time they used alcohol; thus, these response categories are not mutually exclusive.

[3]Some Other Place includes only valid responses from the other-specify questions, including these six most commonly reported locations.

Table 4.2. Mean Number of Drinks Consumed on Last Occasion of Alcohol Use in the Past Month among Past Month Alcohol Users Aged 12 to 20, by Social Context and Location of Last Alcohol Use, Age Group, and Gender: 2006.

Social Context and Location of Last Alcohol Use	TOTAL	AGE GROUP			GENDER	
		12-14	15-17	18-20	Male	Female
TOTAL	4.5	2.8	4.3	4.8	5.3	3.7
SOCIAL CONTEXT OF LAST ALCOHOL USE[1]						
Alone	2.9	2.4	2.8	3.1	3.1	2.6
With One Other Person	3.1	2.0	3.1	3.3	3.5	2.5
With Two or More Other People	4.9	3.1	4.6	5.2	5.8	3.9
LOCATION OF LAST ALCOHOL USE[1,2]						
In a Car or Other Vehicle	5.1	3.2	4.9	5.5	5.7	4.4
At Home	4.0	2.2	3.6	4.4	4.6	3.3
At Someone Else's Home	4.9	3.4	4.7	5.2	5.8	4.0
At a Park, on a Beach, or in a Parking Lot	5.1	4.6	4.9	5.7	5.7	4.6
At a Restaurant, Bar, or Club	4.6	2.1	4.4	4.7	5.5	4.0
At a Concert or Sports Game	6.0	*	5.4	6.6	7.7	4.1
At School	5.1	2.0	5.6	5.3	6.4	3.8
At Some Other Place[3]	5.8	3.1	5.0	6.6	6.9	4.4
Party, Wedding, or Celebration	5.3	2.8	4.5	6.1	6.2	4.6
Outside; location not specified	6.1	4.0	5.0	8.0	7.5	3.4
Hotel, Motel, or Resort	5.7	*	4.9	6.3	7.0	4.9
Camping, Hunting, or Fishing	3.5	*	2.9	4.5	4.2	3.0
Cabin, Cottage, Vacation Home, etc.	5.7	*	5.7	6.4	6.5	*
Dorm Room	4.3	*	*	4.4	5.5	3.2

*Low precision; no estimate reported.

Note: Respondents with unknown responses to number of drinks consumed on last occasion of alcohol use were excluded.

[1] Respondents with unknown responses were excluded.

[2] Respondents could indicate multiple locations for the last time they used alcohol; thus, these response categories are not mutually exclusive.

[3] Some Other Place includes only valid responses from the other-specify questions, including these six most commonly reported locations.

Source: SAMHSA, Office of Applied Studies, National Survey on Drug Use and Health, 2006.

Table 4.3A. Source of Last Alcohol Use in the Past Month among Past Month Alcohol Users Aged 12 to 20, by Age Group and Gender: Numbers in Thousands, 2006.

Source of Last Alcohol Use in the Past Month[1]	TOTAL	AGE GROUP			GENDER	
		12-14	15-17	18-20	Male	Female
UNDERAGE DRINKER PAID	3,269	50	772	2,448	2,052	1,217
Purchased It Himself or Herself	983	9	178	796	640	343
From Store, Restaurant, Bar, Club, or Event	763	7	119	636	508	255
Liquor, Convenience, or Grocery Store	497	7	84	406	356	141
Restaurant, Bar, or Club	254	*	29	225	141	113
Concert, Sports, or Other Event	10	*	5	5	10	0
From Another Person	94	1	35	58	63	30
From Person under Age 21	30	*	18	12	18	12
From Person Aged 21 or Older	63	1	17	45	46	17
Purchased by Someone Else	2,271	40	589	1,642	1,404	868
Parent or Guardian	71	3	16	52	48	22
Another Family Member Aged 21 or Older	254	2	44	208	145	109
Someone Not Related Aged 21 or Older	1,577	22	384	1,170	943	634
Someone under Age 21	310	11	121	178	225	85
UNDERAGE DRINKER DID NOT PAY	7,284	705	2,519	4,061	3,542	3,742
Got It from Parent or Guardian	652	121	253	277	316	336
Got It from Another Family Member Aged 21 or Older	854	93	282	478	465	389
Got It from Someone Not Related Aged 21 or Older	2,637	97	632	1,908	1,200	1,437
Got It from Someone under Age 21	1,449	124	626	698	677	772
Took It from Own Home	396	106	157	132	202	193
Took It from Someone Else's Home	296	47	148	102	157	139
Got It Some Other Way	675	71	278	326	343	332
From Friend or Acquaintance, Unspecified Age and Method	313	35	156	122	140	173

*Low precision; no estimate reported.

Note: Respondents with unknown responses to number of drinks consumed on last occasion of alcohol use were excluded.

Source: SAMHSA, Office of Applied Studies, National Survey on Drug Use and Health, 2006.

Table 4.3B. Source of Last Alcohol Use in the Past Month among Past Month Alcohol Users Aged 12 to 20, by Age Group and Gender: Percentages, 2006.

Source of Last Alcohol Use in the Past Month[1]	TOTAL	AGE GROUP			GENDER	
		12-14	15-17	18-20	Male	Female
UNDERAGE DRINKER PAID	31.0	6.6	23.5	37.6	36.7	24.5
Purchased It Himself or Herself	9.3	1.2	5.4	12.2	11.5	6.9
From Store, Restaurant, Bar, Club, or Event	7.3	1.0	3.7	9.9	9.2	5.2
Liquor, Convenience, or Grocery Store	4.8	1.0	2.6	6.3	6.5	2.9
Restaurant, Bar, or Club	2.4	*	0.9	3.5	2.5	2.3
Concert, Sports, or Other Event	0.1	*	0.2	0.1	0.2	0.0
From Another Person	0.9	0.1	1.1	0.9	1.1	0.6
From Person under Age 21	0.3	*	0.6	0.2	0.3	0.2
From Person Aged 21 or Older	0.6	0.1	0.5	0.7	0.8	0.3
Purchased by Someone Else	21.6	5.3	17.9	25.3	25.1	17.5
Parent or Guardian	0.7	0.4	0.5	0.8	0.9	0.5
Another Family Member Aged 21 or Older	2.4	0.2	1.4	3.2	2.6	2.2
Someone Not Related Aged 21 or Older	15.0	3.0	11.8	18.1	17.0	12.8
Someone under Age 21	3.0	1.5	3.7	2.8	4.1	1.7
UNDERAGE DRINKER DID NOT PAY	69.0	93.4	76.5	62.4	63.3	75.5
Got It from Parent or Guardian	6.4	17.1	8.0	4.4	5.8	7.0
Got It from Another Family Member Aged 21 or Older	8.3	13.1	9.0	7.5	8.6	8.1
Got It from Someone Not Related Aged 21 or Older	25.8	13.7	20.1	30.0	22.2	29.8
Got It from Someone under Age 21	14.2	17.5	19.9	11.0	12.5	16.0
Took It from Own Home	3.9	15.0	5.0	2.1	3.7	4.0
Took It from Someone Else's Home	2.9	6.6	4.7	1.6	2.9	2.9
Got It Some Other Way	6.6	10.0	8.8	5.1	6.3	6.9
From Friend or Acquaintance, Unspecified Age and Method	3.1	4.9	5.0	1.9	2.6	3.6

*Low precision; no estimate reported.

Note: Respondents with unknown responses to number of drinks consumed on last occasion of alcohol use were excluded.

Source: SAMHSA, Office of Applied Studies, National Survey on Drug Use and Health, 2006.

Table 4.4. Mean Number of Drinks Consumed on Last Occasion of Alcohol Use in the Past Month among Past Month Alcohol Users Aged 12 to 20, by Source of Last Alcohol Used in the Past Month, Age Group, and Gender: 2006.

Source of Last Alcohol Use in the Past Month[1]	TOTAL	AGE GROUP			GENDER	
		12-14	15-17	18-20	Male	Female
TOTAL	4.5	2.8	4.3	4.8	5.3	3.7
UNDERAGE DRINKER PAID	5.9	4.8	6.1	5.9	6.8	4.5
Purchased It Himself or Herself	5.7	*	6.0	5.7	6.5	4.2
From Store, Restaurant, Bar, Club, or Event	5.7	*	6.1	5.6	6.5	4.2
Liquor, Convenience, or Grocery Store	6.0	*	6.5	6.0	6.7	4.3
Restaurant, Bar, or Club	4.8	*	5.0	4.8	5.5	4.0
Concert, Sports, or Other Event	9.8	*	*	*	*	*
From Another Person	6.6	*	6.0	7.0	7.2	5.4
From Person under Age 21	8.0	*	5.7	11.5	9.3	6.0
From Person Aged 21 or Older	6.0	*	6.3	5.8	6.4	4.9
Purchased by Someone Else	6.0	4.9	6.1	6.0	6.8	4.6
Parent or Guardian	4.9	*	5.3	4.8	5.5	3.6
Another Family Member Aged 21 or Older	5.2	*	5.4	5.1	6.3	3.8
Someone Not Related Aged 21 or Older	6.1	4.4	6.3	6.1	7.0	4.8
Someone under Age 21	6.1	*	5.7	6.5	6.7	4.6
UNDERAGE DRINKER DID NOT PAY	3.9	2.7	3.7	4.2	4.4	3.4
Got It from Parent or Guardian	2.5	1.7	2.1	3.2	2.8	2.2
Got It from Another Family Member Aged 21 or Older	3.8	2.4	3.6	4.3	4.2	3.3
Got It from Someone Not Related Aged 21 or Older	4.1	3.5	4.1	4.2	4.9	3.6
Got It from Someone under Age 21	4.2	3.1	3.9	4.7	4.7	3.8
Took It from Own Home	2.9	2.5	3.5	2.6	3.3	2.5
Took It from Someone Else's Home	3.8	2.2	4.0	4.3	3.7	4.0
Got It Some Other Way	4.4	3.4	4.3	4.7	4.9	3.9
From Friend or Acquaintance, Unspecified Age and Method	3.9	3.6	4.1	3.7	4.2	3.7

*Low precision; no estimate reported.

Note: Respondents with unknown responses to number of drinks consumed on last occasion of alcohol use were excluded.

[1] Respondents with unknown responses to the questions on source of last alcohol use were excluded

Source: SAMHSA, Office of Applied Studies, National Survey on Drug Use and Health, 2006.

Table 4.5A. Illicit Drug Use in the Past Month and Illicit Drugs Used in the Past Month with Alcohol or within 2 Hours of Alcohol Use on Last Occasion of Alcohol Use among Past Month Alcohol Users Aged 12 to 20, by Age Group and Gender: Numbers in Thousands, 2006.

Drug	TOTAL	AGE GROUP			GENDER	
		12-14	15-17	18-20	Male	Female
	Used Specified Drug Anytime in the Past Month					
ILLICIT DRUGS[1]	3,871	205	1,261	2,404	2,145	1,726
Marijuana or Hashish	3,244	126	1,056	2,062	1,823	1,421
Cocaine (Including Crack)	416	14	77	325	236	181
Heroin	37	5	7	25	24	12
Hallucinogens	423	22	105	295	224	198
Inhalants	234	46	118	70	121	113
Pain Relievers[2]	957	68	280	609	522	435
Tranquilizers[2]	329	9	84	237	160	169
Stimulants[2]	264	15	69	181	123	141
Methamphetamine[3]	101	1	23	77	45	56
Sedatives[2]	39	4	13	23	16	23
ILLICIT DRUGS OTHER THAN MARIJUANA[1]	1,812	124	521	1,167	964	849
Drug[4]	Used Specified Drug with Alcohol or within 2 Hours of Alcohol Use on Last Occasion of Alcohol Use in the Past Month					
ILLICIT DRUGS[1]	1,701	42	523	1,135	1,035	666
Marijuana or Hashish	1,594	37	500	1,058	967	627
Cocaine (Including Crack)	70	2	16	52	42	28
Heroin	2	*	1	1	2	0

Table 4.5A. (Continued)

Drug	TOTAL	AGE GROUP			GENDER	
		12-14	15-17	18-20	Male	Female
Hallucinogens	21	*	10	11	13	8
Inhalants	13	2	10	1	6	7
Pain Relievers[2]	128	4	28	95	70	58
Tranquilizers[2]	26	*	7	20	17	9
Stimulants[2]	15	*	4	11	8	7
Methamphetamine[5]	22	*	4	18	14	8
Sedatives[2]	1	*	1	*	*	1
ILLICIT DRUGS OTHER THAN MARIJUANA[1]	267	9	67	191	157	109

*Low precision; no estimate reported.

[1] Illicit Drugs include marijuana/hashish, cocaine (including crack), heroin, hallucinogens, inhalants, or prescription-type psychotherapeutics used nonmedically. Illicit Drugs Other Than Marijuana include cocaine (including crack), heroin, hallucinogens, inhalants, or prescription-type psychotherapeutics used nonmedically.

[2] Refers to nonmedical use; does not include over-the-counter drugs.

[3] Estimate includes responses to the core Stimulants module with imputations for unknown responses, as well as additional questions in the noncore Special Drugs module for respondents who initially did not report methamphetamine use in the core module because they did not consider methamphetamine to be a prescription drug.

[4] Respondents could indicate multiple other drugs used with alcohol; thus, these response categories are not mutually exclusive. Respondents with unknown responses to questions about other drugs used with alcohol were excluded.

[5] Estimate is based responses to the core Stimulants module *without* imputations for unknown responses, as well as additional questions in the noncore Special Drugs module for respondents who initially did not report methamphetamine use in the core module, as described in footnote 3.

Source: SAMHSA, Office of Applied Studies, National Survey on Drug Use and Health, 2006.

Table 4.5B. Illicit Drug Use in the Past Month and Illicit Drugs Used in the Past Month with Alcohol or within 2 Hours of Alcohol Use on Last Occasion of Alcohol Use among Past Month Alcohol Users Aged 12 to 20, by Age Group and Gender: Percentages, 2006.

Drug	TOTAL	AGE GROUP			GENDER	
		12-14	15-17	18-20	Male	Female
	Used Specified Drug Anytime in the Past Month					
ILLICIT DRUGS[1]	35.8	25.2	37.0	36.4	37.3	34.0
Marijuana or Hashish	30.0	15.5	31.0	31.2	31.7	28.0
Cocaine (Including Crack)	3.8	1.7	2.3	4.9	4.1	3.6
Heroin	0.3	0.6	0.2	0.4	0.4	0.2
Hallucinogens	3.9	2.7	3.1	4.5	3.9	3.9
Inhalants	2.2	5.7	3.5	1.1	2.1	2.2
Pain Relievers[2]	8.8	8.4	8.2	9.2	9.1	8.6
Tranquilizers[2]	3.0	1.1	2.5	3.6	2.8	3.3
Stimulants[2]	2.4	1.8	2.0	2.7	2.1	2.8
Methamphetamine[3]	0.9	0.1	0.7	1.2	0.8	1.1
Sedatives[2]	0.4	0.5	0.4	0.3	0.3	0.5
ILLICIT DRUGS OTHER THAN MARIJUANA[1]	16.74	15.2	15.3	17.7	16.8	16.7
Drug[4]	Used Specified Drug with Alcohol or within 2 Hours of Alcohol Use on Last Occasion of Alcohol Use in the Past Month					
ILLICIT DRUGS[1]	16.0	5.4	15.7	17.4	18.3	13.4
Marijuana or Hashish	15.0	4.6	15.1	16.3	17.2	12.6
Cocaine (Including Crack)	0.7	0.3	0.5	0.8	0.7	0.6
Heroin	0.0	*	0.0	0.0	0.0	0.0
Hallucinogens	0.2	*	0.3	0.2	0.2	0.2

Table 4.5B. (Continued)

Drug	TOTAL	AGE GROUP			GENDER	
		12-14	15-17	18-20	Male	Female
Inhalants	0.1	0.2	0.3	0.0	0.1	0.1
Pain Relievers[2]	1.2	0.6	0.8	1.5	1.2	1.2
Tranquilizers[2]	0.2	*	0.2	0.3	0.3	0.2
Stimulants[2]	0.1	*	0.1	0.2	0.1	0.1
Methamphetamine[5]	0.2	*	0.1	0.3	0.2	0.2
Sedatives[2]	0.0	*	0.0	*	*	0.0
ILLICIT DRUGS OTHER THAN MARIJUANA[1]	2.5	1.1	2.0	2.9	2.8	2.2

*Low precision; no estimate reported.

[1] Illicit Drugs include marijuana/hashish, cocaine (including crack), heroin, hallucinogens, inhalants, or prescription-type. Than Marijuana include cocaine (including crack), heroin, hallucinogens, inhalants, or prescription-type psychotherapeutics

[2] Refers to nonmedical use; does not include over-the-counter drugs.

[3] Estimate includes responses to the core Stimulants module with imputations for unknown responses, as well as additional respondents who initially did not report methamphetamine use in the core module because they did not consider methamphetamine

[4] Respondents could indicate multiple other drugs used with alcohol; thus, these response categories are not mutually about other drugs used with alcohol were excluded.

[5] Estimate is based responses to the core Stimulants module without imputations for unknown responses, as well as additional respondents who initially did not report methamphetamine use in the core module, as described in footnote 3.

Source: SAMHSA, Office of Applied Studies, National Survey on Drug Use and Health, 2006.

End Notes

[1] RTI International is a trade name of Research Triangle Institute.
[2] RTI International is a trade name of Research Triangle Institute.
[3] Prior to 2002, the survey was known as the National Household Survey on Drug Abuse (NHSDA).
[4]SAE is a hierarchical Bayes modeling technique used to make State-level stimates for approximately 20 substance-use-related measures. For more details, see the *State Estimates of Substance Use from the 2004-2005 National Surveys on Drug Use and Health* (Wright, Sathe, & Spagnola, 2007).
[5] Areas were defined using 2000 census geography. Dwelling units (DUs) and population counts were obtained from the 2000 census data supplemented with revised population counts from Claritas (http://cluster1.claritas. com/claritas/Default.jsp).
[6] Census tracts are relatively permanent statistical subdivisions of counties and provide a stable set of geographic units across decennial census periods.
[7] Some census tracts had to be aggregated in order to meet the minimum DU requirement of 150 DUs in urban areas and 100 DUs in rural areas.
[8] For more details on the 5-year sample, see the 2006 sample design report in the *2006 NSDUH Methodological Resource Book* (Morton, Chromy, Hunter, & Martin, 2007).

In: Underage Drinking
Ed: David Edvin and Samuel Harald
ISBN: 978-1-60876-141-8

Chapter 6

UNDERAGE ALCOHOL USE: WHERE DO YOUNG PEOPLE DRINK?*

National Survey on Drug Use and Health

IN BRIEF

- A majority (53.4 percent) of current alcohol users aged 12 to 20 drank at someone else's home the last time they used alcohol, and another 30.3 percent drank in their own home
- The percentage of underage alcohol users who had their most recent drink in a car or other vehicle peaked at 10.1 percent at age 16 (12.8 percent of females and 7.3 percent of males)
- Among 20-year-old current drinkers, 20.0 percent of females drank in a restaurant, bar, or club the last time they used alcohol compared with 10.2 percent of males

In 2006, more than one in four persons aged 12 to 20 in the United States, or about 10.8 million persons, drank alcohol in the past month (i.e., were current drinkers).[1] Nearly one in five persons aged 18 to 20 drove under the influence of alcohol in the past 12 months in 2006,[1] and each year

* This is an edited, reformatted and augmented version of a National Survey on Drug Use and Health publication dated August 2008.

approximately 1,900 people under the age of 21 die as a result of alcohol-involved motor vehicle crashes.[2] In addition, early initiation of alcohol use is associated with increased likelihood of unprotected sexual intercourse and multiple sex partners.[3,4]

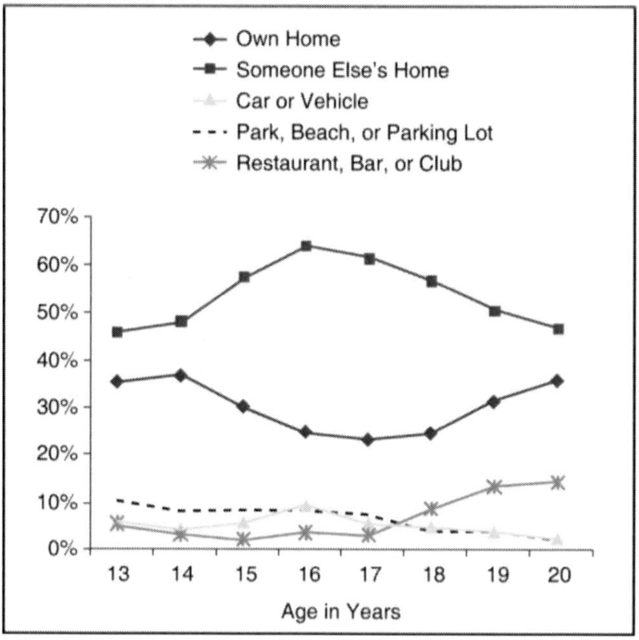

Source: SAMHSA, 2006 NSDUH.

* Standard error (SE) is a measure of the sampling variability or precision of an estimate, where smaller values represent greater precision and larger values represent less precision.

** Estimates for persons aged 18 to 20 include those with unknown enrollment status. Other persons include those aged 18 to 20 not enrolled in college, enrolled in college part time, enrolled in other grades either full or part time, or enrolled with no other information available.

Figure 1. Location of the Most Recent Alcohol Use in the Past Month* among Past Month Alcohol Users Aged 13 to 20, by Individual Years of Age: 2006**.

The 2006 National Survey on Drug Use and Health (NSDUH) asked past month alcohol users aged 12 to 20 how they obtained the last alcohol they drank and where they were when they consumed it. *The NSDUH Report* examines age-related changes in the locations where male and female underage drinkers use alcohol. It also examines differences by college enrollment and living situation for those aged 18 to 20. Findings presented in this chapter are based on 2006 NSDUH data.

How Do Drinking Locations Change with Age?

In 2006, a majority (53.4 percent) of current alcohol users aged 12 to 20 drank at someone else's home the last time they used alcohol, and another 30.3 percent drank in their own home. This overall pattern of last using alcohol in their own home or at someone else's home held for drinkers at each age from 13 to 20 (Figure 1).[5] More than 60 percent of drinkers aged 16 or 17 used alcohol in someone else's home the last time they drank. About 36 percent or more of drinkers aged 13, 14, and 20 last used alcohol in their own homes. In addition, 10.0 percent of 13-year-old drinkers last consumed alcohol in public places (such as a park, a beach, or a parking lot).

The percentage of underage alcohol users who had their most recent drink in a car or other vehicle peaked at 10.1 percent at age 16. An estimated 15.0 percent of those aged 20 last drank in a restaurant, bar, or club. Approximately 7 to 10 percent of alcohol users aged 13 to 17 last drank in public places, with the percentages decreasing to fewer than 4 percent of drinkers aged 18 to older. In contrast, most recent use of alcohol in a restaurant, bar, or club started to increase at age 18 and was at its highest point at age 20.

Do Age-Related Changes in Drinking Locations Differ for Males and Females?

Among male alcohol users, the percentage reporting that they drank most recently in a car or other vehicle did not differ significantly by age between ages 15 and 20,6 but it did differ for females (Figure 2). An estimated 12.8 percent of female alcohol users who were aged 16 last drank alcohol in a car or other motor vehicle, a rate that was 8 times greater than the rate for female drinkers who were aged 20 (1.6 percent). At age 16, 7.3 percent of male current drinkers had their last drink in a car or other vehicle.

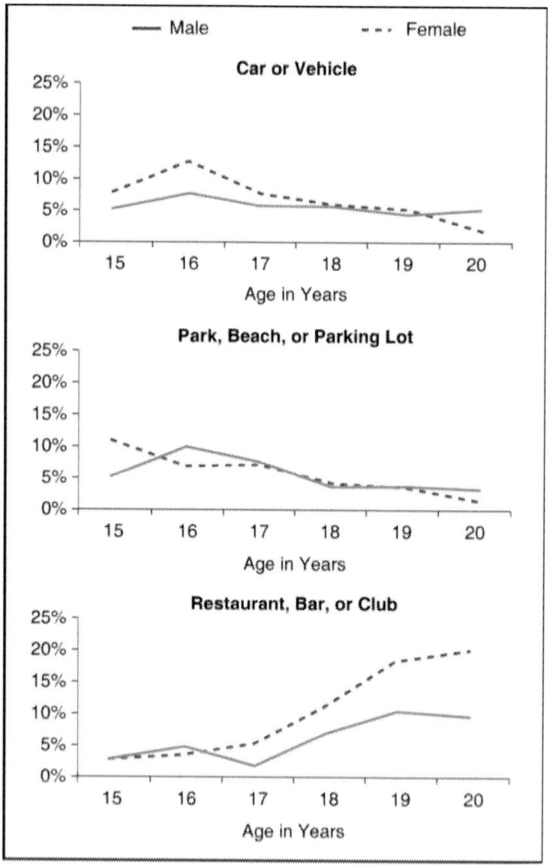

Source: SAMHSA, 2006 NSDUH.

* Standard error (SE) is a measure of the sampling variability or precision of an estimate, where smaller values represent greater precision and larger values represent less precision.

** Estimates for persons aged 18 to 20 include those with unknown enrollment status. Other persons include those aged 18 to 20 not enrolled in college, enrolled in college part time, enrolled in other grades either full or part time, or enrolled with no other information available.

Figure 2. Location of the Most Recent Alcohol Use in the Past Month* among Past Month Alcohol Users Aged 15 to 20, by Gender within Individual Years of Age: 2006**.

Among 15-year-old drinkers, females were twice as likely as males to have last used alcohol in a public place, such as a park, beach, or parking lot (10.6 vs. 5.0 percent). Among males, alcohol consumption in public places peaked at age 16 and then declined. Among females, alcohol consumption in public places declined after age 15.

The proportion of underage current drinkers who consumed their last alcohol in a restaurant, bar, or club generally increased with age. Starting at age 17, female drinkers were more likely than their male counterparts to have consumed alcohol in one of these locations. Among 20-year-old current drinkers, 20.0 percent of females drank in a restaurant, bar, or club the last time they used alcohol compared with 10.2 percent of males.

Table 1. Most Recent Alcohol Use in the Past Month at Home or at Someone Else's Home* among Past Month Alcohol Users Aged 18 to 20, by College Enrollment Status and Parental Living Situation*: 2006**.**

College Enrollment Status/Parental Living Situation	Location of Most Recent Alcohol Use			
	Home		Someone Else's Home	
	%	SE+	%	SE+
Total Aged 18 to 20++				
Living with a Parental Relative	24.3	1.07	55.4	1.29
Not Living with a Parental Relative	42.9	1.90	43.1	1.92
Full-Time College Student				
Living with a Parental Relative	21.2	1.49	56.8	2.03
Not Living with a Parental Relative	33.5	2.28	50.7	2.33
Other++				
Living with a Parental Relative	26.6	1.54	54.4	1.72
Not Living with a Parental Relative	56.9	2.55	31.7	2.47

* Respondents could indicate multiple locations for the most recent time they used alcohol; thus, these response categories are not mutually exclusive.

** Respondents with unknown responses were excluded.

*** Persons with unknown parental living situations were excluded. Parental relatives include a parent, grandparent, or parent-in-law.

Source: SAMHSA, 2006 NSDUH.

Where Do Persons Aged 18 to 20 Drink?

Among drinkers aged 18 to 20, those who were living with a parent or similar relative were more likely than those who were not living with a parental relative to have most recently used alcohol in someone else's home (55.4 and 43.1 percent, respectively) (Table 1). This pattern was more pronounced for drinkers in this age group who were not full-time college students (54.4 percent of those living with a parental relative vs. 31.7 percent of those who were not). However, more than half of underage drinkers who were full-time college students last drank alcohol in someone else's home regardless of whether they were living with a parental relative.

Discussion

Underage alcohol use poses important public health and public safety risks. Knowing the locations where this behavior is most likely to occur can help parents talk with their teenagers more effectively about the dangers of alcohol use and alert parents to times when they need to exercise greater monitoring and supervision. These data also provide prevention specialists with new information to help guide program development or modify existing prevention activities in their communities.

Suggested Citation

Substance Abuse and Mental Health Services Administration, Office of Applied Studies. (August 28, 2008). *The NSDUH Report: Underage Alcohol Use: Where Do Young People Drink?* Rockville, MD.

Underage Alcohol Use: Where Do Young People Drink?

- A majority (53.4 percent) of current alcohol users aged 12 to 20 drank at someone else's home the last time they used alcohol, and another 30.3 percent drank in their own home

- The percentage of underage alcohol users who had their most recent drink in a car or other vehicle peaked at 10.1 percent at age 16 (12.8 percent of females and 7.3 percent of males)
- Among 20-year-old current drinkers, 20.0 percent of females drank in a restaurant, bar, or club the last time they used alcohol compared with 10.2 percent of males

The National Survey on Drug Use and Health (NSDUH) is an annual survey sponsored by the Substance Abuse and Mental Health Services Administration (SAMHSA). The 2006 data used in this chapter are based on information obtained from 31,320 persons aged 12 to 20. The survey collects data by administering questionnaires to a representative sample of the population through face-to-face interviews at their place of residence.

The NSDUH Report is prepared by the Office of Applied Studies (OAS), SAMHSA, and by RTI International in Research Triangle Park, North Carolina. (RTI International is a trade name of Research Triangle Institute.)

End Notes

[1] Office of Applied Studies. (2007). *Results from the 2006 National Survey on Drug Use and Health: National findings* (DHHS Publication No. SMA 07-4293, NSDUH Series H-32). Rockville, MD: Substance Abuse and Mental Health Services Administration. [Available at http://oas.samhsa.gov/p0000016.htm]

[2] Hingson, R., & Kenkel, D. (2004). Social, health, and economic consequences of underage drinking. In R. J. Bonnie & M. E. O'Connell (Eds.), *Reducing underage drinking: A collective responsibility* (pp. 351 -382). Washington, DC: National Academies Press. [Available at http://www.nap.edu/ books/0309089352/html]

[3] Stueve, A., & O'Donnell, L. N. (2005). Early alcohol initiation and subsequent sexual and alcohol risk behaviors among urban youths. *American Journal of Public Health, 95*, 887-893.

[4] Swahn, M. H., Bossarte, R. M., & Sullivent, E. E. 3rd. (2008). Age of alcohol use initiation, suicidal behavior, and peer and dating violence victimization and perpetration among high-risk, seventh-grade adolescents. *Pediatrics, 121*, 297- 305.

[5] Estimates were unreliable for 12-year-old drinkers and were therefore not used.

[6] A lower age limit of 15 years was set for estimates regarding locations of the most recent alcohol use among male and female underage drinkers by single years of age because of the larger sample sizes of male and female drinkers aged 15 to 20.

In: Underage Drinking
Ed: David Edvin and Samuel Harald
ISBN: 978-1-60876-141-8

Chapter 7

UNDERAGE ALCOHOL USE: WHERE DO YOUNG PEOPLE GET ALCOHOL?*

National Survey on Drug Use and Health

IN BRIEF

- More than one quarter (28.1 percent) of persons aged 12 to 20 used alcohol in the past month, including more than half (51.1 percent) of those aged 18 to 20, 25.9 percent of those aged 15 to 17, and 6.1 percent of those aged 12 to 14
- Nearly one third of current alcohol users aged 12 to 20 (30.6 percent) paid for the last alcohol they used, more than one in four (26.4 percent) got it for free from a nonrelative aged 21 or older, 14.6 percent got it for free from another underage person, 5.9 percent got it from a parent or guardian, and 8.5 percent got it from another relative aged 21 or older
- Current alcohol users aged 12 to 20 consumed more drinks on average the last time if they paid for the last alcohol they used (6.0 drinks) compared with those who did not pay for their last alcohol (3.9 drinks)

* This is an edited, reformatted and augmented version of a National Survey on Drug Use and Health publication dated November 2008.

Although the use of alcohol is illegal for persons under the age of 21, its use constitutes one of the principal public health issues for this age group,[1] and reduction of underage alcohol use is a top public health priority of the Federal Government.[2] Many of the efforts to prevent or reduce underage alcohol use attempt to reduce the availability of alcohol to underage drinkers. Data from the 2006 and 2007 National Surveys on Drug Use and Health (NSDUHs) indicate that even with efforts to reduce availability, underage drinkers are still able to obtain alcohol.

The NSDUH Report examines how current (i.e., "past month") drinkers aged 12 to 20 obtain alcohol, by age group and gender. The 2006 and 2007 NSDUHs included items that asked past month alcohol users aged 12 to 20 how they obtained the last alcohol they drank. This chapter also presents data on the prevalence of current underage alcohol use and findings on the average number of drinks that underage drinkers had on their last occasion of alcohol use, depending on where they obtained alcohol. All findings presented are annual averages based on combined 2006 and 2007 NSDUH data.

What Percentage of Young People Are Underage Drinkers?

More than one quarter (28.1 percent) of persons aged 12 to 20 (an estimated 10.8 million persons) used alcohol in the past month. More than half (51.1 percent) of those aged 18 to 20 were current alcohol users compared with 25.9 percent of those aged 15 to 17 and 6.1 percent of those aged 12 to 14. Underage males were more likely than their female counterparts to be current alcohol users (28.8 vs. 27.4 percent).

How Do current Alcohol Users Aged 12 to 20 Obtain Alcohol?

Nearly one third (30.6 percent) of current alcohol users aged 12 to 20 in 2006 and 2007 (an estimated 3.2 million persons) paid for the last alcohol they used, and 69.4 percent (an estimated 7.3 million persons) got the last alcohol they used for free. More than one in four (26.4 percent) got the last alcohol they used for free from a nonrelative aged 21 or older, 14.6 percent got it for free from another underage person, 5.9 percent got it from a parent or guardian, 8.5 percent got it from another relative aged 21 or older, and 3.9 percent took it from their own home without asking.[3]

How Do Underage Drinkers in Different Age Groups Obtain Alcohol?

Among underage current alcohol users, over one third (36.5 percent) of persons aged 18 to 20 paid for the last alcohol they drank compared with 23.5 percent of those aged 15 to 17 and 7.5 percent of those aged 12 to 14 (Figure 1).

Current alcohol users aged 18 to 20 also were more likely than their younger counterparts to have gotten alcohol for free from a nonrelative of legal drinking age (30.5 percent compared with 20.3 percent of those aged 15 to 17 and 13.4 percent of those aged 12 to 14) (Figure 2). However, alcohol users aged 18 to 20 were less likely than those aged 12 to 14 to have gotten the last alcohol they used from a parent or guardian (4.2 vs. 16.6 percent), to have taken it from their own home without asking (2.2 vs. 14.0 percent), or to have gotten it from another underage person (11.1 vs. 18.6 percent).

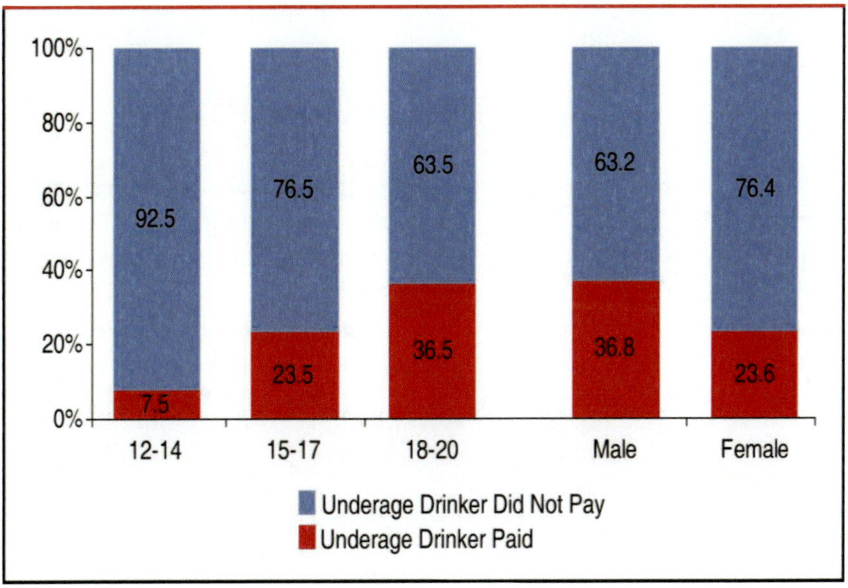

Source: SAMHSA, 2006 and 2007 NSDUHs.

Figure 1. Payment or Receipt of Alcohol for Free for the Last Use in the Past Month among Alcohol Users Aged 12 to 20, by Age Group and Gender: Annual Averages, 2006 and 2007*.

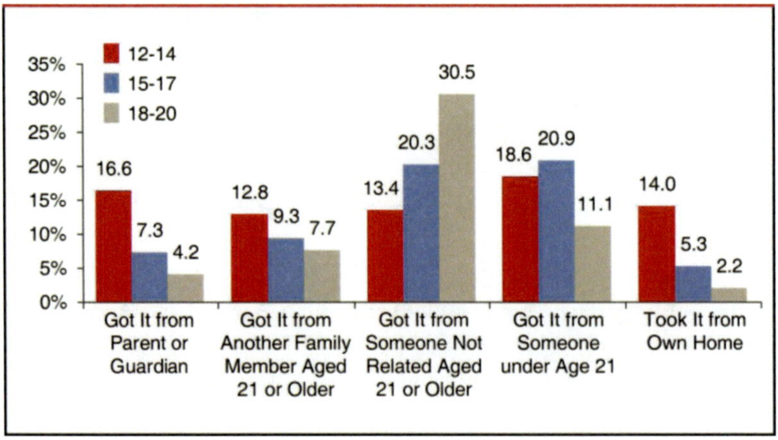

Source: SAMHSA, 2006 and 2007 NSDUHs.

Figure 2. Source of Alcohol Obtained for Free for the Last Use in the Past Month among Alcohol Users Aged 12 to 20, by Age Group: Annual Averages, 2006 and 2007*.

How Do Underage Males and Females Obtain Alcohol?

Underage male alcohol users were more likely than their female counterparts to have paid for the last alcohol they used (36.8 vs. 23.6 percent) (Figure 1). Conversely, more than three fourths of female underage drinkers (76.4 percent) obtained their last alcohol for free compared with 63.2 percent of males. Female underage drinkers were more likely than their male counterparts to have gotten the last alcohol they used for free from a nonrelative of legal drinking age (31.0 vs. 22.1 percent) (Figure 3).

How Many Drinks Do Underage Drinkers Have, Depending on How They Obtain Alcohol?

Current alcohol users aged 12 to 20 consumed more drinks on average the last time if they paid for the last alcohol they used (6.0 drinks) compared with those who did not pay for their last alcohol (3.9 drinks) (Table 1). Underage current drinkers who got alcohol for free from a nonrelative of legal drinking age consumed more drinks on average (4.3 drinks) than those who got the last alcohol they used from a parent or guardian (2.5 drinks).

Table 1. Mean Number of Drinks Consumed on Last Occasion of Alcohol Use in the Past Month among Past Month Alcohol Users Aged 12 to 20, by Age Group and Source of last Alcohol Used: Annual Averages, 2006 and 2007.

Source of Last Alcohol Used in the Past Month*	Total		Age Group					
			12-14		15-17		18-20	
	Mean	SE	Mean	SE	Mean	SE	Mean	SE
Total	4.6	0.05	2.8	0.11	4.4	0.07	4.8	0.07
Underage Drinker Paid	6.0	0.11	**4.8**	**0.50**	6.3	0.18	**6.0**	**0.13**
Underage Drinker Did Not Pay**	3.9	0.04	**2.7**	**0.10**	3.8	0.07	**4.2**	**0.06**
Got It from Parent or Guardian	2.5	0.10	**1.7**	**0.11**	2.1	0.11	**3.1**	**0.19**
Got It from Another Family Member Aged 21 or Older	3.6	0.16	**2.3**	**0.18**	3.5	0.25	**3.9**	**0.23**
Got It from Someone Not Related Aged 21 or Older	4.3	0.07	**3.4**	**0.38**	4.3	0.14	**4.3**	**0.09**
Got It from Someone under Age 21	4.2	0.09	**3.2**	**0.25**	4.0	0.12	**4.5**	**0.13**
Took It from Own Home	3.0	0.18	**2.3**	**0.25**	3.6	0.32	**2.9**	**0.28**

*Respondents with unknown responses were excluded.

** Underage drinkers who did not pay for the last alcohol they used include those who got alcohol from someone else's house, those who got it some other way, and those whose source was missing, as well as the respondents who reported getting alcohol without paying for it from the other sources shown in the report.

Source: SAMHSA, 2006 and 2007 NSDUHs.

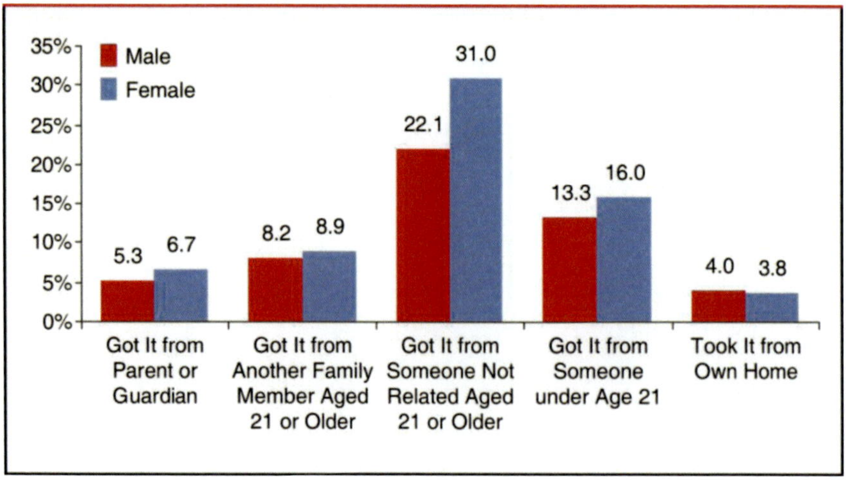

Source: SAMHSA, 2006 and 2007 NSDUHs.

Figure 3. Source of Alcohol Obtained for Free for the last Use in the Past Month among Alcohol Users Aged 12 to 20, by Gender: Annual Averages, 2006 and 2007*.

These patterns also held within individual age groups of underage alcohol users. For example, current alcohol users aged 12 to 14 who paid for the alcohol themselves consumed an average of 4.8 drinks the last time they drank compared with an average of 2.7 drinks if they did not pay for it. These 12 to 14 year olds consumed an average of 3.4 drinks if they got their alcohol from a nonrelative aged 21 or older and 1.7 drinks if they got it from a parent or guardian. Among current alcohol users aged 18 to 20, those who paid for the last alcohol they used averaged 6.0 drinks compared with 4.2 drinks among those who got it for free.

Discussion

Even with increased efforts to reduce the availability of alcohol to young people, data from NSDUH indicate that underage drinkers are able to purchase or obtain alcohol from relatives and friends at an unacceptably high rate. This should be of concern to professionals, policymakers, parents, and others who are attempting to reduce the negative consequences of underage alcohol use.

UNDERAGE ALCOHOL USE: WHERE DO YOUNG PEOPLE GET ALCOHOL?

- More than one quarter (28.1 percent) of persons aged 12 to 20 used alcohol in the past month, including more than half (51.1 percent) of those aged 18 to 20, 25.9 percent of those aged 15 to 17, and 6.1 percent of those aged 12 to 14
- Nearly one third of current alcohol users aged 12 to 20 (30.6 percent) paid for the last alcohol they used, more than one in four (26.4 percent) got it for free from a nonrelative aged 21 or older, 14.6 percent got it for free from another underage person, 5.9 percent got it from a parent or guardian, and 8.5 percent got it from another relative aged 21 or older
- Current alcohol users aged 12 to 20 consumed more drinks on average the last time if they paid for the last alcohol they used (6.0 drinks) compared with those who did not pay for their last alcohol (3.9 drinks)

End Notes

[1] National Institute on Alcohol Abuse and Alcoholism. (2006, January). *Alcohol Alert No. 67: Underage drinking: Why do adolescents drink, what are the risks, and how can underage drinking be prevented?* [Available at http://pubs.niaaa.nih.gov/ publications/ AA67/AA67.htm]

[2] U.S. Department of Health and Human Services. (2007). *The Surgeon General's call to action to prevent and reduce underage drinking.* Rockville, MD: Office of the Surgeon General. [Available at http://www.surgeongeneral.gov/topics/underagedrinking/]

[3] Other sources of alcohol for which underage drinkers did not pay include alcohol from someone else's house, alcohol that was obtained some other way, and situations in which underage persons did not pay for the last alcohol they used but the specific source was unknown.

INDEX

A

B

C

D

E

F

G

H

I

J

K

L

M

N

O

S

Y